1940

1940

By Laurence Thompson

WILLIAM MORROW & COMPANY, INC.

NEW YORK

To Margaret
8 September 1940

Acknowledgments

I am grateful to the Dowager Countess of Halifax, who allowed me access to Lord Halifax's diary for 1940, together with certain other papers, and who has permitted me to quote freely from them.

The Earl of Birkenhead interrupted work on his own biography of Lord Halifax—a kindness which can be appreciated to its fullest extent only by fellow authors—to answer my questions and to draw my attention to a number of points which would otherwise have escaped my notice.

Mr. Malcolm R. Lovell, of Miami, Florida, has made available to me his unpublished contemporary record of the attempt to arrange a meeting between the German chargé d'affaires in Washington and the British Ambassador, Lord Lothian.

Sir Martin Lindsay has allowed me to read and draw upon chapters of his autobiography; Colonel E. G. C. Beckwith, The Sherwood Foresters, has let me make free use of his mimeographed account of the Norwegian campaign; in my description of the French campaign I have been able to draw upon the memories of my friend Mr. H. G. Castle, late of The Royal Sussex Regiment; the Air Historical Branch of the Ministry of Defence made available to me the operations record books of the Battle squadrons of the Advanced Air Striking Force in France.

Chapters Four and Five owe much to that unsatisfactory source for the historian, "private information." I am nonetheless grateful to those who have helped me with these chapters, though protocol forbids that I should name them all. One I can name is Mr. S. Clement-Davies, who passed on to me unstintingly his father's memories of these events.

Among others whose help I can, and most gratefully do, acknowledge, are Earl Attlee, Lord Boothby, Mrs. W. H. Burrows, Mr. L. J. Burt, Sir Nevile Butler, Mr. J. W. Collier, Dame Isobel Cripps, Major General Sir Francis De Guingand, Dr. T. Kingston Derry, Mr. P. V. Emrys Evans, Mr. R. T. Holmes, Sir Ronald Howe, Mr. R. J. Minney, Mr. John Montgomery, Lord Reith, Sir Harold Scott, Major General Sir Edward Spears and the Right Hon. Richard Wood.

Sir Basil Liddell Hart, Marshal of the Royal Air Force Sir John Slessor, and the late Viscount Margesson are among those who have read and commented on certain passages, to my great profit. Any errors of fact and eccentricities of opinion which remain in spite of them are due to my own inefficiency and perversity.

Dr. Henry Durant of the Gallup Poll, and the directors of Mass Observation, have allowed me to quote from their contemporary surveys. The Controller of Her Majesty's Stationery Office has permitted the use of material, copyright of which is vested in the Crown. Earl Baldwin of Bewdley has allowed me to quote from a letter of his father to Lord Halifax.

The following have kindly given permission to quote from other copyright material: Cassell and Company Ltd. and the Houghton Mifflin Company (*The Second World War* by Sir Winston Churchill, and *The Reckoning* by the Earl of Avon); the Public Archives of Canada (*The Mackenzie King Record* by the Hon. J. W. Pickersgill); Doubleday & Company Inc. and The *Chicago Sun-Times* (*The Ciano Diaries, 1939-1943*, edited by Hugh Gibson); Mr. Reginald W. Bell (*The Bull's Eye*); Mr. William L. Shirer (*Berlin Diary*); the literary executors of M. Louise Haskins (*The Desert*); Dr. Fritz Hesse (*Hitler and the English*); Hollis & Carter Ltd. (*The Ruling Few* by Sir David Kelly); The Hutchinson Publishing Group (*Tempestuous Journey* by Frank Owen); Macmillan & Co. Ltd. and the literary executors of the late Richard Hillary (*The Last Enemy*); Constable Publishers London (*The Ironside Diaries* by Field-Marshal Lord Ironside of Archangel).

Finally I must acknowledge my debt to the staff of the British Museum Reading Room and Newspaper Library, the Imperial War Museum, the Librarian of The Reform Club, and the Narrator, Ministry of Defence Library (Central and Army).

List of Illustrations

CONTENTS

1940

Chapter

1

"THE GATE OF THE YEAR"

By decree of the British government, 1940 began quietly. Under the Control of Noises (Defence) Order, the sounding of sirens, factory hooters, whistles, or noisy rattles was forbidden. Sirens, it was believed, might cause general alarm, as well as create confusion in the ranks of those protecting Britain from air attack. Church bells, however, might be rung. Their turn for silence came in June.

In some areas of Central London, a Christmas attempt had been made to mitigate the black-out by experiments with what was called, in the jargon of the day, "amenity lighting" of shops and streets, equivalent to the light of a candle about seventy feet away, and five hundred to fifteen hundred times less bright than what were beginning to be nostalgically remembered as the lights of London. Some Londoners found "amenity lighting" even more depressing than the previous total darkness, and there were ironical cheers in Piccadilly Circus when the Old Year was ushered out —illegally—by the light of a torch shone on the face of a nearby clock.

For the most part, however, merriment was not only muffled, but driven underground. In the brightly lit entrance hall of Piccadilly Circus station, a party of young people, self-conscious in fancy hats, sang that half-tamed relic of the bacchanal, "Knees Up,

Mother Brown." Many of their elders performed the rite of listening to the late night B.B.C. news, perhaps in the half-conscious
hope of hearing an announcement that the events of the past four
months had all been a mistake. But no such announcement was
ever made and, disappointed, they retired to cold and blacked-out
bedrooms.

The British people entered this year, which decisively changed
their lives, with no great expectations. A survey by Mass Observation, a British organization of a kind made familiar by the Gallup
Poll, recorded that 12 per cent were optimists, 22 per cent were
resigned about the future, 20 per cent saw a dark future with a
silver lining, and 46 per cent were gloomy and uncertain. One individual recorded that he felt like a man in a dentist's waiting
room: "It's got to come and will probably be horrible while it
lasts, but it won't last forever, and it's just possible these teeth
won't have to come out after all."

The mood subtly differed from that of September, 1939, when
some had fainted upon hearing Prime Minister Neville Chamberlain's sad, flat voice on the radio proclaim war; others had awakened that night, in terror, from the nightmare of a sky black
with bombing planes wing-tip to wing-tip. A middle-aged school-
mistress in a small country town recalled, "At 11:15 I went up, and
we sat round listening to Chamberlain speaking. I held my chin
high and kept back the tears at the thought of all the slaughter
ahead. When 'God Save the King' was played, we stood."

The endless, sophisticated discussion by politicians and press
about Munich and the government's appeasement policy, had
then presented itself, for many people, in the form of two simple
propositions: "It's got to come, we might as well have it and finish
with it"; and "We can't let old Hitler get away with it again, can
we?"

Heroism, though muted, had been real enough. From former
Prime Minister Baldwin's statement that "The bomber will always get through" to the estimate of the Committee of Imperial
Defence that the opening air attack on London would last sixty
days, with 600,000 people killed and twice that many injured, the
British people had been left with few illusions about what was
going to happen to them if they declared war on Germany. Thousands of papier-mâché coffins were stacked and ready, a million

burial forms had been issued, thousands of hospital beds waited for the injured.

This was the shock people had braced themselves to withstand; and nothing happened, except that the road deaths rose to a record high as a result of the black-out. The British people might have felt—perhaps they did feel—thankful, with a twinge of guilt about Poland, as about Czechoslovakia the year before. They certainly felt resentful, like a man publicly detected in the pose of lifting a heavy weight which turns out to be india-rubber. The politicians had been wrong, the newspapers had been wrong. Publicists like H. G. Wells and scientists like J. B. S. Haldane, with all their warnings of massacre from the air, had made fools of them.

The British are a curious people, who more than most feel the need of moral justification for even their most immoral acts. Secretly, most of them would have agreed with Chamberlain's description of Czechoslovakia as a "far-away country of which we know nothing"; but they had been told repeatedly that it was their duty to go to war on behalf of weaker nations, and they had done so reluctantly, though with a sense of mission. Germany under Hitler had torn up agreement after agreement, had swallowed in turn Austria and Czechoslovakia, and had then invaded Poland. The Russians, of whom they had been inclined to think well, had first of all signed a pact with the Nazis, had then divided conquered Poland with Germany, and in November, 1939, had wantonly invaded their small neighbor, Finland. Mussolini, a figure of fun to most of the British, had invaded Abyssinia and Albania and, though for the moment neutral, was making aggressive noises. Clearly nothing was to be done with such people except to teach them better manners. The British therefore felt themselves to be fighting in a just cause, and wanted to get on with it. For some reason which they could not understand, and could not be told, they were not allowed to do so. The sense of mission began to turn sour, a distrust of any kind of authority—known to the army as bloody-mindedness—began to be born.

Until December, 1939, the war had been a main topic of conversation. By the turn of the year it had almost ceased to be mentioned, except as the tedious background to complaints, or jokes, about rationing, evacuees, air-raid wardens. A majority of people had given up carrying their gas masks, and there was government concern about family air-raid shelters, distributed free, and left to rust unassembled in thousands of back gardens.

Upon the press descended the black-out of censorship, which made serious reporting and discussion of the war virtually impossible. Newspapers were forbidden to name the Lord Mayor of a town "somewhere in England" visited by the King, because the town contained a munitions factory. Pictures of a new British plane were released with instructions that the gun turret must be painted out before they were published; the same pictures were published in German newspapers with the gun turret intact.

From the end of December until mid-February, with only a single break, Britain experienced its coldest winter for forty-five years. The Strait of Dover froze at Folkestone and Dungeness, and for eight miles between Teddington and Sunbury the river Thames was solid ice. In Derbyshire villages, snowdrifts rose higher than cottage roofs. At the end of January, heavy snowfalls put out of action hundreds of miles of telephone and telegraph wires, and snowplows sent to rescue trains were themselves engulfed in thirty-foot drifts. For weeks, the censorship rationed newspaper references to this weather story of the century. When the fact that trains were reaching their destinations 28½ hours late could no longer escape comment, the story was released, with the explanation in one periodical: "It is probable that on January 29, when chaotic transport conditions prevailed over a large part of England, due to snow and ice, Berlin had little idea of the extent of our wintry weather." As a matter of fact, frost gripped the whole of Europe, touching even the Italian Riviera, and once more had caused Hitler to postpone his long-expected offensive against the French and British armies.

In such circumstances, there was inevitably an air of unreality about newspaper accounts of the war. On the first day of the New Year, a *Times* special correspondent with the French forces reported—with considerable thankfulness, one may surmise, for being allowed to report anything at all—a "story of brave adventure," typical of the patroling constantly going on along the Maginot Line, the chain of French fortifications facing Germany from Luxembourg to the Swiss border. A tall, fair-haired French lieutenant in his early twenties and a holder of the Legion of Honor and the Croix de Guerre encountered a German patrol while on reconnaissance in the woods in No Man's Land. "It was our young hero, a

Parisian," said the *Times,* "who led his party round and caught the enemy in the rear." The French took four prisoners, two of them officers, and killed six or seven Germans. One German officer, it was said, had been compelled to divorce his Jewish wife, who had escaped to London. Reportedly, he had English money concealed about him. All four prisoners spoke of misgiving in the German army about the Russo-German alliance "although one young hothead loudly proclaimed his conviction of the Führer's infallibility, until his interrogator reminded him that he bore no wounds."

Such, in January, 1940, was what the British people were allowed to know about a war which, they had been led to suppose, would bring annihilation almost overnight.

Cut off from the real war, the press displayed an almost hysterical air of frivolity.

Mr. Chamberlain, reported the *Times,* had received the gift of a walking stick in the form of a rolled-up umbrella, which an eighty-six-year-old Suffolk shepherd had carved out of elm wood with a pocketknife.

The *Daily Express* dealt faithfully with a Christmas pantomime, "Heil Cinderella," written by Cecil Beaton and John Sutro, with Lady Margaret Drummond-Hay as Prince Charming. It had originally been presented at the Earl and Countess of Pembroke's Wilton House, and was later performed before six hundred officers and men at an R.A.F. station. "On the whole," recorded the *Express,* "the troops were quiet. The coughing was respectful."

An *Express* reporter castigated "Nazi methods"—a guard with fixed bayonet at the dock gates—used to prevent the press from recording full details of the arrival from Germany of Unity Mitford, a self-proclaimed disciple of Hitler, with a mysterious bullet wound in her neck. Her father, Lord Redesdale, lacked at that time the endearing public image which his daughter Nancy was later to create for him as Uncle Matthew of the entrenching tool, grinding dentures, and thoroughly English detestation of "bloody abroad." He and his family were subjected to much petty persecution as Nazi sympathizers, which moved him at last to protest in a dignified letter to the *Times* that, although like many people he had once hoped for Anglo-German understanding, he was no less faithful to his country now than when he had served in the trenches of the First World War.

Such incidents reflected the dangerous currents which flowed beneath much of the surface frivolity. The intellectual climate of Britain between the wars had been for the most part pacifist and socialist. It was Stanley Baldwin who, characteristically, dismissed the intelligentsia as bearing the same relationship to intelligence as gents bore to gentlemen. These intellectuals included many journalists, broadcasters, and popular publicists, whose propaganda, direct and indirect, had been devoted to bringing about social revolution, peacefully if possible, but if not . . . Young intellectuals, who as members of the Left Book Club supported the Popular Front, exercised their limbs at week-ends upon the Sussex Downs, while exercising their minds by endlessly debating whether the British governing class could be expected to surrender power peacefully, and, concluding that it could not, went on to consider what form the consequent revolution was likely to take. They saw Hitler's Nazi government in Germany as the manifestation of counterrevolution, and suspected the British governing class of having more than a little sympathy with it.

The government, on the other hand, feared the effects of Russian subversion exercised through a small number of devoted Communists and the very much larger number of their sympathizers. In March, 1938, Chamberlain referred to "the Russians stealthily and cunningly pulling all the strings behind the scenes to get us involved in war with Germany (our Secret Service doesn't spend all its time looking out of the window)" and almost on his deathbed, he counseled his closest colleague, the Foreign Secretary, Lord Halifax, against placing too much trust in Russia. Fear of a return to the financial crisis of 1931, with the opportunity it had offered for Communist and extreme Socialist proselytizing, conditioned much prewar government thinking. Until March, 1938, the Cabinet had ruled that the course of normal trade must not be impeded by rearmament, and even after that ruling had been rescinded following the Nazi advance into Austria, the Minister for the Coordination of Defence was surprised to be told that the government considered the dangers of a financial crash to be even greater than those of a military debacle.

Distrust ran deep on both sides, though not as deeply as in France, where a state approaching civil war had existed since

1934. "Better Hitler than Blum" had been a slogan coined by French industrialists to express their hatred of the Popular Front government headed by a mild and erudite Socialist littérateur of great charm and, as subsequently transpired, considerable physical courage. Blum's wartime successor, the radical Daladier, arrested many Communists, but was more lenient with those Frenchmen who preferred Hitler to Blum. "I have opened the abscess," he told a questioner, "but it was so deep the scalpel disappeared down it, and had I gone on, my arm would have followed."

To these internal strains in France was added the resentment of having been forced by the British into what many regarded as an unnecessary war over Poland, and to this initial resentment was allied distrust of British intentions to prosecute the war seriously. The French publicly claimed to have mobilized six and a half million men, their British allies not a quarter that number. French industry was so short of men that armament production was seriously disrupted, while the British had about a million and a half unemployed. French suggestions that Britain should export five hundred thousand of these surplus workers to man French industry were coolly received. The French offered to disband ten of their second-line divisions, returning the men to the factories, and handing over their equipment for the training of British troops. Unfortunately, while the British had insufficient equipment of their own, French arms were not up to British standards, and the offer was regretfully declined. Until British formations began manning a sector of the Maginot Line at the rate of a brigade at a time, many Frenchmen were unaware that there was a British Expeditionary Force in France; and some Frenchmen in close contact with the B.E.F.—there were eventually ten divisions—found in the British regular soldier a distressing tendency to looting and lechery, while British officers were said to be standoffish and prickly. "When you went to see the British officially, they would give you perfectly correct answers to any question, but nothing more," noted one French officer who frequently met the B.E.F.*

---

* Marc Bloch, *Strange Defeat*. I have used Bloch's narrative at several points, in preference to other French accounts, first because he was a professional historian, who understood that evidence is not always what it seems, and also because, unlike some of his countrymen, he made a noble attempt to understand the British point of view. He was shot by the Germans in 1944, a reminder that for many Frenchmen the war did not end with Pétain's Armistice.

German propaganda drilled incessantly at the exposed nerve of French fear that Britain was prepared to fight to the last French soldier. From German bombers descended, not bombs, but colored leaves, bearing on one side the message, "In the autumn the leaves fall. So fall the *poilus,* fighting for the English"; on the other side the words, "In the spring the leaves come again. Not so the *poilus."*

The French troops were also subjected to a second front of propaganda from the powerful French Communist party which, since the Nazi-Soviet Pact of August, 1939, had proclaimed that the war was a struggle between capitalists and no concern of the workers.

Under these conflicting pressures the French army, publicly proclaimed as the most powerful in Europe, began perceptibly to disintegrate. Carton de Wiart, a visiting British general, noted that men with too little to do and women left at home with neither husbands nor lovers provided a ripe seedbed for mischief. Lieutenant General Alan Brooke, the commander of the British First Corps, attended a celebration parade mounted by the French General Corap, whose Ninth Army manned the French line north of the Maginot fortifications, along the Luxembourg and Belgian frontiers. Brooke observed that the soldiers were unshaved, their horses ungroomed, their vehicles dirty, and their clothes and saddlery fitted badly. The American Under-Secretary of State, Sumner Welles, touring Europe in the spring of 1940, reported to his government that French officers complained about the lack of discipline among their men. Fears were expressed that, if Hitler delayed his attack on the Western front for long enough, the French rank-and-file would spontaneously disband themselves and go home.

The French were already half-convinced that the British did not intend seriously to fight. Such British generals as the French-born Brooke—though not Lord Gort, the Commander-in-Chief of the British Expeditionary Force, nor Sir Edmund Ironside, the Chief of the Imperial General Staff—afterward claimed to have become convinced that the French would not fight either.

Insulated by their own contempt for foreigners and by what they, but not their neighbors, call the English Channel, the British people were nevertheless subjected to some of the same pressures as the French. The British Communist party, never strong in numbers, had lost support as a result of the Nazi-Soviet Pact and the Russian attack on Finland in December, 1939. Even such a well-known and well-liked Communist as Harry Pollitt could collect fewer than a thousand votes as antiwar candidate in a by-election in the East End of London early in 1940. A member of the Communist party recalls having to flee for his life when he tried to sell the *Daily Worker* in a London working-class suburb. His attackers consisted of an angry mob of drunken women who were sympathetic with the cause of Finland. However, the devoted and hard-working British Communists had a considerable nuisance value. The activities of one party member in North London may be taken as typical of the unspectacular whole. Party instructions were that members must not allow themselves to be isolated, but should take the lead in local activities and inject a note of criticism whenever possible. This party member therefore became a part-time civil-defense volunteer, and led a local campaign of agitation against the government's refusal to provide deep air-raid shelters. By day, he was a conscientious, well-liked foreman at a small factory slowly changing from the peacetime production of light metal goods to the manufacture of seaplane floats and ammunition boxes. Shortly before Christmas, 1939, the firm's owner saw the opportunity of a useful profit by using surplus material from the ammunition boxes to produce multicolored toy bricks. On Christmas Eve, the foreman was invited out by his men for traditional drinks, which they took a traditional pleasure in mixing for him. He returned hilariously to the factory and sprayed paint over the hundreds of bricks while roaring out, "What a —— profitable war effort! Toy bricks!" His previous efforts at the political education of his men had been unavailing; but this was a point they could understand, and the government's popularity in one factory fell just a little.

In a democracy at war, there is a very fine dividing line between legitimate criticism, plain bellyaching, and subversion. No one, for instance, could question the patriotism of the proprietor of the *Daily Express*, Lord Beaverbrook, but at this time he stood far removed from the centers of political power, a situation never wholly congenial to his ardent temperament; and he happened to

have in his employment some of the most brilliant journalists of
their day, who also held Left Wing or antigovernment views. At
the beginning of January, the *Express* felt called upon to defend
its critical attitude toward the government. In a leading article it
pictured The Man in the Train complaining about his favorite
newspaper's carping; but, said the *Express,* it wanted to win the
war, and it was only turning the spotlight on government delays in
mobilizing the war effort.

The spotlight, by accident or design, ranged widely over a number of points of national disunity and discontent. Was it right,
asked the *Express,* that Army Other Ranks should be excluded
from bars used by officers? Were not army rations greater than
those for civilians? An *Express* reporter, detailed to consume as
many calories as were allowed for girls of the Auxiliary Territorial
Service, had to report that, for once, she had failed to complete an
assignment. What were Dr. Arnold Toynbee and his staff doing at
Balliol College, Oxford, where they received £5,000 a month of
the taxpayers' money for examining foreign newspapers and supplying occasional memoranda for government departments? Were
not divisional officers at gasoline rationing stations largely drawn
from retired colonial civil servants and ex-army officers who, lacking in commercial experience, were given to quite arbitrary awards
of supplementary fuel coupons? Had not civil-defense workers
landed themselves safe, cushy jobs at the public expense? The *Express* was happily able to report that in such towns as Southampton
and Coventry, the weekly bills for Air Raid Precautions had been
substantially reduced.

Other popular newspapers contributed their share of such
trenchant criticism; and there were indeed many causes for complaint in a nation turning over, still sluggishly and amateurishly,
from peace to war. By the beginning of 1940, half the families in
the country had one or more members on the move. Wives and
children had been evacuated from the towns at the beginning of
the war, young men were called up for the services, workers moved
from the depressed areas of Tyneside and South Wales to busy
armament centers like Coventry and Oxford. Another two million
young men, warned that they would shortly be called up, found it
difficult to take their civilian jobs very seriously. To what seemed
like an unnecessary breakup of family life were added a multitude

of worries. Government supplementary payments to the wives of drafted soldiers were tardy and inadequate. A correspondent reported to the *Times* that, in a case known to him, a wife with two children was left about a pound—less than five dollars—a week to feed and clothe her family. There was an all too glaring contrast between cases of this kind and advertisements still appearing in the *Times* for "Butler-valet and cook (married couple), Surrey, 10 servants. £160."

The Prime Minister, in a tighten-your-belts speech at the Mansion House early in January, described the sacrifices already made by the wealthy, and called for a halt in wage claims by the workers. But "You don't want to work hard for them, they've got more money than you" was a not untypical worker's reaction to Chamberlain's appeal.

Nor was financial worry confined to the working classes. It was weeks, sometimes months, before recently drafted officers got their pay, and their wives were forced to the indignity of borrowing from friends. Fashionable London doctors joining the services found their incomes suddenly reduced to £400 a year, and owed as much as £700 in back rent for their unused consulting rooms. The government's military advisers, convinced of the danger of an annihilating blow from the air, insisted on the evacuation of many government departments from London. Married men had to leave their families behind, and support two homes on inadequate allowances, living themselves in dreary seaside lodgings or commandeered hotels. There were reports of threatened strikes by civil servants under sentence of evacuation, unless the cost of billeting was met, and the government workers were provided with monthly travel passes to visit their families.

On the outbreak of war, more than a million and a quarter mothers and children had been evacuated from cities and towns. A proportion of them came from the slums of London, Liverpool, Glasgow, Birmingham, Manchester; and people who had been intellectually aware for some time of such abstractions as "problem families," "depressed areas," "the underprivileged," found themselves confronted by the reality in their own sitting rooms. Some of the children were verminous, and quickly distributed the vermin among others. Others had no underclothes, and were sown into canvas shrouds. Some refused to sit at tables, which they had not got in their own homes, but ate "doorsteps" of bread and marge squatting on the floor. One boy, unused to beds, could only sleep lying against the leg of a bed, clinging to it with one hand and resting his head against it. Sanitary habits followed their own conventions. "You dirty thing, messing the lady's carpet. Go and do it in the corner," one Glasgow mother was reported as saying to her six-year-old.

The first outcry was directed against the evacuees themselves. One M.P. from a country area told the House of Commons that his constituents would go to prison rather than take such people in again. Some of the well-to-do were said to have escaped the horror by closing their homes and moving to hotels. Then there was a great searching of conscience as liberal Britain—not for the first or the last time during the war—sprang to the defense of the defenseless, and feeling turned away from the children toward the conditions from which they had come. Much of the welcome given by ordinary people of all political parties to welfare legislation during and after the war stemmed from the personal shock of those early evacuation months; but, meanwhile, blame was heaped upon the government: how had such things been allowed to happen in one of the richest nations the world had ever known?

All these discontents sprouted like mushrooms in the long cold winter's black-out. The black-out headed every list of current grumbles. It was symbolic, as if with war the lights of civilization had indeed gone out forever. No one who had once lived with the black-out can forget the exhilaration of visiting a lighted city, Dublin perhaps, or Durban, where light flooded from the windows like water pouring on a man lost in the desert. One almost bathed in the light, sluiced in it, stood drinking it in, even the vulgarity of cinema and advertising signs. But the black-out also had a physical effect. In a Gallup Poll published in January, no fewer than 18 per cent of those interviewed claimed to have suffered some physical injury because of it, not only in road accidents, but by stumbling over unlit curbs, colliding with sandbagged Air Raid Precautions posts and other obstacles.* A heartfelt letter to the *Times* demanded that running in the black-out should be made a punishable offense.

* Compare this percentage with the 3 per cent who, by October, claimed to have suffered injury in air raids.

At the beginning of the war, the Air Raid Precautions warden in his tin hat, usually a neighbor, had been a father-figure, symbolizing protection. One of them remembers with humility how, conscious of his own amateurishness and of the responsibility which seemed to rest on his shoulders, he went from house to house in the early days, testing gas masks. A policeman, a clergyman, the mother of a baby, all regarded him as if he were the bringer of life itself. But wardens were also responsible for ensuring that no chink of light escaped from a window between dusk and dawn, and by January they were hated, "I loathe every warden, and would like to murder them," was one comment to Mass Observation.

Some extraordinary cases were reported. To extinguish a hundred-watt lamp left burning in a temporarily vacant house, a policeman forced a double-locked door, first with his shoulder, then with an iron bar. The door was of mahogany, framed in oak, and set in concrete. The damage cost £15 to repair; on hearing that, the magistrate considerately reduced the offender's fine from £2 to £1.

A motorist driving a blacked-out car halted cautiously in an alleyway before turning into the main road. A pedestrian walked into the car and injured himself. The county court judge awarded the pedestrian £15 damages and costs, and ruled that, black-out regulations notwithstanding, a person obstructing the highway must either light the obstruction or give other warning, even if the obstruction were only temporary. Few city-dwellers had not experienced, or heard at secondhand, of some such apparent absurdity, and the effect on normally law-abiding citizens was to turn them insidiously against authority.

As if to demonstrate that criminals, too, were patriots, crime figures had fallen at the beginning of the war, but to the criminal classes the black-out provided an irresistible opportunity. With winter came an outbreak of robberies on the public highway. One London gang, waiting at main-line railway stations, pretended to be a party of drunks roistering home. They would throw their arms hilariously around the selected victim, pinning him while one picked his pockets. If he fought back, they beat him insensible, and left him in the road, as likely as not to be run over by a blacked-out car.

Children were assaulted, girls followed. There were whispers of immorality. One Mass Observer reported, "I have heard of two or three cases where young men have boasted of intercourse in a shop doorway on the fringe of passing crowds, screened by another couple who were waiting to perform the same adventure. It has been done in a spirit of daring, but is described as being perfectly easy and rather thrilling."

In spite of such compensations, there was constant pressure to relax the black-out, and envious references to Paris and Berlin, where it was less severe. If the German bombers had come, of course, it would have been different; but they had not come. What was the *point* of it? Did the government merely want to make people miserable, to convince them, against all the evidence, that there was, in the current phrase, a war on? Early in January Sir John Anderson, the Home Secretary, perhaps the greatest administrator of his day, but no hand at public relations, sought to defend it. "One might imagine," he declared, "that the black-out was invented by Bumbledom. Civil servants are as likely as anyone to stumble on sandbags and miss the curb." The public, though not wholly convinced that civil servants shared their sufferings, found the thought gratifying.

Although public speaking was an ordeal to King George VI because of a stammer, he had decided that on Christmas Day, 1939, the first Christmas Day of the war, it was his duty to revive his father's custom of broadcasting a message to his people. He was not a man to shrink from duty, which in the end killed him at the age of fifty-six; and being a simple man as well as a dutiful one, he did not perhaps realize—though his advisers may have been aware— how much people felt drawn to him by their consciousness of his audible fight with, and often-repeated victory over, a painful handicap.

While his Christmas broadcast message was in preparation, a clipping from the *Times* had been sent to Buckingham Palace. It contained some words found written on a postcard in the desk of a dead Bristol doctor. The doctor's daughters had used the words on greeting cards, one of which was received by Mrs. J. C. M. Allen of Clifton, who kept it and, thinking the words appropriate at the outbreak of war, passed them on to the *Times*.

Shortly after three o'clock on Christmas Day, King George's hesitant, upper-class, undramatic voice broadcast them to the world: "A new year is at hand. We cannot tell what it will bring. If it brings peace, how thankful we shall all be. If it brings us continued struggle we shall remain undaunted. In the meantime I feel that we may all find a message of encouragement in the lines which, in my closing words, I would like to say to you: 'I said to the man who stood at the Gate of the Year, "Give me a light that I may tread safely into the unknown." And he replied, "Go out into the darkness, and put your hand into the Hand of God. That shall be to you better than light, and safer than a known way." ' "

In newspaper offices, advance copies of the speech led to a frantic search for the authorship of the quotation, and cables came from New York, seeking enlightenment for the American public. The Poet Laureate advanced the cautious opinion that the lines sounded like G. K. Chesterton. Others attributed them to John Bunyan and Thomas à Kempis. It was not until midnight that the B.B.C. was able to announce the name of the author, sixty-four-year-old Miss Minnie Louise Haskins.

Miss Haskins, a retired lecturer of the London School of Economics, then living at Crowborough, in Sussex, had not heard the King's broadcast, but had been listening during the evening to a B.B.C. summary of the speech, when the words spoken struck her as "oddly familiar." Not until the quotation was finished did she remember that, many years before, she had written something like this in a slim volume of verse called *The Desert,* which had been privately printed in 1908 and sold in aid of Zenana missionary work in India.

Within a few days, despite protests from clergymen that Bunyan and the author of the Gospel according to St. John had said it better, Miss Haskins was famous. Her volume of verse, republished, passed through eight editions, and remained in print until 1943, by which time forty-three thousand copies had been sold. It achieved for her what a lifetime's work in factory welfare and social science had been unable to do: an entry in *Who's Who* and an obituary in the *Times* when she died in 1957.

Perhaps this assessment of its worth was a just one. Miss Haskins' words may not have been the most heroic banner under which to advance into a year which changed the course of world history, but they were not inappropriate for a decent, puzzled, discontented people who had braced themselves to withstand Armageddon, and found themselves instead facing the petty miseries of burst water pipes, a shortage of coal, verminous evacuees, and the dim spiritual erosion of the black-out.

Chapter

2

THE GENERALS' PLOT

The National government upon which so much of the discontent focused commanded a majority of more than two hundred and twenty votes in the House of Commons over its combined Labour and Liberal opponents.

It had reached the zenith of its popularity in the weeks following the Munich agreement of September, 1938, when a pacifically inclined nation had felt itself snatched back at the last moment from what it believed to be the brink of war. An observer of the Prime Minister's return from Munich noted that he had never seen so shameful a sight in his life—the huge crowd seemed ready to roll on the ground like worshipers at the Juggernaut festival to let Neville Chamberlain ride in glory over them.

The inevitable reaction from such an exaggerated sense of relief was an equally emotional sense of shame. Two by-elections, at Oxford City and Bridgewater, revealed the beginning of a public swing of opinion against the government, strengthening the position of small groups of critics on the government's own backbenches which had come together under the leadership of three former ministers, Winston Churchill, Anthony Eden, and Leopold Amery. Two of them, Churchill and Eden, had rejoined the government at the outbreak of war. Churchill became First Lord of the Admiralty and a member of the War Cabinet. Eden, who as

Foreign Secretary had been at the center of power, now found himself only on the fringe of the inner circle, as Secretary of State for the Dominions.

Outside the dissident Conservative groups were an increasing number of government backbenchers, particularly the young, the well-born, and those in the services, who, in a frivolous but revealing reference to the Prime Minister's Victorian dress and provincial background, "couldn't stand those boots and all that Birmingham nonsense." Some sixty members of this largely Conservative House of Commons were in the army, which suffered the greatest shortage of equipment among the three services. Officers were often unable to fire even one practice round from the pistols which were their only personal weapon, and training with live ammunition for Bren guns and rifles was strictly rationed. As the shortages revealed themselves, not altogether friendly looks were cast by their army colleagues at the officer-politicians, and the half-joking inquiry was made, "Well, what are you going to do about it?"

Upon civilian M.P.'s descended a weekly burden of constituency grumbles about food rationing, which was first introduced at the beginning of 1940, about the impossibility of obtaining grain for the backyard hens which the government had enjoined all good householders to keep, about private property requisitioned for government use at the start of the war and since left to stand empty, about evacuees, and the black-out, and the shortage of coal.

The Prime Minister, however, still got his cheer as he left Number Ten Downing Street for the House of Commons, and political commentators noted, some of them grudgingly, that his mastery of the Commons was unchallenged. Invited by the Gallup Poll in December, 1939, to choose between Chamberlain and Churchill as Prime Minister, the public gave fifty-two votes to Chamberlain in proportion to thirty for Churchill.

The War Cabinet consisted of nine men, of whom four formed an inner council which consisted of the Prime Minister himself; the Foreign Secretary, Lord Halifax; the Chancellor of the Exchequer, Sir John Simon; and the Lord Privy Seal, Sir Samuel Hoare.

Two of these four, Chamberlain and Hoare, had held high office almost continuously since the early 1920's. Dapper, a little fussy, the Cabinet's "fixer" of press opinion, Hoare was an able man, though perhaps too well aware of his ability. He had been Secretary of State for Air during the formative years of the Royal Air Force, then, as Secretary of State for India, had achieved a parliamentary triumph by piloting a reforming India Bill through the Commons against fierce opposition from some of his own backbenchers, led by Churchill. As Foreign Secretary, he had supported a plan initiated by Laval, the French Foreign Minister, for conceding Abyssinian territory to the invading Italians, and public outcry had forced his resignation, though he quickly returned to office as First Lord of the Admiralty. First with the India Bill, then with the Hoare-Laval Pact, he had antagonized successively the reactionary and progressive wings of his own party; and he had committed the sin of having been in office for a very long time.

Simon, the Chancellor of the Exchequer, had been Foreign Secretary during the period of Japanese aggression in the Far East and of Hitler's rise to power in Germany, and has some claim to be considered the most disastrous holder of that office in the present century. He was a brilliant though pedantic lawyer, who had a touching personal longing to be liked. One of his colleagues noted that he was constantly trying to secure the friendship of other people on terms more favorable to himself. It was said of him as Chancellor that he seemed primarily concerned with making sure that Britain had enough money left to pay the indemnity after losing the war. The verdict was unfair—Britain was shortly to be saved from bankruptcy only by the help of the United States—but Simon was a man doomed to attract such unfair verdicts, to some extent because he was at such pains to avoid them.

Halifax, the Foreign Secretary, Fellow of All Souls, Master of Foxhounds, a reforming Viceroy of India, was one of those able servants of the state with a truly English gift for backing into the limelight. He never sought high office, but high office was always being thrust upon him, and he conscientiously shouldered the burden. A devout Anglo-Catholic, who saw every problem in terms of Christian morality and went down on his knees to seek guidance in crises great or small, he was not incapable of the kind of ruthlessness shown by his grandfather, the Chancellor of the Exchequer at the time of the Irish famine. Unexpectedly, in a man tall, cadaverous and apparently grave of mien, he had an engaging sense of humor and a skeptical eye for what he regarded as rhetoric or pomposity. Perhaps the most acute verdict on him has been written by himself. Describing in his diary a visit to the remains of a house that had belonged to Lord Gainsborough, which Gainsborough had burnt rather than allow it to fall into the hands of Oliver Cromwell, Halifax noted, "I could not have done that myself, for I should always have hoped to get Oliver Cromwell out again."

Finally, Neville Chamberlain, the Prime Minister, who in 1940 reached his seventy-first birthday, was a man, in the words of a political opponent, of unusual integrity, obstinate courage, and restricted sympathies.* Chamberlain's personality, like his policies, tended to excite extremes of personal involvement. Of his appeasement policy, which has been endlessly criticized, it should be said that the case against it is by no means as clear-cut as has sometimes been made out, and his attempt to detach the Italian dictator Mussolini from his alliance with Hitler was nearly successful enough for the Germany Army Chief of Staff, in January, 1940, to consider it wise to move German troops to the Italian border passes as a precautionary measure.

Chamberlain's personality was complex. He was not, as has sometimes been suggested, a weak man, but a strong one in an uncommon way. One of the notable things about him is the contrast between his public image—the old, feeble umbrella-carrier, hanging onto office "like a dirty old piece of chewing-gum on the leg of a chair," in one elegant Conservative rebel phrase—and the Chamberlain men found when they came to work with him. The trade-union leader Lord Citrine comments on his frankness, once trust had been established; Sir Edmund Ironside, the Chief of the Imperial General Staff, who saw him frequently under stress, remarked on his resilience, imperturbability, efficiency; Lord Attlee, with whom he was not on good personal terms, pays a characteristically laconic tribute: "a good chairman, a good committee man, always very businesslike. You could work with him."

This strength was qualified by certain weaknesses. He was an unusually loyal colleague, though there was about his loyalty more than a hint of arrogance, as if he were saying, "I have selected these men for their offices. How can I be wrong?" Shy and sensitive him-

---

* An anonymous writer in the *New Statesman* of November 16, 1940. Although written as a fairly hostile obituary notice, this still reads as a perceptive summing-up of Chamberlain.

self, he had the shy man's egocentric insensitivity to the feelings of others, and his aloofness even from the upper hierarchy of his own party led him into the kind of minor political blunder which caused one of his backbenchers to describe him as the silliest clever man of his time. A clear-headed and logical thinker within his own rather narrow terms, he was intolerant of what he considered to be muddleheadedness in others; impatient of criticism; sometimes vindictive to those who had opposed him. By 1940 he had made many enemies.

At the beginning of September, 1939, when the Cabinet had agreed to prepare for a war lasting three years, Chamberlain laid his forehead on the table and kept it there for nearly ten minutes. When he looked up, his face was ghastly. He was not a war Prime Minister, and knew it, but continued to believe that as an efficient chairman of committees, an experienced manipulator of men, he could guide the country more ably than any other potential leader. Though vanity and obstinacy may have had their human share in this appreciation as well as the laudable desire to serve his country, the appreciation itself, at the beginning of 1940, was not entirely wrong. The practical alternatives, if he had resigned on the outbreak of war, would have been Hoare, Simon, or conceivably Halifax. But as a war Prime Minister he had two disadvantages which overrode his many good qualities: he was logical, but not quite logical enough; and he was not, as the phrase goes, a lucky general.

Of the five War Cabinet members outside this inner circle, two, Admiral of the Fleet Lord Chatfield and Lord Hankey, were not professional politicians, a situation always liable to induce a feeling among professionals not in office that they could do the job better. In particular, Chatfield, Minister for the Coordination of Defence, suffered from the disadvantage that his nominal political junior, Churchill, had been First Lord of the Admiralty twenty-five years before when Chatfield himself had been a comparatively junior naval officer. Chatfield was a distinguished sailor, a former First Sea Lord and Chief of Naval Staff, Hankey an equally distinguished civil servant who had won his reputation as Secretary of the War Cabinet under Lloyd George in the First World War. "Neville put Hankey into the War Cabinet instead of me because he thought that it was Hankey who had won the war," commented that distinguished veteran, with characteristic malice.

Coordinated by Chatfield were the three service ministers. Sir Kingsley Wood, the Secretary of State for Air, was a solicitor by profession, a pillar of Wesleyan Methodism, whose cherubic look of an elderly choirboy did not entirely conceal what the *Times,* in its obituary of him, called, "a thorough understanding of current political values." He had been Chamberlain's Parliamentary Secretary at the Ministry of Health in 1924, and had climbed the political ladder under Chamberlain's patronage.

Leslie Hore-Belisha, the Secretary of State for War, and youngest member of the War Cabinet, was also largely Chamberlain's creation. He had been a dynamic Minister of Transport with a flair for public relations when, in 1937, Chamberlain sent him to the War Office to reorganize an army starved of money and bogged down in controversy over its future role. Hore-Belisha was a Jew and an admirer of Disraeli; he saw no reason why a Jew should not, for a second time in history, guide the destinies of his country. He was not a Conservative, but, like Simon, a National Liberal, and as the politically weakest link in the group about Chamberlain, he had at least once previously been used as a target by Conservative critics seeking to bring down the Chamberlain government.

The third member of this service triumvirate, *primus inter pares,* was the First Lord of the Admiralty, a man of sixty-five, burning with a sense of destiny, who saw the minutes, hours, years ticking coldly away while he grew older, and lesser men continued to hold the center of the stage.

Winston Churchill, at the beginning of 1940, was known as an erratic politician, suspect to all parties. To Conservatives, he was the man responsible for the tragedy of Gallipoli, who had twice crossed the floor of the House, and had shown his disloyalty by publicly opposing first Baldwin, then Chamberlain. He had won some support on the Conservative backbenches as a prophet of the coming Armageddon, then forfeited much of it as a result of his characteristically impetuous charge to the rescue of King Edward VIII at the time of the abdication crisis. After Munich, Conservative loyalists had turned their backs when he passed them in the corridors of the House, and his constituency association had come close to passing a motion of no confidence in him. To most Labour members he was a dangerous warmonger, the man who had returned Britain disastrously to the Gold Standard, making inevitable a general strike in which he had wanted to fight the trade unions to a finish. One of the excuses given for Chamberlain's reluctance to recall Churchill to office until the outbreak of war was that this would have achieved the remarkable effect of antagonizing both Hitler and the British Labour party.

Among members of a War Cabinet not notably warlike, he resembled a huge, cigar-smoking cuckoo in a nest of hedge sparrows, this legendary and uncomfortable figure from another age who had charged with the Twenty-first Lancers at Omdurman; this last of the Whig grandees among sisal-planters and Wesleyan Methodist solicitors. "A child's emotion and a man's reason" was how Halifax, always skeptical of Churchillian rhetoric, summed him up. Others, with good cause, often doubted his judgment, and found him, according to their temperaments, voluble, irrelevant, ardent, inspiring, tempestuous, or just a plain bloody nuisance, determined to poke a finger into every pie.

As soon as Churchill was installed at the Admiralty, he began bombarding the Prime Minister with a series of daily letters, often several pages long, exploding with ideas, ranging far beyond the legitimate concern of his department. Chamberlain sent for him, told him that his proper course was to raise these various matters with the Cabinet colleagues concerned. Churchill contritely agreed, swore that he was wholeheartedly behind Chamberlain, sought no extended powers for himself. "I believe all this was quite genuine," the Prime Minister noted. Others of his colleagues were less sure about the extended powers.

The first of the hedge sparrows to get pushed out of the nest was the smallest and weakest, the Secretary of State for War, Hore-Belisha. In so far as opinion polls are a guide, Hore-Belisha ranked only after Eden—always the popular favorite—and Churchill in public popularity. Newspaper photographs and newsreels frequently showed him chatting to the troops, drinking beer in sergeants' messes, tasting with apparent enjoyment the products of army cookery. He was associated in the public mind with a campaign to "democratize" the army, improving pay and conditions for the ordinary soldier, commissioning men from the ranks. When he visited a military establishment, the Other Ranks genuinely cheered. He was one of the few politicians who would be recognized with a shout of "Good old H-B" when his car stopped at traffic lights.

When Hore-Belisha went to the War Office in 1937, Britain, inventor of the tank, was in the process of painfully forming its first home-based armored division. Asked to recommend a commander for this division, Sir Cyril Deverell, then the Chief of the Imperial General Staff, put forward the name of the fifty-nine-year-old Inspector of Cavalry and Commandant of the Army Equitation School. The new Secretary of State, who had been appointed with an express brief to deal with obscurantist generals, rejected this expert on horseflesh, and suggested that a general with at least some experience with tanks might be desirable. He was told that cavalry officers could not be asked to serve under an officer from the comparatively new mechanized branch; besides, it would not be possible for the wives of cavalry officers to call on the one tank officer otherwise qualified, because, some ten years before, he had been divorced. The Secretary of State and the C.I.G.S. eventually compromised on an artillery officer, Major General Alan Brooke; and the Secretary of State made up his mind—perhaps had made up his mind even before he reached the War Office—that he and the C.I.G.S. must part company.

The obvious successor to Deverell was the General Officer Commanding-in-Chief at Aldershot, Sir John Dill, but Dill, who was later to stand up to more than a year of Churchillian battering, was considered to be tired and in poor health. Wavell was passed over as too inarticulate. Casting about, Hore-Belisha hit upon what he believed to be a brilliant coup. He would assure the public that the new broom at the War Office was sweeping very clean by promoting a comparatively junior man, who was, moreover, a V.C. of the First World War and a hereditary viscount. At the same time, the appointment of this junior but popular and respected general would soothe the army's feelings which had been upset by the summary dismissal of Deverell. Hore-Belisha's appointment as Chief of the Imperial General Staff was Major General Lord Gort, V.C., D.S.O., M.C., aged fifty-one, and at that time serving as Military Secretary to the Secretary of State, a position which afforded him opportunities for urging his own claims.

As it turned out, the appointment was disastrous for Hore-Belisha and unfortunate for Gort. Not the least of Gort's qualifications, in the Secretary of State's eyes, was that he could be used to provide an imposing façade, floodlit by Hore-Belisha, while other people did the real work behind the scenes. This was not a position Gort was prepared to accept, and it led to constant friction, exacerbated by Hore-Belisha's methods of working. Like Lloyd George, he would not read government documents, but had them read to him, sometimes in his bath, while dressing, or eating breakfast. Particular offense was caused to the army by his practice of summoning Gort to his house at Wimbledon and talking to him from his bed. In his anxiety to secure for the army a public regard which had been lacking—and thus obtain for it more money, more men, more equipment—he was accused by the War Office hierarchy of in effect issuing a false prospectus on the army's preparedness for war. He listened a great deal—though not enough —to the advice of one known to some in the War Office as "that damned writing feller," Captain B. H. Liddell Hart, now more generously recognized as the most able military thinker of his day, whose doctrines, largely ignored in his own country, formed the basis for the Germans' overwhelming victory in France.

Hore-Belisha was intensely publicity-conscious. The War Office was not. Elderly generals kept London dinner tables amused with stories of the publicity-seeking Secretary of State visiting Aldershot accompanied by his own photographer,* and even his devoted Military Assistant De Guingand, who at first disliked him but later held him in high regard, found him susceptible to the slightest newspaper pressure. Hours would be spent over a letter in the *Daily Mirror* from a soldier, complaining that he could not be expected to live on half a sausage for breakfast.

Finally—and in this respect it might be claimed that he was at last hanged with a rope he had fashioned himself—he took a step which made him many enemies, not only among army officers, but in the noncommissioned ranks. With the laudable desire of easing the passage into army life of conscripted or volunteer civilians, he let it be known that if any soldiers' families had problems, they might write to the Secretary of State himself at the War Office. National servicemen, and some regular soldiers, quickly realized that "family problems" could, with a little ingenuity, be stretched

---

* Rommel, too, had a personal photographer. It does not seem to have diminished his efficiency.

to include their own grievances, real or imaginary, thus bypassing the service channels through which King's Regulations decreed that complaints must be made and, it was claimed, seriously undermining discipline.

Politically, Hore-Belisha stood in a dangerously vulnerable position. He was a Jew and a National Liberal, an unpopular combination among the Anglo-Saxon Conservatives who made up the bulk of the government majority, and he had no political backing except that of the Prime Minister himself. Chamberlain in his rearmament program had deliberately given priority to the Royal Air Force and the Royal Navy, with the army taking what was left when air and sea demands had been, if not satisfied, silenced. It had been assumed that the British army would not again fight a continental war. As a sop to the French this decision was changed in the spring of 1939, less than six months before war broke out. Hore-Belisha himself risked his political life by forcing upon a reluctant Prime Minister a measure of conscription and the doubling, on paper, of the size of the Territorial Army, although these purely political decisions made little military sense, and faced the army with problems of equipment and supply which could not conceivably have been solved in the time available.

Hore-Belisha was very nearly a great Secretary of State. Chamberlain called him the best since Haldane—the competition, it must be remarked, is not formidable. He was, however, aggressively tactless, and unlike Haldane he was not a good organizer. Gort was not the man to redress the balance. With his look of an anxious bulldog, the new C.I.G.S. has generally been depicted as a brave, simple infantry brigadier, promoted above his capacity, who knew all about his men's boots and the tactics of a battalion in attack. This was true enough as far as it went, but it did not go the whole way. Brave he certainly was, but also obstinate and resentful of criticism. Once installed as C.I.G.S., he was quick to recognize that new brooms can sweep clean only once, and that the Secretary of State could dismiss him only at grave risk to his own political head. He became almost as obstructive to Hore-Belisha's intended reforms as his predecessor had been. Above all Gort was ambitious, with no balancing interest outside the army and his career, and his ambition lay in a passionate desire to gain distinction by commanding an army in the field.

With the approach of war, he pressed Hore-Belisha to appoint him as Commander-in-Chief of the British Expeditionary Force which was to be sent to France. Hore-Belisha by that time was glad of an excuse to get Gort out of the War Office. There was, however, a difficulty. According to the precedent set in the First World War, command of the B.E.F. went to the Inspector General of the Forces, who in 1939 was General Sir Edmund Ironside. Ironside was so certain that he was to command the B.E.F. that he sent his staff down to Aldershot to mobilize G.H.Q., while he waited in London for what he regarded as the formality of appointment. Hours, days passed, and no word came to him. On the evening of September 3, some hours after Britain had declared war, the Secretary of State summoned him, and there took place an extraordinary interview, described by both Hore-Belisha and Ironside, which may be regarded as characteristic of Hore-Belisha's insensitivity in handling men.

The Secretary of State informed Ironside that Gort was to be Commander-in-Chief of the B.E.F. and Ironside Chief of the Imperial General Staff. He went on to tell the new C.I.G.S. that he was said to be unreliable, given to talking too much, and likely to upset the Chiefs-of-Staff Conferences. Nevertheless, he had the Secretary of State's complete confidence and could forthwith dismiss the conversation from his mind.

In these circumstances a man disappointed in obtaining the field command on which, like Gort, he had set his heart, took up an appointment for which he believed himself to be temperamentally unsuited. The British army entered the war with a Secretary of State, a Commander-in-Chief, and a C.I.G.S. who were not, to put it mildly, in happy accord.

The new C.I.G.S. was fifty-nine, six feet four inches tall, inevitably nicknamed Tiny, and said to be the original of John Buchan's Richard Hannay. His widowed mother had had to make substantial sacrifices to send him to Tonbridge, Woolwich, and into the Royal Field Artillery. He had had a varied military career —South Africa, France, Brigadier General Staff to the Allied Expedition to Archangel in 1918—but for periods between the wars his ship had lain becalmed. He was not a wealthy man, and had a young son to educate.

Ironside had desirable qualities of forcefulness and imagination. Being human, he also had defects. He was ambitious, and said to be an intriguer; what was worse, an unskilful one. He would appear in the Secretary of State's office with a paper embodying, no doubt, strategic truths, which somehow came down to emphasizing the desirability of an appointment for himself, or, slightly more subtly, a potential rival who would be better serving in India or the Middle East. The forcefulness of his character was more often apparent to his subordinates than to his superiors. To his subordinates he spoke of the War Cabinet as "the old gentlemen," the Secretary of State as "that little monkey," and he told his staff that when Hore-Belisha had appointed him, he had threatened to get rid of him if he found the Secretary of State going behind his back or speaking against his advice on military matters. In the Secretary of State's presence, however, he was not quite so forthright, "oozing charm and friendliness," in the words of one witness. Although his strategic views sometimes showed prescience, they were not always very stable. He would leave for a visit to France, breathing fire against the Allied Commander-in-Chief, the French General Gamelin—a nice little man, according to Ironside, in a well-cut pair of breeches—but would return as an impassioned advocate of French views, having accepted all that Gamelin laid down.

There is a fascinating picture, in Ironside's very honestly edited published diary, of a clever man at work playing, then landing, this valuable if simple fish. Churchill and Ironside had known each other in South Africa, and in 1937, Churchill asked to meet Ironside again. At that time, Ironside held the biggest home command in the army, and Churchill was the government's most formidable critic on defense. They came together at a Norfolk country house. Churchill expressed himself as "horrified" that Hore-Belisha had not seen Ironside before deciding on Gort as C.I.G.S. He himself, he promised, would see the Secretary of State and impress upon him that Ironside was not to be thrown over. Ironside, he was certain, had a great future before him. Ironside was exhilarated by the talk; it was a wonderful thing to have said to him by such a great man. Before long, he was confiding to the government's principal critic that neither the Cabinet nor the War Minister had any idea what the army was wanted for, that they were groping about for a solution and hadn't even begun to formulate a policy.

Not surprisingly, there had been stiff Cabinet opposition to Ironside's appointment as C.I.G.S. It had been forced through by Hore-Belisha, with Churchill's support. As C.I.G.S., Ironside remained in touch with Churchill, and he, Churchill, and Grigg, Permanent Under-Secretary at the War Office and formerly Churchill's Private Secretary at the Treasury, were in the habit of meeting from time to time. War had not long been declared before the Secretary of State for War was having to repel boarding operations from the Admiralty, carried out either by the First Lord in person, or through the intermediation of the C.I.G.S.

In November, 1939, Anthony Eden, the Dominions Secretary, conducted a party of Dominion ministers on a visit to the British Expeditionary Force. A number of them, accustomed to the trenches of the First World War, commented on what seemed to them the inadequacy of British defenses, and this criticism reached Hore-Belisha. The War Minister was a professional politician, very conscious of his exposed position. He himself had recently been to France, and had criticized the strength of the British defenses to Gort on apparently amicable terms. His characteristic reaction to the Dominion ministers' criticism, however, passed on by Eden to the Prime Minister, was that he was being "got at" by political enemies, and he in his turn sharpened his criticism of Gort.

It is worth remarking at this point that the discussion of defenses on the existing B.E.F. lines was to some extent academic. On November 9, after weeks of discussion, the War Cabinet had reluctantly accepted French proposals for an advance into Belgium in the event of a German attack through the Low Countries, and in this eventuality the B.E.F. defenses would be abandoned. There is evidence to suggest, however, that some of the British generals, notably Gort's Chief of Staff, Pownall, had made up their minds on the outbreak of war that, for the army's sake, Hore-Belisha would have to be got out of the War Office, and one cannot resist a surmise that, for some at G.H.Q. and in the War Office, the subject of disagreement rapidly became less important than the disagreement itself; that a welcome chance was taken to work on Gort's resentment of criticism to force the personal issue.

At the end of November, Ironside went over to France, for the purpose, as he said, of settling what by now had blown up into a major row. Banging about in his forceful way, Ironside often managed to kick up such a dust that he vanished utterly within the resulting smoke screen, and it is not at all clear who asked him to go to France. The Secretary of State seems to have thought it was the Prime Minister, the Prime Minister thought it was the Secretary of State, and in his diary Ironside claimed the initiative for himself. He was in any event the last man to be entrusted with the delicate mission of restoring strained relations between the Secretary of State and the Commander of the B.E.F. Although in the Army Council before his departure he had been forcefully rude about Gort, he returned an ally of the Commander-in-Chief, reporting that he had found all G.H.Q. "in a devil of a rage" over Hore-Belisha's criticism. He told Hore-Belisha and Chamberlain that Gort was threatening to resign; and he told his subordinates that the Secretary of State would have to go, adding, "It's time we had a better chap in the War Office."

At a very early stage of the controversy Ironside, according to his diary, had used a curious phrase to the Secretary of State: "I had to tell Belisha that he must be careful how he dealt with his C-in-C. He was put in by the King and must not be monkeyed about."

Early in December, the King visited the B.E.F. His brother the Duke of Gloucester, with the rank of major general, was Chief Liaison Officer at G.H.Q. and, accompanied by Gloucester, the King arrived at G.H.Q. on the evening of December 4. There he was given G.H.Q.'s views on the defense issue and, in the words of his biographer, "found that they bitterly resented Mr. Hore-Belisha's strictures, which they regarded as unwarranted, unsubstantiated, and unjust." Haig's direct approaches to King George V during the First World War have been generally censured. There seems no reason to place in a different category this direct approach of Gort to King George VI.

On his return, the King discussed the situation with Chamberlain. No one can question his constitutional right, which he jealously preserved, to advise, to encourage, and to warn. More questionable is his decision to entertain Gort's complaints in the first place, instead of sending him about his business with the kind of outsize rocket that would have greeted most subordinates bypassing authority. There is the further question of the King's wisdom in allowing himself to become involved in such a dubious affair at all. He had succeeded to the throne less than three years previously, in circumstances which had given the institution of British monarchy the severest shaking it had experienced for a century. Like Churchill, he had not yet established for himself the right to the popular respect which his subsequent conduct won for him.

When, a little later, Hore-Belisha resigned his office, the reaction of the popular press reflected the frenetic suspicion of the time that somebody, somewhere, was conspiring against democracy. Among the wilder assertions were that Hore-Belisha had been fired, at the instigation of British friends of the Nazis, because he was a Jew; that he was the victim of High Society intrigue to replace him by Oliver Stanley, son of the Earl of Derby; that the brass-hats were determined to get rid of him so that they could set up a military dictatorship. It is not too difficult to imagine what the reaction would have been if the King's part in the affair had become known, or of the damage which must have been done to national unity, and to the throne. From these possibilities, however, the King and the country were saved by the discretion of a man whom the King's generals regarded as a publicity-seeking bounder.

Three days after the King's return from France, Chamberlain sent for Hore-Belisha. He said the King had asked him to see Ironside, and added in a puzzled way that he did not really know what it was all about. Had Hore-Belisha confidence in Gort, and in Ironside? Hore-Belisha had doubts about them, but was now the prisoner of his own unfortunate appointments. He might perhaps have brought about the dismissal of one, but to change both the C.I.G.S. and the Commander-in-Chief at this point would clearly have given the government's political enemies the opportunity they were seeking to bring it down. He therefore replied that he had confidence in both of them. The Prime Minister assured the Secretary of State that he had only to tell him if he wanted a change. He added that Ironside was a tactless man.

On December 16, Chamberlain himself arrived in France. A visit to the B.E.F. by the Prime Minister had been discussed for some time, but there is no doubt that its date was decided by what Chamberlain had learned from the King. Gort again expressed his views with the utmost force, and the Prime Minister found that, by now, criticism of Hore-Belisha was not confined to the small circle of G.H.Q., but had been allowed to spread.

Notwithstanding this, Chamberlain saw the King on his return from France, and told him he was not thinking of removing Hore-Belisha from the War Office. On the same day, December 20, Chamberlain saw Hore-Belisha and discussed with him the situation he had found in France. According to Hore-Belisha, Chamberlain ended by saying that the Secretary of State had his complete confidence.

Also on December 20, Eden dined, among other guests, with Churchill. After dinner, Churchill and Kingsley Wood, who was also a guest, spoke about a pending reconstruction of the government, and Churchill "repeated his desire" that Eden should go to the War Office. "The project that I should go to the War Office was strongly pressed, particularly by Churchill, within the next week or two," Eden noted in his diary.*

Hore-Belisha admired Churchill and, with a simplicity unusual in a tough, professional politician, believed his friendship to be reciprocated. He was generally to be found supporting Churchill in the War Cabinet, although he had also strenuously resisted a number of attempts by the First Lord to meddle in War Office affairs. The final *casus belli* seems to have come over the arrival in Britain in December of two Canadian divisions, which the War Office wanted kept secret, but which the First Lord of the Admiralty, without consultation, had announced in a broadcast. Hore-Belisha was also involved in hostilities with Kingsley Wood, the Air Minister, over the principle of close support for the army by the R.A.F. A friendless man, he had indeed raised up for himself by the end of the year a multitude of powerful enemies.

What pressure the Prime Minister was under to get rid of Hore-Belisha can only be surmised; but he noted in his own diary that if a favorable opportunity came to move Hore-Belisha from the War Office, he had better take it and not wait for another crisis, since in wartime nothing could be worse than perpetual friction between the Secretary of State and the Commander-in-Chief.

The opportunity came—or was made—by changes in the government involving the resignation of the Minister of Information. On January 4, the Prime Minister asked Hore-Belisha to see him. His

* Lord Avon, *The Reckoning*.

intention was to ask him to exchange the War Office for the Ministry of Information, but shortly before the interview, this move was vetoed by Halifax, on the grounds of Foreign Office advice that it would have a bad effect on neutral countries, both because Hore-Belisha was a Jew and because his methods would lower British prestige. At the last moment, therefore, the offer was changed to the Presidency of the Board of Trade. To Chamberlain's apparent surprise, Hore-Belisha did not immediately accept the offer, but asked for time to consider it.

Hore-Belisha's first thought on leaving the Prime Minister was to consult Churchill and enlist his support. He telephoned the Admiralty, and was surprised to learn that the First Lord had left after a Cabinet meeting that morning for a visit to France.* His second thought was to telephone another friend, Beaverbrook. Beaverbrook was a specialist in politics by way of the backstairs. His maneuverings had played a part in the downfall of Asquith in 1916, and he had for some time been talking about the need of a "palace revolution" to bring Chamberlain down.

He advanced upon the Admiralty, demanding in his harsh Canadian voice: "Get Bracken." Brendan Bracken, Churchill's Parliamentary Private Secretary, was obediently produced. Beaverbrook commanded: "Get Churchill." Together, Bracken and Beaverbrook left urgent messages for Churchill to telephone them at Hore-Belisha's house, and there, at two o'clock the following morning, the First Lord at last came through. Beaverbrook picked up the telephone and asked if Churchill knew about Hore-Belisha. Churchill answered laconically that he did. There was a silence full of meaning. Beaverbrook sadly began to hang up, convinced that this particular palace revolution lacked its Lloyd George. Hore-Belisha, however, took the telephone from Beaverbrook and said hopefully, "You know what's happened. Max has been wondering if you and I could do something about it."

The rich Churchillian tones reverberated over the wire so that those waiting in the room could hear them: "Tell me, Leslie, what forces can you muster in the House of Commons?"

"You know I've always been a lone wolf like yourself." Hore-Belisha replied.

* Where, it may be noted, the subsequent news of Hore-Belisha's resignation was received without surprise. See Ironside's diary.

"Very difficult, very difficult," came the answer. A pause, then, "I advise you to accept the Ministry of Information"—which, of course, owing to Halifax's intervention after Churchill had left for France, had not been offered.

Early that morning, when he was alone, Hore-Belisha wrote to the Prime Minister telling him that, in the circumstances of apparent mistrust, he could not take the proffered post, and would return to the backbenches. Still hankering after his palace revolution, Beaverbrook pressed Hore-Belisha to make a frank resignation speech in the House of Commons. There was even stronger pressure by the Prime Minister—including, it is said, the offer of return to office at a later date—for Hore-Belisha not to do so. He chose the latter course, except for one oblique reference: "One of the traditions—and indeed the regulations—of the Army for which I have always had the greatest respect, and which has seemed to me to furnish the securest safeguard against the abuse of position or rank, is the requirement that any complaint or grievance can be directed to a superior officer, if desired for transmission to the highest authority; and this is none the less so if the superior officer is the Secretary of State. I mention this because I desire to clear those who have worked with me of an aspersion. I am reluctant to believe that any of the high officers with whom I have been associated would have been so unfaithful to the code, which imbues the whole Army, as to make any representation irregularly, or that, if he had done so, it would have been countenanced." It was generally assumed that, if the passage meant anything at all, it was a reference to rumors that the generals had been complaining about the Secretary of State behind his back to the Prime Minister. The "highest authority" of the army, however, is not the Prime Minister, but the Monarch.

With characteristic self-esteem, Hore-Belisha made his resignation speech from Churchill's old seat below the gangway. After it, he joined the two dissident ex-ministers—Amery, Duff Cooper—and the younger Conservative rebels, Richard Law, Ronald Cartland, Harold Macmillan among them, who were harrying the government's flanks. They did not particularly welcome Hore-Belisha, but his criticisms, as an ex-minister, obviously carried weight. The popularity of the Prime Minister fell, according to a Gallup Poll, from 64 to 56 per cent, a fall to which Hore-Belisha's resignation made a substantial contribution. In the War Cabinet, the First Lord of the Admiralty found the new Secretary of State for War, Oliver Stanley, for the time being at least rather more amenable to his suggestions than Hore-Belisha had been. In France there was some rejoicing; and soldiers of the British Expeditionary Force did what they could, amid snow and ice, to strengthen the defenses which they were to abandon as soon as the real war started.

It was now the turn of Lord Chatfield, the Minister for the Coordination of Defense, to find that, as he put it, political land mines were being laid in his path. He was strongly criticized in the press, and in the House of Commons a critical voice was raised by Admiral of the Fleet Sir Roger Keyes, V.C., National Conservative M.P. for Portsmouth North, and a friend and admirer of Churchill.

At the beginning of April, Chatfield was summoned to the Prime Minister who, after reminding him that he had offered his resignation the previous October, when it had been refused, now asked him to take a post outside the country. "Mr. Chamberlain seemed embarrassed," Chatfield has recorded in his memoirs, "and it seemed as if forces other than himself were moving him to end my political career."

No new coordinating minister was appointed in Chatfield's place. Instead Churchill, while remaining First Lord of the Admiralty, became chairman of the Military Coordination Committee. He was thus in effect Minister of Defence, although he has pointed out that he had no formal power to enforce decisions upon the other service ministers or upon the Chiefs of Staff. If he had no formal power, however, he had powers of personality and experience which were considerable and which were certainly enough to overwhelm the Chiefs of Staff.

But the Cabinet reshuffle in which Chatfield was displaced scarcely created a state of harmony in the Military Coordination Committee. Kingsley Wood, whose good relations with Churchill had surprised some observers, was replaced as Air Minister by Churchill's old enemy of the India Bill debates, Hoare. Churchill, Lord Avon has recorded, was "saddened and disgusted" by this appointment.

The new situation was thus at once an advance and a check for

Churchill. How far this was deliberate policy on Chamberlain's part can, of course, only be surmised, but it seems probable that this was the Prime Minister's intent. Distrust of Churchill's unfettered judgment was still profound even among the friendliest of his colleagues. Eden confided to Halifax in March that "however much people admire Winston's qualities, that admiration is constantly balanced by fear of him if he was loose."

Among the less friendly ones the thought may have occurred that the way to deal with Winston was to give him enough rope to let him hang himself. In a nation so ill-prepared for war, such a thought, if there was one, was to prove very nearly correct.

Chapter

3

FIRST ENCOUNTER

"Let us remember," Lord Tweedsmuir had told a war-time audience in a ringing phrase, "that in this fight we are God's chivalry."

The British people, far from remembering that they were God's chivalry, began to show such a detachment from what was variously called the Bore or Phoney War that the government became seriously worried. The Prime Minister recorded in his diary that, with the government intent only on the prosecution of the war, the M.P.'s and the newspapers were left free to exploit and publicize every grievance. Mass Observation, commissioned to carry out a survey of the effectiveness of government publicity, reported that it was almost totally ineffective. A member of the government told Mass Observation, "If we're going to find out things as unpleasant as this, we'd better not find out anything at all." Ministers dutifully made speeches and radio broadcasts but, lacking the common touch, lowered rather than raised the temperature.

With some knowledge of what was happening in France, the ministers had real cause for concern, for the problem was indeed a serious and, to a considerable extent, a new one. At any moment, so far as they could tell, the country was likely to be subject to a devastating attack from the air. What would be the effect on the morale of civilians, finding themselves in the front line for the first time, if, as seemed to be the case, they refused to regard the war as any affair of theirs?

On the other hand what could they be told, in the face of the enemy, about the serious situation underlying the apparent calm? Vast sums of money had been voted for rearmament; but what was not readily grasped, and could scarcely be emphasized, was the time lag between the allocation of money, and the mass production of a tank or airplane. The design of the Spitfire, for instance, began in 1930. The first contract was placed in 1935, the first Spitfire flew a year later, but by the beginning of the war only nine squadrons had been equipped with them. Disagreement over the design and role of tanks had left the army with a single armored division which was not fully equipped or trained. By 1941, if nothing disastrous happened meanwhile, the outlook would be different. But the public could scarcely be informed of the true situation without also informing the enemy. Ministers fell back upon a series of meaningless, but vaguely reassuring statements: the B.E.F. was as well, if not better, equipped than any similar army; tank production was greater than at any time during the First World War; plane production was 100 per cent higher than in the previous year.

In these circumstances any minor feat of arms, which could be built up for morale-raising purposes, was seized upon with joy and acclamation. Such a feat occurred in the middle of February, with the boarding of the German supply ship, "Altmark."

The "Altmark" incident capitalized the enthusiasm raised by the brilliant action of two British cruisers, "Ajax" and "Exeter," and a New Zealand cruiser, "Achilles," in bringing the German pocket battleship "Admiral Graf Spee" to bay off the South American coast and, although outgunned, forcing her into the neutral harbor of Montevideo, where her captain scuttled her. "Graf Spee" had been commerce-raiding in the South Atlantic since the outbreak of war, and no fewer than four British battleships, fourteen cruisers, and five aircraft carriers had been deployed to catch her. The action by Commodore Harwood's cruisers off the Río de la Plata in December, 1939, was regarded as a sign that, whatever might be the defects of the other services, the Royal Navy still ruled the waves; and helped to establish the First Lord of the Admiralty, Churchill, in the public mind as by far the most active member of the government.

After the battle, "Graf Spee's" supply ship "Altmark" was believed to be making for home with a number of merchant seamen from British ships sunk by the "Graf Spee." The First Lord of the Admiralty gave orders that a special watch was to be kept for "Altmark," and on February 14 she was sighted by aircraft inside Norwegian territorial waters. An overwhelming force of destroyers under Captain Philip Vian, commander of the "Cossack," was sent to intercept her, and when she took refuge in a narrow fjord about a mile and a half long, "Cossack," in a remarkable feat of seamanship, first drove her aground, then boarded her.

About three hundred men of the British Merchant Navy were released from the holds of what newspapers quickly called the Hell-Ship. The story of their hardships lost nothing in the telling, and when four of the ex-prisoners appeared on the platform of the Labour candidate in an East End by-election, they scarcely needed to open their mouths to excite a hitherto unknown violence of anti-German feeling. "If I saw a German drownding," said one woman voter, "I wouldn't save him. Not after that, I couldn't." One of the principal complaints of the prisoners appeared to be that the captain of the "Altmark" always saw to it that preference was given to colored over white British prisoners at mealtimes.

Tucked obscurely away in a few—by no means all—newspaper accounts of the rescue was an exchange between the prisoners and the boarding party: "Meanwhile our boys were opening up the hatches. One of them shouted: 'Are there any English down there?' There was a yell of 'Yes!' You should have heard the cheer when our men shouted back: 'Well, the Navy's here.' "

It needed the greatest headline-writer of them all to seize upon this phrase rejected by most of the skilled practitioners of Fleet Street, and transmute it into glittering rhetoric: "To Nelson's immortal signal of 135 years ago, 'England expects that every man will do his duty,' there may now be added last week's not less proud reply, 'The Navy is here.' "

Spoken at a Guildhall reception for the crews of "Ajax" and "Exeter," this sentence of Churchill's gripped the public mind. It was felt that, dull and unenterprising though the conduct of the war might be on land and in the air, the navy was indeed eternally there; and so it heroically was, bearing with the Merchant Navy the heaviest current burden of the war. In Coventry, Oxford, and similar towns of a great seafaring tradition, men went more cheerfully about their work, women looked a little less morosely at rising shop prices, because of the exploit of Captain Vian and "Cossack's" crew.

The "Altmark" incident had, however, a more important effect than provision of a splendid phrase for the First Lord of the Admiralty, and causing a slight increase in production in British factories. The British government at this time was conducting negotiations with the Swedish and Norwegian governments for the passage of British and French troops to aid Finland in her war against Russia. The Scandinavians, terrified of being crushed between Russia and Germany, would no doubt have rejected these overtures in any event, but the boarding of "Altmark" in Norwegian waters provided them with a convenient excuse for turning down the British demands.

The incident also redirected German eyes toward the north. Vidkun Quisling, a former Norwegian War Minister, had convinced Hitler in December that the Norwegian and British governments were conspiring to cut off German supplies of iron ore from the Swedish mines at Gällivare. The ore was being shipped from the Norwegian port of Narvik, and transported for a greater part of the way to Germany within the safety of the Leads, the deep-water channel running continuously in Norwegian territorial waters from the North Cape to Stavanger. Hitler had already given orders for the study of operations against Norway and Denmark, and the "Altmark" boarding played at any rate some part in convincing him that, if the British were prepared to violate Norwegian neutrality for such a comparatively small prize, they were unlikely to be deterred when the prize was the much more important iron-ore traffic. Five days after the "Altmark" boarding, Hitler appointed General von Falkenhorst to command operations against Norway and, a few days later, signed the order for their execution.

Quisling and the Germans had not been entirely misled about British intentions. Since the outbreak of war, the First Lord of the Admiralty had been pressing for action to cut off the iron-ore traffic, even though in the course of the operation "a breach of Norwegian neutrality might be necessary." Churchill's tempestuous

NORWAY INVADED: The British heatedly debated whether they should capture Narvik and halt the delivery of ore mined in Gällivare, Sweden, and shipped to Germany through the Leads, a deep-water channel running along the Norwegian coast. The Germans meanwhile attacked Oslo, Trondheim, Bergen and Narvik, surprising the British who began landing troops. Eventual British defeat in Norway led to Chamberlain's downfall and almost scuttled Churchill's chance of becoming Prime Minister.

pressure met with resistance inside the War Cabinet, some members of which believed themselves to be fighting for the rights of small nations such as Norway, which Churchill proposed to violate if necessary. In addition, they were sensitive to the effect on American opinion of the First Lord's proposed coup, and doubtful whether British resources were strong enough to withstand determined German reaction. And yet the prize seemed to be great, the First Lord's advocacy was advanced with his customary ardor, and at a length and frequency which wore down all but the stoutest resistance.

At the beginning of December, 1939, Churchill was able to deploy a new argument. Russia had invaded Finland, Russia was Germany's partner in the Nazi-Soviet Pact, and to detestation of Russian communism was added an exhortation by the League of Nations to give Finland such help as lay in the power of the member states. Churchill could justifiably claim to have been a stauncher supporter of the League than other members of the British War Cabinet. He now saw no reason why the Allies should not uphold the League by sending troops to Finland by way of Norway and Sweden and, *en passant* as it were, seizing Narvik and the Gällivare mines. This new pressure, too, met with resistance, there now being added to the War Cabinet's other fears the stark possibility that Allied troops sent to Finland were likely to involve Britain and France in war with Russia.

For weeks the argument raged. The British government sent limited supplies of arms to Finland, and encouraged the formation of a small force of volunteers, clad for snow warfare in white overalls bought from a chain store, and wearing nonintervention badges left over from the Spanish Civil War to denote their international character.

The Allied commander-in-chief, Gamelin, supported by Gort, at first opposed the diversion of Allied troops from the Western Front, but the French government saw considerable advantage in the venture. A militant gesture against Russia might assuage the French Right Wing, which was now both noisy and troublesome, and a war in the north might conceivably be extended to divert German strength from France itself. There was the added factor that exaggerated reports of Russian military inefficiency in Finland seemed to hold out the promise of cheap victories which might halt the growing demoralization of the French army. With what now seems incredible lightheartedness, plans were made to bomb Russian oil fields in the Middle East, and in February the Allied Supreme War Council agreed to send to Finland two British divisions and some 50,000 "volunteers" from the French army. British units had been earmarked, and some hundreds of men—mostly officers who had volunteered to serve in the ranks—were sent off to Chamonix for training in winter warfare. Diplomatic pressure was put on Norway and Sweden to allow the Allied Expeditionary Force passage through their territories, and, according to Sir John Slessor, then Director of Plans at the Air Ministry, grossly exaggerated promises were made of Allied aid in the event of German or Russian reaction.

But as Allied pressure mounted, so did the alarmed Scandinavians put pressure on the Finns to conclude peace with Russia. Finally, under a threat of resignation from Daladier, the British War Cabinet reluctantly agreed to land an expeditionary force for Finland in Norway, if necessary in the face of armed Norwegian resistance.

Ironside has left a memorable picture of these decent, peace-loving men steeling themselves to bloody resolution: Halifax recoiling from the shedding of innocent Norwegian blood, Chamberlain inquiring what effect an eight-inch shell would have on a troop transport, then advancing the opinion that he was prepared to risk a four-inch shell, but not an eight-inch. The Cabinet was saved from such horrors by the Finns, who on the night of the final decision to force a landing in Norway announced that they had accepted Russian terms.

Although Churchill kept up his pressure for action against Narvik even without the excuse of aiding Finland, Gort wanted his divisions in France, and the Prime Minister ruled that the Allied Expeditionary Force should be disbanded.

Churchill now revived the claims of a previous plan—called Operation Wilfred because, in comparison with his other proposals, it was small and innocent—for mining Norwegian waters, and occupying the principal Norwegian coastal towns, including Narvik, if the Germans reacted. This plan, too, went through endless processes of Cabinet discussion before being accepted. Preparations were made for the mine-laying, and five battalions of British

Territorial troops were again put under orders. One of these battalions, the fourth battalion of The King's Own Yorkshire Light Infantry, understood it was going for garrison duties to Bergen, Norway, and, though lacking artillery, armor or transport, had its full complement of office equipment, quartermaster's ledgers, and peacetime accounting forms.

Of these complex maneuvers the British people remained unaware. After the long, harsh winter, Easter came at the end of March with an unusually welcome promise of spring and better times ahead. The war, such as it was, seemed no reason for abandoning the traditional four-day holiday, and seaside resorts were crowded. Blackpool landladies had one of the best Easters in their history. Two hundred would-be visitors were turned away from a Weston-super-Mare hotel. Traffic to the seaside at Brighton was almost as heavy as that found on a peacetime Easter Sunday. The East Coast was particularly popular. Many holiday-makers announced that they had come to look for the war, and they were much on the alert for sounds of explosions or gunfire at sea.

On April 4, the Prime Minister gave what Halifax described in his diary as a "very successful" address to the Central Council of the National Union of Conservative and Unionist Associations. With no particular thought of the Norwegian adventure in his mind, Chamberlain said, "When war did break out, German war preparations were far ahead of our own, and it was natural then to expect that the enemy would take advantage of his natural superiority to make an endeavour to overwhelm us and France before we had time to make good our deficiencies. Is it not a very extraordinary thing that no such attempt was made? Whatever might be the reason—whether it was that Hitler thought he might get away with what he had got without fighting for it, or whether it was that, after all, the preparations were not sufficiently complete—however, one thing is certain: he missed the bus." * In the context

---

* The phrase rankled with both Hitler and Mussolini. When Chamberlain died, Mussolini asked Ciano to be sure to record in his diary the Italian dictator's mot "This time he definitely missed the bus."

of the anticipated knockout blow from the air, it is difficult now to say that Chamberlain was wrong; but the phrase was to haunt him until death, and after.

On the same morning as the reports of the Prime Minister's speech appeared, the *Daily Express*, under the rousing headline, "Come on Hitler! Dares Ironside," published an exclusive interview with the Chief of the Imperial General Staff, in which he was quoted as saying, "We would welcome a go at him. Frankly we would welcome an attack. We are sure of ourselves. We have no fears." This too was characteristic of the ill-luck—or bad management—of this unhappy government. Some days before, Ironside had been persuaded by the Ministry of Information to give an interview to an American journalist. He understood that he was talking off the record, and that by some means circulation of what he said could be restricted to the United States. The Ministry had asked him to paint as rosy a picture as possible, and he did. The talk was published in America as an interview. The *Daily Express*, owning the British rights, reprinted it. The rest of the British press complained bitterly at the *Express*'s apparent privilege in having an exclusive interview with the C.I.G.S., and Ironside had to say it all over again for their benefit, though at the second attempt the picture was a little less rosy.

On the evening of April 6, the main German naval forces and troops for an invasion of Norway sailed from north German harbors. Concealed in empty ore ships and merchant vessels, other German troops lay off the Norwegian coast, or in Norwegian ports. In the light of the words of the Prime Minister and the Chief of the Imperial General Staff, how could the British public doubt that all this had been skilfully anticipated?

Norway was a country with a strong antimilitarist tradition and, even as the German invasion was taking place, there was anguished debate whether to resist or to surrender with no more than the formality of protest, as Denmark had done when similarly invaded. The country's main air strength, nineteen Curtis fighters recently bought from America, lay in crates on Oslo airfield. There was no standing army, and Norway's half-trained militiamen were mobilized only in the north. It is possible that, if the Germans had not made the mistake of trying to force upon the Norwegians a government led by the discredited Quisling, Norway would have gone the way of Denmark. As it was, the advocates of resistance used as an argument in their favor the massive Allied assistance promised in February, which many believed was already on the way as the result of repeated reports of a British invasion plan.

Not only the Norwegians were deceived. In British newspapers over the early days of April appeared a series of optimistic stories; British troops had captured Bergen, the Norwegians had retaken Trondheim, the British fleet had forced the Kattegat and commanded the entrance to Oslo. The *Times* wrote of Hitler's Peninsular War, the *Express* of the British storming of Narvik, which had "an Elizabethan ring to it. It ranks with Cadiz, where we singed the King of Spain's beard." British troops were reported to have landed at points on the Norwegian coast and "it may be mentioned that, great as was the haste, the climate was not forgotten, and that sheepskin coats, sealskin caps and sleeping-bags were issued, together with petrol suitable for the intense cold." The *Daily Mirror* was able to add the detail that pack saddles for reindeer had also been provided. According to Sir John Reith, the then Minister of Information, much of this early optimism emanated from the Admiralty. At a Cabinet meeting on April 9, the First Lord expressed the view that "we had the Germans where we wanted them." At a later meeting, Reith said pointedly that people were anxious to hear what the navy was doing. The Prime Minister, however, looked at the First Lord in vain.

Not until April 26 did a number of newspapers quote a dispatch from an American correspondent, Leland Stowe. He reported that two British battalions, described as The King's Own Royal Light Infantry, had been dumped in Norway, badly armed and undertrained, without antiaircraft guns, fighter cover, or field artillery. After four days' fighting, nearly half of them had been killed, wounded, or captured. The rest had been driven back, and an officer was quoted as saying, "We've simply been massacred." The War Office rather testily described the report as "an obvious distortion of the facts." There was, after all, no such regiment in the Army List as The King's Own Royal Light Infantry.

It is necessary to follow in some detail the adventures of the five Territorial battalions which landed in Central Norway between

April 17 and 19, partly because they helped to persuade the British people that war was a serious business for which they were ill-prepared, but also because of the part they played in the fall of the Chamberlain government. The five were county battalions of The King's Own Yorkshire Light Infantry, The Royal Lincolnshire Regiment, The York and Lancaster Regiment, The Royal Leicestershire Regiment, and The Sherwood Foresters. Both officers and men were in the nature of things conservative, if not Conservative; among them were Conservative party officers and workers from their constituencies, who had voted and actively worked for the return of a largely Conservative government in 1935. In a very real and bitter sense, it was their own government which had betrayed them among the snow-covered hills of Norway. When the House of Commons voted at the end of the Norway debate on May 8, sixty-five of the government's usual supporters deliberately withheld their support. It is perhaps not a coincidence that twenty-six of the absentees represented constituencies in the counties of the five Territorial battalions, and another seven government supporters from those areas voted against it. These volunteer soldiers who nine months before had been farmers, bank clerks, estate agents, haulage contractors, architects, may have done little against the Germans, but among their battle honors they might be allowed some claim to "Westminster, May 8, 1940."

On April 6 and 7, in accordance with the plans agreed for Operation Wilfred, these five battalions had embarked on cruisers at Rosyth, ready to anticipate German reaction to the mining of Norwegian waters. They were organized and equipped on as light a scale as possible, since it had been envisaged that they would be landing in friendly ports, or at worst in the face of half-hearted Norwegian resistance. Captain S. W. Roskill, the official naval historian, has advanced the opinion that, if they had been allowed to sail for their planned destinations, they might at least have captured the vital airfield at Stavanger and could possibly have maintained a hold on better port facilities than were later available. The German invasion of Norway, however, took the British authorities completely by surprise, and on April 7 the first intelligence of it led the Admiralty to suppose, wrongly, that the German fleet was making a break northward for the open Atlantic. On the First Sea Lord's orders, the troops were disembarked from their cruisers at Rosyth, their equipment in some cases being literally hurled onto the quay, and the ships sailed without them to aid in the interception of the German fleet.

The troops forlornly sorted out their battered equipment on the quayside and marched twelve miles to camp at Dunfermline. There information reached The King's Own Yorkshire Light Infantry that their role was likely to be more warlike than they had been led to suppose, and the regimental quartermaster spent the next sixty hours, almost without sleep, trying to re-equip his battalion. He was not helped by the fact that the camp did not contain a single telephone; and he was in any event almost entirely unsuccessful.

On April 11, the three battalions forming 146 Brigade—The King's Own Yorkshire Light Infantry, Lincolns, and York and Lancaster—moved to Glasgow and embarked at Gourock. They still did not know where they were going, but thought it was Narvik, in the far north of Norway. So at this point it was. Two days previously, the Joint Planning Committee—"that machinery of negation," as Churchill scornfully called it when it pointed out to him unwelcome logistic facts—had put up a recommendation to the Chiefs of Staff to ignore Narvik and its iron ore, and go for the tactically more important port of Trondheim, some four hundred miles to the south. The same evening, the Military Coordination Committee, under Churchill as its new chairman, decided to ignore this recommendation and instead to go for Narvik. For Narvik, therefore, 146 Brigade sailed on April 12, together with the picked regular troops of the Guards Brigade.

In London, meanwhile, a new factor had entered the situation: urgent pleas from the Norwegians for an attempt to recapture Trondheim, the ancient capital, where King Haakon and his government, chased from point to point by German aircraft, hoped to find a permanent base from which to organize resistance. Churchill has recorded that he continued to be in favor of ignoring Trondheim and concentrating limited British and French resources upon Narvik, but "serving as I did a loyal chief and friendly Cabinet," he allowed himself to be persuaded into undertaking the capture of Trondheim as well as Narvik.

However friendly the Cabinet may have been at the start of the campaign, it is apparent that amity did not long survive the im-

pact of events. By April 15, Churchill had to appeal to the Prime
Minister to relieve him of the chairmanship of the Military Coordination Committee. One member of this committee, Hoare,
was later to place on record his view that the Norway expedition
was one of the chief mistakes of the war. Briefed by his Air Staff,
who were gravely concerned by an apparent indifference, even hostility, at the Admiralty to their emphasis on the importance of air
power, Hoare seems unlikely to have brought any burning enthusiasm to the venture. Another member of the Military Coordination Committee, Oliver Stanley, had not been hostile to Churchill
on his first appointment to the War Office, but his attitude had
hardened and he was later to refuse office in Churchill's government because, according to Halifax's diary, he had seen so much
of Churchill in the previous two months that he felt he could not
serve him loyally. The remaining member of the Committee,
Leslie Burgin, the Minister of Supply, carried no guns of importance.

Of other members of the War Cabinet, Halifax makes clear in
his diary that "unless we were to refuse the Norwegian appeal to
have a shot for Trondheim, we were bound to try and do what was
always recognized to be a very hazardous thing." His diary gives no
confirmation to rumors current at the time that he had threatened
to resign if the Norwegian appeal were ignored, but the existence
of such rumors suggests that he strongly supported the Trondheim
operation.

In agreeing to try for Trondheim, therefore, Churchill was under considerable pressure. Having agreed, he flung himself with
characteristic determination into the venture. Admiral Forbes, the
Commander-in-Chief Home Fleet, who was doubtful about the
effect of air attack on his ships in the narrow waters of Trondheim
Fjord, was prodded into having more favorable second thoughts;
and at two o'clock on the morning of April 14, Churchill entered
Ironside's room at the War Office and instructed him to divert 146
Brigade from the Narvik convoy to Namsos, three hundred miles
farther south, where it was to be used as the northern half of a
pincer movement in support of a naval assault on Trondheim.
Ironside protested that troops could not be made available for
Namsos until Narvik had been taken, and that to divert half the
Narvik force would imperil that operation. The protest was over-

ruled. When Ironside asked Churchill if he was giving the order in his capacity as chairman of the Military Coordination Committee, Churchill replied that he was. In these circumstances Ironside, still protesting, accepted the order.

The decision to attack Trondheim was basically a sound one. The German invasion of Norway, meticulously planned in contrast to the hasty British improvisations, depended a great deal on luck, and Hitler seems to have been ready to call it off in the face of resolute opposition. If Trondheim could have been captured and held, the German troops advancing from the south would have been halted, and the German garrison in Narvik, already shattered by naval assault, could have been reinforced only by sea. In his diary for April 21, William L. Shirer, then C.B.S. correspondent in Berlin, recorded: "What the Germans fear most I gather is that the British navy will go into Trondheim Fjord and wipe out the German garrison in the city before the Nazi forces from Oslo can get there. If it does, the German gamble is lost." One may accept this appreciation, subject to the important proviso that, if British forces had got to Trondheim, they would still have been faced by the problem of staying there in the face of German air superiority.

These, then, were the circumstances behind the order which reached 146 Brigade when it was within a hundred and thirty miles of Narvik, to change course for Namsos, three hundred miles farther south. The commander, Brigadier C. G. Phillips, was not with his brigade, but in another ship of the convoy, and he, like the brigade's antiaircraft guns, went on to Narvik with the Guards. The troops had been, as the newspapers said, issued with a variety of Arctic equipment. What the newspapers did not say was that all this gear took time to load and unload, and when the troops wore it, they could scarcely move. Reindeer saddles they might have, but not skis, the one essential item, and they were unable to move off the few Norwegian roads without bogging to the waist in soft snow. Nor, in the time available, had the combined resources of the War Office and the Admiralty been able to ascertain whether small Norwegian ports like Namsos could maintain an expeditionary force of any size.

The General Officer commanding what now came to be called Mauriceforce was Major-General Adrian Carton de Wiart, a V.C.

of the First World War, who with his black eye patch and single hand resembled in appearance, and a little in character, Evelyn Waugh's Brigadier Ritchie-Hook. Carton de Wiart had the experienced field commander's sardonic eye for the eccentricities of the War Office, and when he had been telephoned in the middle of the night to report for special duty in the morning, he rightly assumed that, since Norway was one of the few parts of the world in which he had not lost some portion of his anatomy, Norway was where the War Office would send him. He was not allowed to take the troops he had been training in the West Country, and he elected to leave with no more than a single staff officer, who was wounded in an air raid on landing. Carton de Wiart immediately enlisted two officers of the Military Intelligence branch who were on the spot, Captain Peter Fleming and Captain Martin Lindsay, and with these men as his entire staff, got his inexperienced brigade ashore. To the British Territorial Brigade was presently added a demibrigade of French Chasseurs Alpins, who were equipped and trained for snow warfare, but whose usefulness was impaired by the fact that they lacked a vital ski-strap.

The port of Namsos, and Steinkjer, the railhead at which Carton de Wiart concentrated his small force, were quickly obliterated by German bombing. It was indeed one of the many bitter ironies of the Norwegian campaign that the Norwegian civilians, whom the British had ostensibly come to save from the Germans, learned to dread a British arrival, since this usually meant that their small towns and villages, built largely of wood, were quickly razed to the ground by German bombers.

Carton de Wiart was too old a hand not to have a nose for the smell of disaster, and when he received a signal from the War Office promoting him acting Lieutenant General, he did not bother to change his insignia. Ordered to push on as rapidly as possible down the single road to Trondheim, ready to support a naval assault on that port, he did as he was told. The War Office, while punctiliously informing him of his promotion, omitted to keep him informed of the innumerable changes in the plan for the naval assault. German destroyers came up Trondheim Fjord and shelled his troops, who had nothing but rifles, a few Bren guns, and some two-inch mortar smoke bombs with which to repel them.

Better-armed German soldiers were landed in the British rear, and the British had to fall back through unknown country, across hills covered with eighteen inches of snow.

Mauriceforce was eventually evacuated, reaching Scapa Flow on May 5, eighteen days after it had set out, and in time for Captain Lindsay, one of Carton de Wiart's two staff officers, to seek an interview with the Leader of the Opposition in the House of Commons. Lindsay had been prospective Unionist candidate for a Lincolnshire constituency, and he was afterward a Conservative M.P., but on the morning of May 8, it was to the Leader of the Labour Opposition that he took his account of happenings in Norway with the deliberate intention of doing what he could to bring down Chamberlain's government.

The two other Territorial battalions, one of The Royal Leicestershire Regiment and one of The Sherwood Foresters, forming 148 Brigade, sailed for Norway on April 17. On the previous February 5, they had been put under orders for a more or less peaceful occupation of Stavanger airfield. On April 7, they had embarked at Rosyth for Trondheim or Bergen; disembarked at an hour's notice; and later been told they were going to Namsos. When they embarked again on April 14—still for Namsos—they were at first distributed between two cruisers and a transport, the S.S. "Orion." At the last moment, it was decided that "Orion" could not be risked without air cover off the Norwegian coast, and her troops were transferred in the black-out to two additional cruisers.

The only guides these two battalions had were a dozen tourist maps of the whole of Norway, which had been hurriedly distributed between the four cruisers at the last moment. Two companies and half the headquarters company of the Foresters were with their commanding officer in one cruiser. Brigade headquarters and the other half of the battalion, under its second-in-command, were in a second cruiser. In the confusion of embarkation and re-embarkation, field telephones had been loaded in one cruiser, the cable for them in the second. Other equipment was similarly divided. The two halves of the battalion did not see each other again until almost a week later.

One half the battalion of the Leicesters was distributed between two cruisers while the other half was temporarily left behind. Neither battalion had any transport or tracked Bren carriers—these were to follow later—or arms heavier than three-inch mortars, and the greater part of the mortar ammunition had been lost at one stage or another of embarkation.

Shortly before the convoy sailed, orders reached Brigadier H. de R. Morgan that his brigade's destination was not Namsos, but Andalsnes, and its role was to operate northward and take offensive action in the Trondheim area. There was a subsidiary, and contradictory, order that he was to make contact with Norwegian Army Headquarters, believed to be in the Lillehammer area far to the south, and do what he could to prevent the isolation of Norwegian forces operating toward Oslo. When Brigadier Morgan disembarked at Andalsnes, he was almost immediately told that the Norwegians were in desperate straits near Lillehammer; that his force had been placed under the orders of the Norwegian Commander-in-Chief; and that, instead of attacking northward toward Trondheim, he was to hurry his men south with all possible speed.

At 1 A.M. on April 20, in a snowstorm, two companies of the Foresters reached Nykirke, some fifteen miles southwest of Lillehammer, two hundred miles and in the opposite direction from their supposed objective, Trondheim. They were told the Germans were "somewhere down the road," with nothing but a Norwegian ski patrol in front of them, and left to get on with it. By 10:45 P.M., having received neither orders nor information for some hours, they began to feel a little forlorn. The two company commanders decided to risk security and put a call through on the public telephone to the Hotel Victoria, Lillehammer, which they had heard—they had not been officially informed—was battalion headquarters. An English voice answered them with the cheering words, "Lucky you rang. We were just wondering what was happening to you."

The other half of the Foresters were cut off from these two companies by lake and river. Together with two companies of the Leicesters, the Foresters were put under orders to relieve the exhausted Norwegians. In front of them were two German infantry battalions, a motorized machine-gun battalion, a battery of artillery, and some smaller units, totaling about four thousand men.

The Germans had skis, the British none. The snow, three feet deep, was like a bog to walk through, and the British, unable to move off the roads and tracks, had to face the constant scorn of the Norwegians, whom they had supposedly come to save.

There was a suspicion that some of the Norwegians were fifth columnists. Norwegian and German uniforms were indistinguishable at a distance, and the British, seeing ski troops on their flanks, would take them for Norwegians until a machine gun opened fire. In one such ski foray, the Germans almost captured brigade headquarters, which had to evacuate without its papers. Among these were undistributed copies of operation orders for the proposed occupation of Stavanger in February, of which German propagandists later made skilful use in proving the existence of a British plan to occupy Norway.

In face of such superior forces, the British could only retreat. They had no maps, no transport except civilian cars and lorries, and the Norwegian drivers spoke no English. There were no communications except by runner or motorcycle. Company commanders had no time to reconnoiter, and, bringing up the rear as each position was abandoned, they found on arriving at a new position that their leading platoons had already been placed in position by senior officers, and their first task was to wade through the snow to find their own men.

One platoon, sent on outpost guard, waited from 2 P.M. until dusk without any communication from company headquarters. As darkness fell, men asked the platoon commander, "When do we go home, Sir?" By that time, the Germans were ten miles behind them. Captain Martin Redmayne, a future Conservative Chief Whip, was looking for his company when he heard the exhaust of a motorcycle. He realized rather suddenly that it was not one motorcycle, but many, and that the many were German. He hastily went over the edge of the road on one side as the Germans equally hastily went over on the other. Redmayne was lucky enough to fall about ten feet into a kind of cave. The Germans threshed about overhead for a bit and then went on. "It was not a very brilliant performance on either side," he has since recorded.

The British fell back along winding mountain roads, amid a landscape of steep snow-covered slopes and gray masses of pine forest, among which it was impossible to tell accurately whether machine guns were firing in front of them or in their rear. On Sunday, April 21, the ship carrying their transport and Bren carriers was torpedoed off the Norwegian coast, and on the following day they learned that their own navy had been unable to prevent the Germans getting tanks ashore at Oslo.

On April 23, St. George's Day, an irony which did not escape them, the Foresters and the Leicesters were reunited for the first time since they had sailed from Scotland. They took up a position at Tretten, with orders that they must hold for at least one clear day, to give the Norwegians time to regroup behind them.

In summer a brook tumbles down the mountain slopes and under the road beside a farmhouse called Rindheim. In April the brook was frozen and covered, like everything else, with snow. To the north of the brook and almost under the shadow of a great bluff behind it, was a field, snow-covered, dotted with piles of frozen manure ready for spreading in the spring. Here, in the first serious encounter of the war between British and German troops, the German tanks caught up with them; perhaps no more than three, according to the official British historian of the Norwegian campaign. These British Territorials were the first to discover in action that the antitank rifle, with its savage kickback, did not penetrate heavy armor. There was then little for them to do but retreat into the woods, from which German mortars forced them out again into the path of the tanks. By nightfall, 148 Brigade, reduced to an effective strength of nine officers and three hundred men, had virtually ceased to exist as a fighting formation.

As dusk fell, a party of mostly wounded men sat by the roadside with the Foresters' medical officer, hoping for transport. A tank rounded the corner from the south, and they scattered into the trees. A voice from the tank called in English, "Come out, Englishmen, it is all right." A Foresters officer came out of cover, revealing the party's position. A shot from the tank killed him. The medical officer ran forward to help him, and was shot down. The tank's machine gun opened up, spraying the edge of the wood from which the men had come. Few of the party escaped.

Some officers and men of the two battalions, in scattered parties and without maps, set out across the snow-covered hills for Andalsnes, a hundred and twenty miles away. Listening to the radio in mountain farmhouses, they heard that Andalsnes had been evacuated, and wearily changed direction for the Swedish border, only to be captured before they reached it.

On April 26, a captured subaltern, an N.C.O., and a private of the Foresters were flown to Berlin, and paraded before the German Chancellor like Ancient Britons at a Roman triumph. A German staff officer officiously demonstrated to Hitler the difference between an officer's and an N.C.O.'s uniform and then asked if he wished for a tin of British bully beef to be opened. Hitler seemed particularly interested in the frail antitank ammunition, which he tried, apparently without success, to crush between his fingers. Then with a baleful look he said in German, "This war was not necessary. You can thank your government for it," and left them to their captivity.

British losses in the Andalsnes operations, mainly from these two battalions, have been given as four officers and seventeen other ranks killed; twenty-one officers and a hundred and twenty-eight other ranks wounded; seventy-six officers and one thousand one hundred and fifty-six other ranks missing. When the missing returned from their prisoner-of-war camps five years later, and read the dispatches of the campaign, unpublished until 1946, many of them were surprised to learn that they had formed part of something grandly styled the North-Western Expeditionary Force commanded (from the War Office) by Lieutenant General H. R. S. Massy.

On St. George's Day, the Chief of the Imperial General Staff returned in high fettle from a successful meeting of the Supreme War Council in Paris. Winston, it was true, had been a bit difficult, but there had been complete agreement at the Council to continue the build-up in Norway as fast as possible. At the War Office, Ironside found his Secretary of State, Oliver Stanley, and his new deputy, Sir John Dill, sitting very glum, talking about evacuation. "I find people talking about 'desperate situations' and of 'evacuation' as if it had to be carried out in a minute," he wrote in his diary with soldierly irritability. "Too many damned strategists who all have a finger in the pie, all amateurs who change from minute to minute and are either very optimistic or very

pessimistic. Very difficult to make war under such circumstances.
We must get back to allowing the soldiers to make decisions."

The situation at the levels of the Chiefs of Staff and the War
Cabinet had indeed undergone many transformations since the
brave days of early April, when Churchill had confidently told the
Cabinet that "we had the Germans where we wanted them."

On April 9, it will be remembered, the Joint Planning Committee had recommended an attempt to recapture Trondheim,
which had been ignored in favor of Narvik. On April 13, the
planners were told to plan the seizure of Trondheim. On April 15,
they recommended a pincer movement by land on the town, but
that evening the Chiefs of Staff decided on a naval assault, supported by the land forces. On April 18, Churchill has recorded, a
"vehement and decisive change in the opinions of the Chiefs of
Staff and the Admiralty" had occurred, due to urgent warnings
from the Air Staff of the grave risk involved in committing heavy
ships to Trondheim Fjord in face of almost complete German
command of the air. By the night of April 19, the naval assault
had been abandoned in favor of the land pincer movement. By
April 23, however, according to Slessor, the naval assault was back
in favor, and on April 25 orders were given through Churchill for
the operation to be undertaken. In less than twelve hours these
orders had been canceled, and a decision to evacuate had been
made.

An offer by Sir Roger Keyes to lead the assault on Trondheim
in old ships of war brought only a threat of resignation from the
First Sea Lord, Sir Dudley Pound, if it were accepted. It was the
resignation over Gallipoli of the First Sea Lord, Lord Fisher,
which had helped to bring about Churchill's downfall in 1915,
and it is not straining the imagination too far to surmise that the
nightmare shadow of Gallipoli must have haunted Churchill at
every turn of the Norwegian campaign, affecting his judgment and
perhaps his nerve.

In a post-mortem entry in his diary for May 3, Halifax recorded:
"Great efforts are being made to represent the Norwegian business
as the result of timid colleagues restraining the bold, courageous
and dashing Winston. As a matter of fact the exact opposite would
be at least as near the truth, and on Winston certainly rests the
main responsibility for the abandonment of the naval attack on

Trondheim. I do not blame him for he reached his opinion in concurrence with the Chiefs of Staff, and owing to necessities the orders for the change were given in the middle of the night after the P.M. had been consulted by telephone at Chequers, before the Cabinet could be informed."

But if some measure of blame for the Norwegian fiasco does rest on Churchill, it certainly does not rest on him alone. One of the main contributions to a probably inevitable failure was amateur staff work at every level, including that of the Chief of the Imperial General Staff. Ironside's appointment had been forced upon a reluctant War Cabinet by Hore-Belisha and by Churchill. He had already played his part in the fall of Hore-Belisha. It would have been irony indeed if his defects had now aided the fall of Churchill, as they very nearly did; for it became apparent during the Norwegian campaign that Ironside was not in his element with even such comparatively small-scale planning, and Dill was hurriedly brought over from France as Vice-C.I.G.S. to instill some coherence into the War Office. Opportunities for agreeing wholeheartedly with Hitler are limited, but one cannot quarrel with his verdict on the British campaign in Norway: "From the military point of view it can only be described as frivolous dilettantism."

The final inescapable truth, however, was a belated realization at the Admiralty, as by the War Cabinet, that the British Fleet was to a considerable extent helpless in face of German command of the air. Germany held the inner ring of communications, German forces had captured the only usable Norwegian airfields. It was this fact which had forced the navy's abandonment of any surface attempt to cut off German reinforcements by controlling the Skagerrak, and, later, of the naval assault on Trondheim. Norway, in fact, marked the end of an era; not the brief incidents of so-called appeasement, or the Twilight War, but the span of one hundred and thirty-five years from the Battle of Trafalgar, during which command of the sea enabled a small island, as much as any nation could, to control not only her own destiny, but also that of others. Sea power was no longer enough without air power, and the combined cost of the two was more than all but the richest nation-states could afford.

On April 26, faced by these unpalatable facts, the War Cabinet accepted with obvious relief the Chiefs of Staffs' recommendation to evacuate central Norway. But now there was another difficulty. Reynaud, the new French Prime Minister, had been urging on the Norwegian operations with all his considerable zest, looking to them to help him with his own internal difficulties, and to draw more and more German troops to a front far away from France. The French had offered to take over responsibility for Norway, and had been somewhat haughtily rebuffed by the British. What, now, were the British to tell the French? What happened was considerably less than perfect frankness between Allies. The British did not consult the French about the decision to evacuate, but presented them with the information that this was what they were forced to do. A hastily summoned meeting of the Supreme War Council agreed to the principle of evacuation, but the French were still left in the dark as to its details. Its suddenness took them by surprise, and still further shook French confidence in British determination to wage serious war.

And in Britain, for the first time since the outbreak of war, public opinion turned massively against the government. The navy had been there, but apparently helpless. The army had not lived up to Ironside's confident words. The Secretary of State for Air, in a broadcast, had unwisely allowed himself to become airborne on wings of poesy rather than fact. "Today," Hoare had told the nation, "our wings are spread over the Arctic. They are sheathed in ice. Tomorrow the sun of victory will touch them with its golden light."

In a Gallup Poll taken in March, 57 per cent had supported Chamberlain as Prime Minister, 36 per cent were against him. In May, after Norway, only 32 per cent were in favor, 58 per cent against.

On the day the evacuation of Andalsnes was announced, Amery, the principal Conservative rebel, telephoned Hoare and told him angrily, "The Government must go." What force there was behind the ultimatum remained to be seen.

Chapter

4

NEMESIS

The Norwegian campaign, from the British point of view, was far from being an unmitigated disaster, for the German naval losses sustained in it made virtually impossible a cross-Channel invasion later in the year. This, however, was not an advantage readily apparent in April, 1940, and in all other respects the completeness of the defeat was emphasized in the public mind by the optimism of the early newspaper reports.

The effect on world opinion may be judged from a tirade to which Joseph Kennedy, the American Ambassador, treated Halifax and Reith, the Minister of Information. The service departments, labor, and England generally, Kennedy told them, were inefficient and degenerate, and a meeting of United States attachés had agreed that England was going to lose the war. This was an opinion long held by Kennedy. The conduct of the Norwegian campaign did nothing to offset his propagation of it in the United States, and the effects were not easily reversed.

The man who stood most exposed to blame for this fiasco was the First Lord of the Admiralty. It was he who had pressed the venture in its various forms upon a reluctant War Cabinet; and it was he who had taken the first decision in favor of Narvik rather than Trondheim, and with all the weight of his formidable personality had urged on or overridden service chiefs with what they regarded as insufficient consideration for logistic realities. He did not lack enemies, and over dinner tables and in clubs and lobbies there began to be whispered the significant word, "Gallipoli."

Churchill himself has written that it was a marvel he survived. He attributes the fact that he did so to his years in the wilderness, uttering ceaseless warnings then unheeded but now remembered. A less subjective observer may advance a more immediate reason for his survival: the support of Chamberlain who, to reverse Lloyd George's famous phrase, turned himself into an air-raid shelter to keep the splinters of the Norway debate from hitting the First Lord of the Admiralty.

The relationship between Chamberlain and Churchill during these first months of the war is fascinating. When Churchill had been out of office each had savagely attacked the other,* and neither was of a forgiving nature. With Churchill's recall to the government, a subtle change became apparent. "To me personally Winston is absolutely loyal," Chamberlain recorded, "and I am continually hearing from others of the admiration he expresses for the P.M." This latter statement one may take with several pinches of salt, for Churchill knew that, until he had secured substantial support in the Commons, his political existence depended on Chamberlain, and no doubt he took steps to ensure that his gratitude was known. It is a mistake frequently made, however, to judge politicians as if they were inhumanly capable of any emotion greater than self-interest, and it would be wholly wrong to ignore the strong vein of chivalry in Churchill's nature, or his genuine gratitude to the man who had at last restored him, however reluctantly, to the center of affairs.

On Chamberlain's side, the war exposed in him an unexpected streak of bellicosity. No one reading the extracts from his diary quoted by Sir Keith Feiling can doubt the depth of his personal hatred of Hitler, and while one part of his mind remained coolly aware of British deficiencies which made an aggressive policy unwise, another part urged him to strike and wound. After Hore-Belisha's departure, he was often to be found as almost the only Cabinet supporter of Churchill's sometimes ill-judged schemes for a more vigorous prosecution of the war.

---

* "The undertaker from Birmingham" was one of Churchill's choicer descriptions of Chamberlain.

It is interesting, if vain, to consider what might have happened if Chamberlain had decided, after the Norway campaign, to throw Churchill overboard. The First Lord would have gone down with all guns firing, and they were formidable guns; but it is not at all certain that he would have been able to sink the government. The Conservative backbenchers' distrust of Churchill would have been fed by discreet hints and "leaks" about what had really happened over Norway.* The extent of the Labour party's support for him is unknown, because its members were never given an opportunity to express their opinion; but contemporary evidence suggests that it was confined to a handful of well-liked but scarcely influential eccentrics such as Josiah Wedgwood. The government would certainly have been badly shaken by the dismissal of Churchill, the image of national unity would have been seriously damaged, but one may venture the opinion that, for the time being and with weakened authority, Chamberlain could have remained in control.

None of this happened. In the days between the decision to evacuate central Norway and the debate in the House of Commons, the official guidance firmly given to the press and in the Commons lobbies was that the War Cabinet stood or fell together, that there was no truth in reports of divided counsels over Norway, that no one minister was more responsible than any other for what had happened. In particular, it was made known that there would be no reconstruction of the government under Chamberlain's leadership.

Putting Chamberlain's motives for this campaign at their lowest, one may read into them a considerable degree of self-interest. The government knew that the targets of its small band of dissident backbenchers were Hoare, Simon, Kingsley Wood, and Chamberlain himself. Chamberlain could probably have saved himself for the time being if he had sacrificed the other three before the Norway debate. But by casting his mantle over Churchill he faced the dissidents with the tactical problem of pressing the immediate case over Norway without involving Churchill in the government's downfall, and he was thus protecting himself and the others by

---

* I have been told that Hoare was indeed "intriguing" against Churchill at this time. The "intrigue" seems to have consisted of suggestions that Churchill was not wholly blameless for the fiasco—a proposition with which, surely, it is difficult to quarrel.

protecting Churchill. But this, as in the case of Churchill, would leave out of account the loyalty Chamberlain had shown to Churchill in the past months and was to show in the future. "To a very large extent I am in your hands—and I feel no fear of that," Churchill was to write to him after returning from Buckingham Palace as Prime Minister. This confidence was amply justified.

At first the consequences of Chamberlain's decision seemed unlikely to be fatal. When Reith told Margesson, the government Chief Whip, at the end of April that within a week or two the government would either fall or have to be drastically reconstructed, Margesson dismissed the suggestion as nonsense. Respected as a firm disciplinarian rather than liked, Margesson knew his own backbenchers—or believed that he did—and was confident that in the last resort they would come to heel, as they had always done. "I don't think my enemies will get me down this time," Chamberlain himself noted, only three days before the Norway debate in the Commons; and as late as May 6, the day before the debate, Halifax recorded in his diary: "Considerable political clamour, but I doubt whether this, at present at all events, will amount to much."

The explosion of the mine beneath the government's apparently impregnable fortress took almost everybody by surprise, including the sappers who had been working so assiduously to place it in position. A number of the tunnelings have already been noted: post-Munich reaction, a general feeling of dissatisfaction among the younger and more ardent Conservative M.P.'s with the Prime Minister's aloofness and stuffiness, shortages of equipment brought personally home to service members, the slow attrition of grumbles on the Home Front. To these had now been added a humiliating defeat in the first large-scale encounter with the enemy.

The actual membership of the dissident groups was small—perhaps no more than thirty. The principal one, at first known as the Eden Group, had been formed in 1938, after Eden's resignation as Foreign Secretary. It was not immediately joined by those Conservatives who disagreed with Eden's hostility to Italy, but these came in after Munich, and they included Amery and another minister who had resigned from the Chamberlain government, Duff Cooper. When Eden rejoined the government at the beginning of the war, Amery took over the Group's leadership. Churchill had his own handful of the faithful, some of whom were also members of the Eden Group. Yet another small group met under the leadership of Clement Davies, an Independent Liberal M.P., who was a devoted supporter of Churchill and who during the crucial days leading up to and after the debate worked indefatigably on his behalf.

These forces had not been formidable in the past, and there seemed no particular reason why they should be so now. Under Amery's leadership, however, they began to concentrate on two constructive demands which had been gaining in popularity over the past months. The first was for a smaller War Cabinet of ministers free of departmental responsibilities, who would be able to give their full time to the over-all strategy of the war. Chamberlain rejected the demand. The second was for a genuinely National government drawn from the best men of all parties, regardless of their status in the party hierarchy. Chamberlain turned down this demand also, until it was too late, and this was the demand which wrecked him.

Chamberlain was temperamentally antipathetic to the idea of coalition government. One of his first actions on becoming Prime Minister had been to raise the political temperature, deliberately kept low by Baldwin, with a speech attacking the League of Nations, and the idea of collective security, which had outraged the Labour party and the supporters of the League. When Chamberlain returned from Munich, Halifax suggested to him a coalition including Churchill and Eden, as well as Liberal and Labour leaders. Chamberlain, however, only looked surprised, and no more was heard of the idea. At the beginning of the war, the Prime Minister had invited the Labour and Liberal leaders, Clement Attlee and Sir Archibald Sinclair, to bring their parties into the government, but their formal refusal was apparently received without surprise though with some resentment, and it is difficult to decide who disliked and distrusted the other more, the Opposition or the Prime Minister. In April, there had been some discussion among Labour leaders about joining the government, but the unanimous feeling was that they could not do so under Chamberlain. In the light of this past history, it is difficult to believe that any dissident Conservative seriously thought that Chamberlain had much chance of forming an all-party government. Nevertheless, this was the demand which the dissidents began forcefully to press for.

It is not easy to trace where these demands came from at this particular moment, but they were certainly both propagated by a small but influential Watching Committee formed in the middle of April under the imposingly respectable chairmanship of the fourth Marquess of Salisbury. Lord Salisbury, frock-coated, a sympathizer in his later years with the cause of Moral Re-Armament, was a Conservative elder statesman who had begun his ministerial career in 1900, when his father was Prime Minister, and had ended it as Lord Privy Seal and Leader of the House of Lords under Baldwin. His forthright opposition to the Munich settlement had led to a physical assault from one of Chamberlain's loyal supporters. Lord Salisbury was a Cecil, seventy-eight years old, quite impervious to any sanction the government could impose upon him. His son, the present Marquess, sat in the House of Commons as Viscount Cranborne. He had been Eden's Under-Secretary at the Foreign Office, had resigned with him and was widely supposed to be the iron hand in Eden's velvet glove. The Salisbury Committee drew its secretary, Paul Emrys Evans, and some of its members, from the former Eden Group now led by Amery.

The Salisbury Committee did not lack influential channels through which to make its views known. On April 24, when things were going disastrously in Norway, Salisbury saw Halifax at the Foreign Office. Halifax noted in his diary: "Jem Salisbury had been to see me earlier about a new ginger group of notables in both Houses that he has formed to give expression to what he says is great dissatisfaction with the Government. I told him very politely that I wished he was sitting where I was: that my experience was that in a war everybody who was not running it thought they could run it better than the people who were. The upshot was that I am to meet them all on Monday and be cross-examined. As far as I can make out it mostly comes down to a desire to plunge into indiscriminate bombing. This mixed up with a lingering strong suspicion that, somehow or other, the P.M. is going to land them all into another Munich. It is a strange clash and mixture of emotion and reason."

The Monday meeting was not, according to Halifax, a success: "Lord Salisbury and what he calls his Watching Group in thoroughly critical mood, and nothing I said had the least effect upon them."

According to Sir Edward Spears, who was a member both of the Amery Group and the Salisbury Committee, the Committee began to press the demand for a National Government after the announcement of the evacuation from Norway on May 2, though Emrys Evans, for one, had been urging it for some time. Halifax's diary entry of May 5 notes: "The Sunday papers are excited, as I knew they would be, about Norway and about reconstruction of the Government. A good deal of this inspired by personal prejudice against the P.M. I fancy the movement for including Labour will grow, but whether they will serve under him or not remains to be seen."

But if not under Chamberlain, then under whom? The name which began to be put about at the beginning of May was that of Halifax. This, too, was an idea which had been floating in the air for some time. Geoffrey Dawson, editor of the *Times*, had been privately propagating it in March.* But who, at the beginning of May, set the Halifax lobby in powerful motion? One of the earliest public references to Halifax as potential Prime Minister appears in the *Evening Standard* of May 6, and is associated with the name of Lord Salisbury: ". . . The all-party group of critics want a complete reconstruction of the Government with the inclusion of Liberal and Socialist leaders, and they have their own very definite ideas of the Ministers they think should be dropped. I understand that a long statement of their case has been presented by Lord Salisbury to the Prime Minister. If Mr. Chamberlain refuses to make the changes, they say that there should be a new Prime Minister. And the man they select is Lord Halifax. They believe that Lord Halifax could select a new and effective team. And they think that the Socialists, who have refused office under Chamberlain, would be amenable if Halifax was in command."

The existence of some such memorandum or statement by Salisbury to the Prime Minister seems to be confirmed by contemporary reports in the *Times*, the *Daily Telegraph*, and the *Man-*

---

* Lord Dalton in *The Fateful Years* records that Sir Campbell Stuart, who was among other things a director of the *Times*, "had suggested to me, and no doubt to others, that Halifax should be P.M. and Attlee lead the Commons." Sir Campbell tells me that he has no recollection of having made such a statement to Dalton or anyone else.

chester Guardian, but it was not made on behalf of the Watching Committee, whose attitude to Halifax was ambivalent. Some of them—certainly not all—wanted Churchill. Others were prepared to support Halifax as a fly to entice the Labour party, who were believed to be unwilling to swallow Churchill at any price, and also those growing numbers of Conservatives dissatisfied with Chamberlain but still distrusting Churchill. It would be reasonable to assume a calculation in some minds that the primary aim was to dislodge Chamberlain. If that could be done, Halifax would not long survive, and then Churchill's path to the premiership would be clear, provided he had not been too heavily compromised in the Norwegian fiasco or some later disaster.

The Labour party, under Attlee's leadership, was not without its own schisms. Before the war it had been weaned with difficulty from its practice of voting against any measure of rearmament, but it retained a pacifist Socialist element which Lord Attlee has described, perhaps a little acidly, as seeming to think that an inefficient army was less wicked than an efficient one. When in 1931 Ramsay MacDonald formed the National Government, he had split the parliamentary Labour party and driven it to electoral disaster. As a result, he had left some of its members with a distrust of coalition government, and there existed a party conference decision which, it could be argued, precluded the parliamentary party from joining a National Government without the authority of a party conference.

Nor was Attlee's leadership unchallenged. Although he had been elected in 1935 by a substantial majority over Herbert Morrison, an uncertain number of Labour M.P.'s continued to believe that Morrison was the more able man, and Morrison himself had never accepted his defeat. Several attempts had been made to have Morrison replace Attlee, the most recent during the autumn of 1939, when Attlee had been ill.

On May 6, the day before the debate in the House of Commons, Halifax had an appointment to see Morrison about the possibility of Labour joining a coalition. Halifax's diary contains no information about this meeting beyond the fact of the appointment, and Morrison's surviving papers are discreetly silent on the subject. The meeting was certainly unknown to Attlee and to a number of members of the Parliamentary Executive of the party.

On the following morning, the first day of the Norway debate, a letter appeared on the front page of the *Daily Mail*—it had been rejected by the *Times,* presumably on the grounds that the writer would not allow his name to be published—signed by "A British Politician," in fact Sir Stafford Cripps K.C., who, though he had been expelled from the Labour party for his Popular Front activities before the war, retained some influence in the party. Cripps had recently returned from a long visit to Russia and China, coming back by way of the United States, where the effect on informed opinion—he had seen Roosevelt, among others—of the Royal Navy's failure to prevent the German invasion of Norway had made a deep impression on him. He had certainly been in touch with Halifax to report his impressions, and he had been working behind the scenes to bring together the Liberal leader, Sir Archibald Sinclair, probably Morrison, and a somewhat reluctant Lloyd George, to join with Amery and the dissident Conservatives in support of a coalition.

Cripps's letter in the *Daily Mail* repeated the demands being put forward by dissident Conservatives for an all-party government and a small, nondepartmental inner Cabinet. The Prime Minister suggested was Halifax, and the inner Cabinet was to consist of Churchill, Lloyd George, Eden, and Morrison, with Attlee relegated to an "outer" post as Chancellor of the Exchequer.*

It has been suggested that Cripps's *Daily Mail* letter was an example of the kind of political aberration to which he was prone. It can be said with fair confidence that it was not, and that he knew what he was doing, which was to try to secure at almost any cost a coalition government under the most widely acceptable Prime Minister, and with Morrison replacing Attlee, not as Leader of the Labour party, which for the moment was constitutionally impossible, but as principal Labour representative in a coalition government. Although Morrison had played a part in securing Cripps's expulsion from the party, there was no personal animus between them, and Cripps was certainly one of those who had a high regard for Morrison's ability.

---

* It is interesting to note that Cripps, an eminent lawyer if sometimes politically naïve, saw no overwhelming difficulty about Halifax's peerage. "It would be necessary," he wrote, "to make a change in the Standing Orders of the House of Commons by resolution or Act of Parliament to enable the Prime Minister to sit and speak in that House."

These, then, were some of the political crosscurrents flowing when, on Tuesday, May 7, 1940, the House of Commons began to debate the formal motion, "That this House do now adjourn."

The order of government speakers in the debate is interesting. It was opened by the Prime Minister, with Churchill speaking at the end of the debate on the second day. At least one political commentator noted that, from a tactical point of view, the government would have been better advised to have the First Lord of the Admiralty speak at the end of the first day, with the Prime Minister pulling his side together at the end. Morrison, speaking for the Labour Opposition, made the point that they had asked for Churchill to be heard earlier. "We took the view that the First Lord was the Prime Minister's principal witness. He had a considerable responsibility—not the entire responsibility—for the operations, and the Opposition think that he should have been heard early so that the House might have as much as possible of the facts from the point of view of those mainly concerned with the conduct of operations . . . He is the chief witness who refused to go into the box."

Chamberlain, in his opening speech, pointed out that Norway was no Gallipoli, the forces engaged had not been nearly as great. He described as "unworthy and unfounded" the suggestion that one minister of those directly responsible for the war was more responsible than his colleagues for what had happened. He defended the Norway operations with his usual cold logic, and apparently without a great deal of heart. It was noticed that he seemed to lack his usual easy command of the House; and it is probable that he had been brought to realize, too late, how exposed was the position in which he had placed himself.

The first open sign of trouble from his backbenches came when the Speaker called Sir Roger Keyes. Before the debate, Keyes had talked to Carton de Wiart, fresh back from Namsos, and he had been the beneficiary of some useful advice from dissident Conservatives. Duff Cooper had encouraged his desire to come down to the House in admiral's uniform, with six rows of medal ribbons and the Grand Cross of the Bath. He was an appalling speaker, and Harold Macmillan had advised him to write out what he had to say and to read it in defiance of the conventions of the House.

Incoherently, sometimes inaudibly, Keyes sailed into the government, and particularly into the First Lord of the Admiralty, for their pusillanimity in refusing to undertake the naval assault on Trondheim. His attack carried the more conviction because he was a known friend of Churchill, and his very inarticulateness appealed more to the government backbenches than Amery's over-polished rhetoric which was to follow. One of the sins imputed to Amery and Duff Cooper by loyal Conservatives was that their dissidence was at least partly inspired by desire for place. No one could suspect Keyes of that. When he sat down, it is probable that Chamberlain could no longer have avoided reconstructing his government.

The effect of Amery's speech was different. He was called during the dinner hour, in an almost empty House. Clement Davies, who had constituted himself unofficial Whip of the dissident groups, went around smoking room, dining room and lobbies, drumming up an audience for him, but while the Opposition benches filled, those on the government side remained half-empty, since Amery, a small, intense man, had the reputation of being a most boring speaker.

For a time, most of the applause came from the Opposition while Amery skilfully deflected the attack away from Norway and Churchill to Chamberlain and the general conduct of the war. As he continued, he began slowly to gain some sympathy among the government backbenches. He quoted Cromwell's words to John Hampden: " 'Your troops are most of them old, decayed serving men and tapsters and such kind of fellows . . .' " He paused for the briefest moment, making a lightning assessment of the mood of the government benches. In looking up the Cromwell quotation he had come upon another. If he used it, he might risk losing the sympathy he had won with difficulty, but his own rhetoric swept him on: "I have quoted certain words of Oliver Cromwell. I will quote certain other words. I do it with great reluctance, because I am speaking of those who are old friends and associates of mine, but they are words which, I think, are applicable to the present situation. This is what Cromwell said to the Long Parliament when he thought it was no longer fit to conduct the affairs of the nation: 'You have sat too long here for any good you have been doing. Depart, I say, and let us have done with you. In the name of God, go!' "

The Opposition benches took up the cry, though the Conservative benches remained silent. Chamberlain was not present to hear the words, but they were reported to him. He was an old friend of Amery, who had been an ardent admirer of Chamberlain's father, Joseph Chamberlain. They were fellow members from Birmingham constituencies. There is no doubt in the minds of some of those close to Chamberlain at the time that it was Amery's brutal assault which finally broke his nerve.

When the Prime Minister saw the King that evening, he said, though smilingly, that he had not come to resign, and had not yet abandoned all hope of reconstructing his government on the basis of a national coalition in which Labour would join. The King offered to intervene with Attlee, an offer which Chamberlain declined, saying that Attlee would be more certain of the attitude of his followers after the annual conference of the Labour party, which began the following week at Bournemouth. He still seems to have seen the crisis as developing slowly, allowing time for the full formalities of negotiation and bargaining.

On the morning of May 8, the Parliamentary Executive of the Labour party met to consider its tactics during the second day of the debate. That morning's *Daily Herald*, official newspaper of the Labour Opposition, carried a forecast by its political correspondent, Maurice Webb, that "Sweeping reconstruction of the Government, involving the possible resignation of Mr. Chamberlain, is now widely regarded as inevitable in the near future. . . . Events will not take this drastic turn at once. Indeed, as I have previously stated, the Government will get through the present debate without immediate disaster. . . . It has been suggested that the Labour Party should either put down a vote of censure or force a division on a motion for the adjournment. The view may be taken, however, that this would be an unwise tactic. . . . The view taken by the most experienced critics of the Government is that the debate should be allowed to end without any direct challenge."

Maurice Webb was very much in Morrison's confidence. The political correspondent of the *Star*, who was close both to Morrison and to Hugh Dalton, forecast confidently that Labour would not divide the House at the end of the debate.

There had been an understanding through the "usual channels" of the Whips' offices that Labour would not force the House to vote; though the Labour Chief Whip, Sir Charles Edwards, had often had to break such arrangements in the past with an apologetic, "It's a very difficult party to manage, you know." Attlee, however, had come to believe after the events of the previous day that there was a possibility of persuading a substantial number of Conservatives to vote against the government. At the meeting of the Parliamentary Committee, he proposed from the chair that the Labour Opposition should force a division. His proposal was opposed by several members, notably Dalton. Morrison's memoirs give the impression that he strongly favored a division, but this is not an impression confirmed by all those present at the meeting, one of whom describes his support for the motion as "reluctant." Attlee's proposal was, however, carried, and later approved by a meeting of the parliamentary party.

The Conservative rebels had met the previous evening and decided not to table a motion hostile to the government at that stage. Without the decision by Attlee and the Labour party, therefore, it seems unlikely that the opinion of the Commons would have been tested by a vote.*

The *Times* of May 10 rebuked the Labour party: "It was common knowledge after the first day's debate that a large body of opinion, more than large enough to compel a complete reconstruction of the Cabinet, would have been ready to declare itself by way of direct communication to the Prime Minister. When the Labour Party ran up its flag this movement was thrown into confusion." It is interesting to speculate what might have been the relative positions of Morrison and Attlee in a Cabinet so reconstructed—if, indeed, Attlee and what might be described as the "official" Labour party had joined the government at all. When Churchill formed his government, with Attlee inside the War Cabinet and Morrison outside it, Morrison, according to Dalton, was "not very pleased," and even seems to have had thoughts of refusing office.

When the Norway debate continued on the late afternoon of

* There was an understanding between three women M.P.'s, the Conservatives Lady Astor and Mrs. Mavis Tate, and the Socialist Ellen Wilkinson, that if nobody else forced a vote, they would do so. I hope I shall not be accused of antifeminism if I suggest that a division sponsored from such a quarter would not have been taken entirely seriously. Lady Astor at this time appears to have been grooming Lloyd George to succeed Chamberlain. (See Thomas Jones, *A Diary With Letters*, p. 457.) Lloyd George had some support outside the House, but very little inside it.

May 8, it fell to Morrison's lot, as first Opposition speaker of the day, to announce to a crowded House that the Opposition intended to force a division, the first notification, so far as is known, that the government had had of such a possibility. Morrison had had at any rate some sort of contact with Halifax. A conscientious objector of the First World War, a fact which government supporters did not let him forget, he had attacked government inefficiency in waging the present war in a speech which had gained much telling detail from notes made by Attlee of a lunchtime talk that day with Martin Lindsay, Carton de Wiart's staff officer at Namsos. The cockiness of Morrison's debating manner, which was that of a fatherly schoolteacher lecturing a particularly backward class, was calculated to get under the skin of the most even-tempered opponent.

Any or all of these things may have accounted for the Prime Minister's obvious anger as he rose to answer Morrison's attack. Chamberlain's intervention was unprepared, and it was a moment when, with opinion on his own backbenches hanging in the balance, it was essential that his every word should be exactly right. His opening was statesmanlike enough, but then for a few fatal moments the party politician, the too-experienced debater, took over: "It may well be that it is a duty to criticise the Government. I do not seek to evade criticism, but I say this to my friends in the House—and I have friends in the House. No Government can prosecute a war efficiently unless it has public and parliamentary support. I accept this challenge. I welcome it indeed. At least I shall see who is with us and who is against us, and I call on my friends to support us in the Lobby tonight."

The loyalist majority cheered, but a number of government supporters sat stunned. It was not, perhaps, the Prime Minister's fault that the events of the past weeks had become the subject of party maneuver. It was his fault that he had failed to lift the argument above such a level.

Following Chamberlain's intervention, the government had put up Hoare, an experienced practitioner in the art of lowering fevered temperatures. As he talked on, the Chamber began to empty and it seemed to some of the dissidents that the effect of Chamberlain's words might drain away. Lloyd George had left the Chamber. Clement Davies hurried after him, caught him in the corridor, and urged him, in Welsh, to return and take part in the debate. Lloyd George was unwilling, claiming to have been insulted by a Conservative backbencher. In fact, he feared that he could not effectively intervene without involving his old friend and colleague Churchill. The two argued volubly for a while, then Lloyd George went back to the Chamber.

When Hoare sat down, Lloyd George launched a furious onslaught on Chamberlain. There was loathing between these two, dating back to the time of the First World War, and Chamberlain once more allowed himself to be provoked into a sneering intervention. Lloyd George seized the opening to thrust home the full force of Chamberlain's ill-judged appeal to his friends: "It is not a question of who are the Prime Minister's friends. It is a far bigger issue. The Prime Minister must remember he has met this formidable foe of ours in peace and in war, and he has always been worsted. He is not in a position to appeal on the ground of friendship. He has appealed for sacrifice. The nation is prepared for every sacrifice, so long as it has leadership. . . . I say solemnly, that the Prime Minister should give an example of sacrifice, because there is nothing which can contribute more to victory in this war than that he should sacrifice the Seals of Office."

At the end of Lloyd George's speech, Churchill was overheard saying to Kingsley Wood, "This is all making it damned difficult for me tonight." It was indeed. When the First Lord rose to end the debate, at least one observer watched him curiously. "The ostensible issue was Norway," Reith noted in his diary. "He was at least as much responsible as any other Minister; but Norway was incidental. I wondered if any speaker had ever been in a more equivocal position: wondered if he would defend Chamberlain, knowing what Chamberlain's enemies wished to happen. He was obviously ill at ease."

Churchill did his best, but in a sense, the better that best was, the worse for Chamberlain. Tempers were running high, and Churchill allowed himself to become involved in a shouting match with the Labour backbenches. To his claim that British and French shipping losses had almost been replaced by captured ships and new building, Emanuel Shinwell, sitting in the shadow of the gallery, cried, "Oh!" Churchill rounded upon this favorite enemy: "I daresay the honourable member does not like that. He would

like me to have a bad tale to tell. That is why he skulks in a corner." There were cries of "Withdraw!" and appeals to the Speaker
to know whether "skulking" was a parliamentary expression.
Churchill continued to shout above the uproar: "All day long we
have had abuse, and now you won't listen. You dare not listen to
the argument. It's deliberately barracking the argument. It's not
fair. It's not British."

His friends feared, his enemies hoped, that he had now irrepar-
ably ruined his chances of Labour support.

Throughout the evening, in the committee rooms above the
Chamber, and in the long corridors, excited groups of government
backbenchers met to discuss their course of action in the face of the
Labour challenge. During the evening, a new urgency was lent to
their discussions by a report—one of many received during previous months—that the long-awaited German attack through the Low
Countries was expected within the next forty-eight hours. It may
have been that this news was deliberately spread by the government in the hope that it would reunite the party behind Chamberlain, but in many cases it had an opposite effect. If the government
had so mishandled Norway, how could the same government be
trusted to face this greater danger? But the news also swung opinion to an increasing extent behind Churchill; an effect which
Hitler in timing his attack can scarcely have anticipated but is
unlikely to have wished to achieve.

Messengers from the government passed to and fro among the
backbench groups. Lord Dunglass, the Prime Minister's Parliamentary Private Secretary, saw several members of Amery's group,
telling them that the Prime Minister would meet them next morning. To one group of service members, meeting under the chairmanship of Victor Cazalet, the Prime Minister sent warning of the
serious consequences of their defection, and a request to know
their terms. The brusque message returned was that Hoare, Simon,
and Kingsley Wood must go, and that if the Prime Minister did
not like that, he could go himself.

The Whips did their best to stem the flood, using such persua-
sion as is open to men who serve under the Patronage Secretary, in
an era when Conservative politicians sought to enter, rather than
leave, the House of Lords. In at least one case, a recalcitrant mem-

ber was threatened with the dire penalty of having Churchill as Prime Minister if the government went down. But discontent had perhaps been too efficiently dammed up in the past and could no longer be contained.

In the Opposition division lobby, Conservative members, a number of them in uniform, mingled with pacifists and anti-imperialists from the Labour backbenches. There were enough of them, together with abstainers, to raise hopes among the dissidents that the government might even have been defeated, and cheers of relief came from the loyalists when, after the division, the government Chief Whip was seen to be standing on the right, an indication that the government had won. Margesson read out the voting figures. The government's potential majority had fallen to eighty-seven. Thirty-three Conservative members had voted against the government: the hard core of the dissidents, Amery, Duff Cooper, Richard Law, Boothby, Harold Macmillan, Spears, Emrys Evans, Lord Wolmer, Ronald Tree; but also serving officers like Quintin Hogg, John Profumo, and a future chairman of the powerful Conservative caucus, the 1922 Committee, Major William Anstruther-Gray. Hore-Belisha voted against the government, as did Lady Astor, Harold Nicolson, Clement Davies, Lord Winterton. At least another thirty had only voted for the government on the understanding that there would be far-reaching changes.

As the effect of the figures sank in, there was tumult. The Conservative member for Stockton-on-Tees, Harold Macmillan, said to the Labour member for Newcastle-under-Lyme, Josiah Wedgwood, "We ought to sing something." Together they struck up "Rule Britannia," not ironically, Wedgwood explained afterward, but with hope and thankfulness. They started on too low a note, and the duet ended ignominiously almost as soon as it had begun. There were chants of "Who missed the bus!" and "In the name of God, go!" To one observer, some of the proceedings seemed ill-mannered and indecent.

On the government front bench Simon ostentatiously patted Chamberlain's back. The Prime Minister rose, smiled his frosty smile at one or two of his supporters, and passed through the door behind the Speaker's chair. One of the rebels, Boothby, watched the tall, straight figure walking alone down the long corridor toward the Prime Minister's room. There Chamberlain told his friends that he intended to resign.

Chapter

5

HALIFAX OR CHURCHILL?

Chamberlain's actions of the next two days have sometimes been presented as nothing more than a selfish attempt to maintain himself in office: "Incorrigibly limpet, always trying new tricks to keep himself firm upon the rock," as Dalton put it. It would be fairer to see his conduct in the context of Churchill's handling of the Norwegian campaign, which had seemed to confirm the general suspicion of his judgment and to increase the very real fear of what he would do if he were given supreme power.

At some point on May 9, Chamberlain made a formal attempt to save the government by inviting Amery to join it and bring his supporters with him. Amery took the now-familiar line: would it be an all-party government? After the maneuvers of the previous days, Chamberlain seems to have learned that he had nothing to hope for from the Labour party. He answered bleakly, "I hope that won't be necessary," and on those terms Amery refused office.*

At ten o'clock, Halifax saw Chamberlain. Halifax had a report from R. A. Butler, Under-Secretary at the Foreign Office, on soundings taken among Labour leaders the previous night. Dalton had

* This offer is not mentioned in Amery's memoirs or in his diary. He did, however, later tell Dr. A. L. Rowse that Chamberlain had offered him office, and with that support I have accepted the story as recorded by Dalton in *The Fateful Years* and attributed to a "good Tory source."

said that Labour would join a coalition under Halifax, but not under Chamberlain or in the company of Simon. Morrison had told
Butler that the idea of Labour joining the government was "coming along well," * but only on the conditions described by
Dalton. Dalton, according to Butler's report, said that there was no
choice but Halifax. Churchill must stick to war, and the Home
Secretary, Sir John Anderson, who had been mentioned as an
alternative, was not well enough known.

Chamberlain told Halifax that he did not think the situation
could be left as it was, and that the only way to restore confidence
in the government was by having all parties in. He pressed Halifax
to succeed him, implying that he would be willing to serve under
him. "The evident drift of his mind," Halifax noted, "left me with
a bad stomach ache. I told him again, as I had told him the day
before, that if the Labour people said that they would serve only
under me I should tell them that I was not prepared to do it, and
see whether a definite attitude could make them budge. If it failed,
we should all, no doubt, have to boil our broth again." Chamberlain and Halifax agreed to meet, with Churchill and Margesson,
the government Chief Whip, at half-past four that afternoon.

Eden, lunching with Churchill, was surprised to find Kingsley
Wood as a fellow guest, apparently on excellent terms with
Churchill and primed with information and good advice about the
afternoon meeting. Kingsley Wood, who was close to the Prime
Minister, was able to warn Churchill that Chamberlain would
want Halifax to succeed him, and would want Churchill to agree.
"Don't agree," Kingsley Wood advised, "and don't say anything."
The advice was excellent, but Eden was shocked that it came from
one so much in Chamberlain's confidence.

One cannot help wondering, as Churchill approached this fateful meeting, whether his mind went back to that summer day almost exactly twenty-five years before when, as First Lord of the
Admiralty in Asquith's government, he had gone confidently down
to the Commons, full of new plans, to be told that, because of
Conservative opposition to him over Gallipoli, he had lost the

* It was not. Neither Attlee nor the Parliamentary Executive had yet been formally sounded. A suggestion in the *Times* of May 10, that the Labour leaders might
be prepared to come in under Chamberlain, but without "at least two prominent
members of the present War Cabinet," seems to have no foundation.

Admiralty. The situation now was not so very different, except that he was twenty-five years older, and it was the highest office that was at stake. No government, it will be remembered, could be formed without the support of the Conservative backbenches, who remained substantially loyal to Chamberlain, who in turn supported Halifax; and no coalition government could be formed without the support of Labour, where also Halifax appeared to have substantial backing.*

The meeting began with a recapitulation by Chamberlain of the situation as he saw it. He said he had made up his mind to go, and that the succession lay between Halifax and Churchill. For his part, he would serve under either. It would be necessary to see the Labour leaders before they went to their Bournemouth conference and ask them formally whether they would be prepared to join a government either under Chamberlain, or under some other Prime Minister.

Margesson agreed that unity was essential and did not think this could be secured under Chamberlain. He said he was not prepared at the moment to pronounce definitely between Halifax and Churchill as Chamberlain's successor, at which, Halifax noted in his diary, "my stomach ache continued."

Chamberlain looked expectantly at Halifax, sitting on his left. According to Churchill's account of this meeting, there was then a silence, which lengthened until it seemed to him longer than the two-minute silence on Armistice Day. According to Margesson, the silence was in fact a short one, broken almost immediately by Halifax urging Churchill's greater fitness for leadership in war, and drawing a comparison between the uneasy relationship of Asquith and Lloyd George during the First World War, and what his own relationship was likely to be with Churchill, who would be running defense from the real center of power in the Commons. "The inevitable result would be," Halifax noted in his diary, "that, outside both these points of vital contact, I should speedily become a more or less honorary P.M., living in a kind of twilight just outside

* According to Sir Edward Spears, whose account of this incident seems more probable than Amery's, Attlee had told Brendan Bracken on the previous day that he was not very favorable to serving under Churchill, but would under Halifax. Lord Attlee has said that he has no recollection of this supposed conversation with Bracken, and that he acted throughout the crisis only in accordance with formal decisions of the Labour party.

the things that really mattered." Only after Halifax's refusal did Margesson reveal a swing of opinion which had revealed itself during the day among the Labour leaders against a Prime Minister in the Lords.

With, according to Halifax, suitable expressions of regard and humility, Churchill said he could not but feel the force of Halifax's arguments. Chamberlain reluctantly, Churchill less reluctantly, accepted Halifax's verdict. The succession was settled.

Although Halifax's refusal of the succession was absolute, and he never afterward expressed regret, his attitude to the premiership remains in one respect enigmatic. While there was a chance of Chamberlain staying, he undoubtedly remained completely loyal, as he afterward did to Churchill. But during the crisis he had given at least one person to suppose that he would not refuse the succession if it were offered to him, although believing that Churchill would get it. His final decision, like that of many Conservative M.P.'s the night before, seems to have been influenced by the timing of the German offensive.

If he had decided differently, would Churchill have served under him? His friends would have pressed him not to—had indeed tried to dam the tide flowing in Halifax's favor by putting it about that he would not—but he had told Bracken, according to Spears, that he would; and one wonders whether, if Halifax had grasped the offered chance, Churchill could have borne to tear himself away from the center of events. And as second man, responsible but without full powers, would he have been finally swept away in the disaster of a greater Norway?

It was a bright, sunny afternoon, and these two figures of history, Churchill and Halifax, sat drinking tea together in the garden at Number Ten Downing Street, awaiting the arrival of the Labour leaders, and talking of nothing in particular. One would give a great deal to know what they were thinking.

Before going to Downing Street, Attlee and Arthur Greenwood, the deputy leader of the Labour party, met Clement Davies at the Reform Club. According to Davies' account of this meeting, Attlee was in favor of Chamberlain staying temporarily in office, in view of the expected German attack. Greenwood on the whole was not.

They argued with Attlee for two hours before apparently convert-
ing him.

During the First World War, Attlee had served in the Gallipoli
campaign, and had suffered an infantry officer's view of the effect of
the delay in reaching important military decisions which had re-
sulted from the long drawn-out bargaining between Conservatives
and Liberals over the formation of Asquith's coalition government
in 1915. He was determined that, so far as it lay in his power, a
similar situation would not be created now. It was in this frame of
mind that he went to the meeting with Chamberlain, Halifax, and
Churchill.

The Prime Minister and his two colleagues sat on one side of the
table, the Labour men on the other. No hint was given of what had
gone before, but both Halifax and Churchill loyally pressed upon
the Labour men Chamberlain's claim to their support.

Greenwood, according to an account of this meeting given by
Clement Davies, interrupted Churchill in full flow: "We haven't
come here to listen to you orating, Winston. Whatever we ourselves wish to do in these circumstances, we've no choice but to
refuse, because members of our party have got absolutely no confidence in the Prime Minister." Attlee, more laconic, was even more
brutal: "I'm bound to tell you, Prime Minister, that in my view
our party will not serve under you, nor does the country want
you."

Attlee and Greenwood agreed, however, to put before the party
executive at Bournemouth on the following day two formal questions: would the Labour party serve under Chamberlain? Would it
serve under another Prime Minister? Attlee was to telephone "Yes"
or "No."

The usual explanation given of Chamberlain's insistence that
these questions should be formally answered by the Labour party,
although he had already made up his mind to resign, is that he had
to justify his resignation to his own loyal followers—still a substantial section of the Commons—and could do so only by confronting
them with a Labour refusal to serve under him, emphasizing the
national disunity which would follow if he stayed in office. This explanation, however, leaves a number of questions unanswered. It
has been suggested, for instance, that Chamberlain still desperately
hoped for Labour support. Those close to him at the time believe

that he had no illusions about that. What he may have hoped for was a Labour refusal to serve under either himself or Churchill, which would have enabled him to put renewed pressure on Halifax to change his mind. It was for this, not support for himself, that he was prepared to hang on as long as possible.

According to Dalton's account of the meeting, as related to him by Attlee on the following morning, Chamberlain then asked whether, pending answers to these two questions, the Labour leaders would send a message saying that the Labour party supported the government at this grave crisis of the war. Whatever reservations Attlee may still have had after his earlier meeting with Davies, the answer Chamberlain got was that Attlee and Greenwood would consider this. Lord Attlee is certain that he had no further communication with Chamberlain. In Halifax's account of the Labour leaders' attitude at this meeting, however, he suggests that they were "a bit evasive," and it is conceivable that a misunderstanding arose which became important on the following day.

In the early hours of Friday, May 10, the Prime Minister was awakened by the ringing of his bedside telephone. The long-awaited German invasion of Holland and Belgium had begun. Shortly before six o'clock, he was told that the Dutch Minister was on his way to see him. He rose, dressed, received the Dutch Minister and the Belgian Ambassador, promising them all possible British assistance, as Poland and Norway had been promised. The British Expeditionary Force already stood at six hours' notice to leave its prepared positions on the Belgian frontier and move forward to the line of the River Dyle, east of Brussels.

For a moment it is possible to catch a glimpse of Churchill as he was on this day when he assumed power, before the mists of legend engulf him, along with Alfred who burned the cakes but beat the Danes, Bruce and his unconquerable spider, all the other figures of a history blocked out for him in strong, certain masses of black and white, in a way only possible to one almost totally immune from the disadvantages of education.

At six o'clock that morning, summoned by the news from Holland and Belgium, Hoare found Churchill at the Admiralty, smoking a large cigar and eating fried eggs and bacon, as if he had just

returned from an early morning ride. Despite the disasters of Norway, the hazards of debate and political negotiation, he was ready
with confident advice about the new campaign.

At eight o'clock the War Cabinet and the Chiefs of Staff met
urgently to consider the situation on the Continent. Winston,
Ironside noted, had a new toy—a homing antiaircraft fuse—he
would just show the Cabinet, it wouldn't take a minute. While the
war waited, the Cabinet heard all about Winston's homing antiaircraft fuse.

"I have seldom met anybody with stranger gaps of knowledge, or
whose mind worked in greater jerks," Halifax noted of Churchill
in his diary on the following day. "Will it be possible to make it
work in orderly fashion? On this much depends."

It fell to the lot, first of Chamberlain and Halifax, then of Eden,
to try to make Churchill's mind work in an orderly fashion. Lord
Avon has movingly testified that it was a task as difficult, if reward-
ing, as the harnessing of genius must always be. On those who undertook it much did indeed depend.

Shortly before a midmorning Cabinet meeting on May 10, Reith
saw Chamberlain. The Prime Minister was in good form, stimu-
lated by the news from the Low Countries, and ready for action if
he was encouraged and authorized to act. According to Reith's
diary note, he said that he had seen Attlee and Greenwood again
that morning, after the news of the invasion, and had understood
that they were prepared to defer the political crisis in view of the
military one; but there was a Labour conference at Bournemouth
next day, and they would have to conform to decisions made there.

Halifax's diary notes: "The P.M. told the Cabinet what had
passed on the Home Front, and said that he thought it would all
have to wait until the war situation was calmer . . . The P.M. told
me that he had a feeling that Winston did not approve of the delay,
and left me guessing as to what he meant to do."

Eden's diary for the day contains this passage: "After 11:30 Cabinet N.C. made statement to us of what had been his intention, as
W[inston] had told me. Added that new attack must cause hold-up,
only temporary. He had communicated with Attlee in this sense,
who had accepted. He had asked Attlee to put out notice which
would include support of Government *pro tem,* but when an-

The Prime Minister, Mr. Neville Chamberlain, on his 71st birthday,
March 18, 1940.

Above left, the Secretary of State for War, Mr. Leslie Hore-Belisha, and Lord Gort, Commander-in-Chief of the British Expeditionary Force, inspecting British defenses in France. Above right, Sir Edmund Ironside, Chief of the Imperial General Staff. Below, King George VI and the Duke of Gloucester with Gort in France.

Mr. Winston Churchill, First Lord of the Admiralty, addresses men of H.M.S. "Exeter" on her return to Portsmouth, February 15, 1940, after taking part in the destruction of the German pocket battleship "Graf Spee."

Above, British troops en route for Norway relaxing on the promenade deck of S.S. "Oronsay." Below, what remained of Namsos after German bombing. Bottom, British troops preparing to re-embark from the blitzed quay at Namsos.

Above left, Lord Salisbury. Above right, Mr. L. S. Amery. Below, Mr. Churchill, flanked by two of his supporters, Sir Kingsley Wood and Mr. Anthony Eden, after the morning Cabinet meeting on May 10, 1940.

Above, Dunkirk, photographed by an aircraft of R.A.F. Coastal Command. Below, the return from Dunkirk.

Above left, Lord Lothian, British Ambassador in Washington. Above right, Mr. Malcolm R. Lovell, unofficial peacemaker. Right, Dr. Hans Thomsen, German chargé d'affaires in Washington.

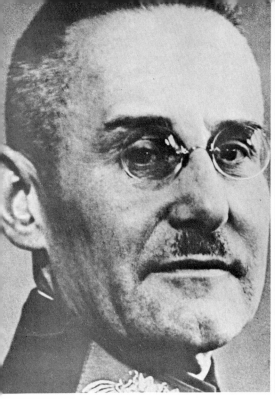 

Above left, General Franz von Halder. Above right, Admiral Erich Raeder. Below, German invasion barges waiting at Boulogne.

nounced on tape it did not say more than support of war effort."

The message had, in fact, been drafted that morning by Dalton who, suspecting Chamberlain's intentions, had deliberately made it as unhelpful as possible. When the news-agency tape of the message was handed in during the Cabinet meeting, Chamberlain's adviser, Sir Horace Wilson, noted on it that it seemed to leave things just as they were "before the war blew up," and passed it to Reith. Reith at least received an impression that more might be expected.

The unexpected delay seems to have precipitated something approaching a Cabinet revolt. During the morning Kingsley Wood told Chamberlain that he must go. Eden records that just before the Cabinet, he was talking to Hankey when Simon came up and said he understood that, despite the German attack, Churchill was pressing for early changes. Simon, says Eden, was indignant; but the usually mild Hankey commented, "Personally, I think that if there are to be changes, the sooner they are made the better."

Ripples of uncertainty spread from Downing Street through Westminster and Fleet Street. There is some indication that Lord Salisbury felt them and brought his weight to bear. Clement Davies felt them and urgently telephoned the Labour leaders, who had gone by train to Bournemouth, warning them that Chamberlain was seeking to stay in office.

Spurred by this warning, and by a report that the Germans were bombing Canterbury,* the National Executive of the Labour party met in a basement room of the Highcliff Hotel, Bournemouth. They resolved that the Labour party would not enter a government under Chamberlain, but would serve under a new Prime Minister. Dalton deemed it wise to have written into the minutes that the resolution was a decision of the National Executive, not a recommendation which the party conference might overturn if it proved hostile when it met on Monday.**

* A single German plane dropped bombs near Petham and Chilham, a few miles from Canterbury: the first German attack of the war on the British mainland. There were no casualties. The fact that Dalton records the rumor may be taken as an indication of the extent to which the threat of the knockout blow from the air still haunted British thoughts.

** However, the conference gave no trouble, apart from impassioned speeches against an imperialist war from such forcing grounds of revolution as Chislehurst and Norwood. It endorsed the Executive decision by 2,413,000 votes to 170,000. Would it have been managed so easily if the German attack had not begun when it did?

There was no discussion of who the new Prime Minister was to be, and therefore no indication of what attitude the Executive, with its pacifist and Socialist members, might have taken to Churchill. Attlee left Bournemouth with a blank check in his pocket and did not know until he arrived back in London, and was asked to go to the Admiralty, what the final choice had been.

At about five o'clock, just as Attlee and Greenwood were leaving for London with the answers to the Prime Minister's two questions, Chamberlain's private secretary rang. Attlee read the Executive resolution to him over the telephone.

According to Halifax' diary note, the Prime Minister had already decided not to wait and had arranged to see the King that evening to advise that Churchill should take over; but he appears to have had the Bournemouth message when his full Cabinet assembled. He told them that he was resigning, and asked formally for their own resignations. He spoke with evident emotion and shook hands with each minister in turn. Then he drove to Buckingham Palace.

The result of the Commons debate, King George VI's biographer tells us, had caused the King displeasure. He thought Chamberlain had been treated "grossly unfairly," and suggested Halifax as his successor. Chamberlain replied that Halifax was not enthusiastic because of the peerage difficulty, upon which the King suggested that Halifax's peerage could be placed in abeyance for the time being. He finally accepted without evident enthusiasm Chamberlain's advice to send for Churchill. The meeting between the King and the champion of the King's abdicated brother passed off, however, with no more than a mild misunderstanding over an intended joke. Churchill, the King noted, was "full of fire and determination to carry out the duties of Prime Minister."

Almost at once there was difficulty. Chamberlain remained Leader of the Conservative party, he retained the support of some two hundred members of the House of Commons, and while in theory a government could have been formed without him, in practice it was impossible. Churchill offered him the post of Chancellor of the Exchequer, with Leadership of the Commons. When this became known, there was consternation. Attlee and Greenwood, despite some pressure from Bournemouth, accepted Chamberlain's presence in the War Cabinet as inevitable. They protested, however, that he could not be given Leadership of the Commons.

The Conservative dissidents, too, were aghast, and Amery, Lloyd George, Clement Davies, and Duff Cooper met urgently at Amery's house to consider what pressure they could bring to bear. As they entered Amery's study Lloyd George murmured, "I presume, my dear Leo, that this must have been the room where my downfall was conspired twenty years ago?"

"Yes, sir. It was," Amery answered succinctly; and the four set to work upon a letter to Churchill which would encompass the further downfall of Lloyd George's ancient enemy. While the letter was being typed, Duff Cooper excused himself and left the house. Amery had already in principle accepted office in the new government. When he took the letter round to the Admiralty, a belligerent Churchill seemed to be expecting him. Without opening the letter, he said, "Thank you, Leo, and I'll take your resignation at the same time."

Churchill was indeed in a difficult situation, dependent for support on Conservatives who had remained loyal to Chamberlain, and who were already angry at the supersession of their leader as the result of a Labour and rebel Conservative alliance. To give way further to dissident or Labour demands might have wrecked the coalition before it had been formed.

Into this impasse the redoubtable Lord Salisbury advanced for the last time. Hearing about Churchill's offer to Chamberlain, he telephoned Amery's house and spoke to Clement Davies. Davies told him the situation. "The man's a menace!" Lord Salisbury is said to have exclaimed with reference to Chamberlain; and promised to telephone Churchill at once. Under these combined pressures, Chamberlain gracefully surrendered the Leadership of the House and the Exchequer, and entered the new War Cabinet as Lord President of the Council. The Labour leaders accepted this compromise, though not without some rumblings from Bournemouth.

The Exchequer went, to the astonishment of all, to Sir Kingsley Wood. His was one of the heads the dissident Conservatives had most insistently called for; but he had, as the *Times* said, "a thorough understanding of current political values." Before the end of the year he was back in the War Cabinet, last survivor of the eight hedge sparrows who had received the cuckoo into their nest at the beginning of the war.

Under the pressure of events, and with his natural impetuosity, Churchill completed his Cabinet within four days. This speed, and the need to maintain a balance of party loyalties, sowed seeds of future dissension. On the day following the Norway debate, government supporters who had voted against Chamberlain had met and agreed, among other things, to give their support to a Prime Minister, whoever he might be, who "should choose his colleagues on merit, and not on the recommendation of any party manager." In spite of this resolution, the new War Cabinet of five consisted of the two official leaders of the Labour party, Attlee and Greenwood, together with three members of the previous War Cabinet, Churchill, Chamberlain, and Halifax. There was no place for Morrison, nor for Amery, who at one point had had the government at his mercy and who accepted the comparatively minor post of Secretary of State for India only after some hesitation. Duff Cooper was given a political death sentence by being appointed the Minister of Information, and a handful of dissidents, Boothby, Macmillan, Richard Law, Harold Nicolson, had undersecretaryships. No post was found for Clement Davies, who was offered a peerage, which he declined.

Hoare was dropped, but Simon retained office, if not power, as Lord Chancellor, and nearly a score of senior members of the previous Cabinet remained in the new one. The Liberals were dissatisfied because their leader, Sinclair, though becoming Secretary of State for Air, was not in the War Cabinet. The loyal Conservatives were dissatisfied because their leader had been cut down.

The Norway debate is often quoted as an example of the power of a vote in the House of Commons to bring down a strong government, even under conditions of modern party discipline. The claim is only partly justified. It is true that Chamberlain fell, though it seems possible that he was persuaded to resign at least as much by Amery's speech as by the Commons vote. But he fell only to make way for Halifax, who could certainly have formed a government, though how long that government would have lasted is another question. Churchill in fact came to power through the self-abnegation of Halifax; and it could be said that the only major effect of the Norway vote was to install the official Labour leaders, Attlee and Greenwood, in the War Cabinet, instead of Morrison and perhaps Eden. It is somewhat doubtful if this was the result the fomentors of revolt hoped to achieve.

On Whit Monday, May 13, while German armor was forcing a passage across the Meuse, Churchill met a special session of the House of Commons for the first time as Prime Minister. When the new Prime Minister entered the crowded House, chin characteristically squared to meet the challenge of destiny, the packed Labour benches cheered. The Conservative benches remained silent. Their enthusiasm was reserved for the fallen Chamberlain.

In the first and perhaps the greatest of his speeches as leader of a nation at war, Churchill told the now-silent Commons that he had nothing to offer but blood, toil, tears, and sweat; that his only policy was to wage war, his only aim victory. Again, the Labour benches cheered him, the Conservatives did not, though even on the Labour benches there were silent reservations about the value of Churchillian rhetoric in stopping German tanks.

But publicly, the statement was welcomed by H. B. Lees-Smith on behalf of the Labour party, by Sir Percy Harris for the Liberals, by Lloyd George, and one of the Independent rebels, Austin Hopkinson.

The loyal Conservative backbenches spoke through the voice of Sir William Colfox, member for Dorset West. It would have been very much better in the interests of the country, said Sir William, if Mr. Chamberlain had remained Prime Minister of a reinforced government; but it was essential that there should be national unity, and as his Leader was a member of the new government, he would do all he could to support it.

Conservative anger that the wrong man had been shot over Norway continued for many months; indeed in some quarters it still persists. The lasting sense of insecurity which this hostility induced in Churchill himself may be illustrated by a story said to have been told to Clement Davies by Lord Horder, Chamberlain's doctor.*

At the beginning of October, Chamberlain, still Leader of the

---

* It is right to say that the present Lord Horder had not heard this story, and has pointed out to me a number of reasons why he believes it improbable. On the other hand, Clement Davies had a retentive memory, he told the story in circumstantial detail, and there seems no credible reason why he should invent it.

Conservative party, though he had resigned from the government, lay at his Hampshire home, wasting away with cancer. Horder had to pronounce upon him almost immediate sentence of death. Chamberlain did not wince, but asked Horder to deliver a letter to Churchill in London. Horder, deeply moved by what he had seen, hurried to London, told the Prime Minister that Chamberlain had not much longer to live, and handed over the letter. Churchill took it and, without opening it, asked, "Did he say anything about the Leadership?"

Horder, who had not the responsibility of conducting a nation's affairs in war without any firm basis of party support, was able to afford the luxury of feeling shocked.

Chapter
6

THE BATTLE OF THE MEUSE

On the evening of May 9, while the attention of the British and French governments was partially distracted by internal crises, Colonel J. G. Sas, the Dutch military attaché in Berlin, ate a farewell dinner with his friend Major General Hans Oster, chief assistant to Admiral Canaris, the head of German Military Intelligence. Six days previously, Oster had warned Sas that the German attack through Holland and Belgium would begin on May 10, and after their farewell dinner together Sas confirmed the warning to his government in a dramatic message: "Tomorrow at dawn. Hold tight!"

This was by no means the first warning of an attack which the Allies had received from German or Italian sources, and so many false alarms throughout the winter had blunted the impact. But in so far as the warning had any effect at all, it served to concentrate British and French eyes more firmly on the northern front.

Oster's warning may have been well intentioned; and yet there must remain a question-mark against it. Both he and his chief, Canaris, were associated with the constantly changing groups which, under the leadership of a former Army Chief of Staff, General Ludwig Beck, and a former mayor of Leipzig, Carl Gördeler, provided most of whatever opposition to Hitler there was inside Germany. Chamberlain seems at one time to have placed some faith in the German opposition's ability to carry out a coup d'état, with the apparent connivance of Göring, who hoped to succeed Hitler at the head of the German government. There were constant attempts to keep in touch with the German dissidents, at least once frustrated by the discovery that instead of negotiating as they thought with the representatives of German generals opposed to Hitler, British intelligence agents were in fact talking to a representative of Himmler's Gestapo. The situation was further complicated by the eagerness of amateur diplomats, British, Swedish, German, and American, to plunge with greater enthusiasm than skill into the curious and complex underworld of peace feelers and plots. One sympathizes, indeed, with Halifax, who is recorded as muttering under his breath, "It's a tricky business" when approaches from the German opposition through two different intermediaries were reaching him at the same time.

It has to be emphasized that any opposition to the Nazi regime, with its powers of arbitrary arrest, torture, and sudden death, required physical courage greater than is possessed by most of us; but that said, there is no evidence that Beck, Gördeler and their associates were any more representative of national opinion than, say, Mosley in Britain or Quisling in Norway. In any event, they were helpless without the support of the army, whose Commander-in-Chief, Brauchitsch, and Chief of Staff, Halder, had both been implicated in conspiracies against Hitler, but whose efforts, unlike those of British generals, had failed to claim even such a comparatively humble scalp as that of a Hore-Belisha.

Before the start of the Norway campaign, the German opposition had tried to secure an undertaking from the British government through the Vatican that the Allies would not take advantage of an attempted coup d'état by attacking Germany from the west. Both Brauchitsch and Halder had by that time lost whatever enthusiasm they might previously have had for overthrowing Hitler. Halder wrote to Gördeler at the beginning of April that since Britain and France had declared war on Germany, it would have to be fought through and a compromise peace was senseless. When information about the Vatican negotiations reached Brauchitsch, he brushed it aside on the grounds that it was impossible to organize a successful military coup in the middle of operations. From this point it seems clear that he and Halder had decided that the quickest way to peace was to win the war; and they afterward claimed to be helpless in the face of Hitler's triumphant progress in Norway and France.

It was the delaying tactics of the Army High Command, however, which had initially prevented a German attack in the west during the autumn of 1939, and later the icy weather caused further delays, in the course of which the German plan had been changed. The main weight of the assault was now to be delivered, not through Holland and Belgium, but through Luxembourg and Belgium south of Liège.* There would be an attack in the north, but this was to some extent a decoy, designed to draw the French and British armies forward and keep them engaged while they were encircled from the south.

It is difficult to believe that the head of German Military Intelligence and his chief assistant did not know about this change of plan, but no hint of it seems to have been communicated by Oster to his friend Sas, and one must therefore continue to harbor a suspicion that Oster's warning, like Colonel Meinertzhagen's famous "haversack ruse" which deceived the Turks about British intentions in Palestine in the First World War, was part of a deliberate deception, designed to keep Allied eyes fixed on the north.

When, at first light on May 10, 135 German divisions rolled forward on a front extending from the North Sea to the Swiss frontier, Gamelin, the Allied Commander-in-Chief, had no hesitation in putting into operation the Allied counterplan for an advance into Belgium. Nine divisions of the British Expeditionary Force—a tenth was on garrison duty in the Maginot fortifications, and three more Territorial divisions, not fully equipped, were being used as pioneer labor in base areas—advanced in line with French armies on either flank. For some days the censored and misleadingly briefed British press reported this Anglo-French advance as if it had been a victory. On May 11, the *Times* military correspondent announced that "This time at least there has been no strategic surprise," and on May 13, the *Times* news report was headlined, "British Forces Moving Across Belgium. Successful Encounters With The Enemy. . . . BEF Sweeps On."

Reaction on the German side would not have confirmed these

* Both conception and execution of the new plan owed much to an Englishman, Captain B. H. Liddell Hart. The plan's principal author, Manstein, said it had been suggested to him by an article of Liddell Hart's pointing out the possibility of armored warfare in the Ardennes. The most able German tank general, Guderian, frankly avowed himself Liddell Hart's disciple.

optimistic pronouncements. "I could have wept for joy: they'd fallen into the trap!" Hitler afterward said, according to the records of his Table Talk. "It had been a clever piece of work to attack Liège. We had to make them believe we were remaining faithful to the old Schlieffen plan, and they *had* believed it."

The combined French, British, Belgian, and Dutch armies had a numerical superiority over the Germans of 156 divisions to 135. They had some four thousand tanks, mainly French and better armored though less mobile than the Germans' 2,800 tanks. The French tanks were mostly split up for infantry support and not concentrated in armored divisions.* Only in the air did the Germans hold a clear advantage. But the German dispositions had ensured that, while north of Liège Bock's Army Group B was numerically inferior to the Allies, Rundstedt's Army Group A in the south concentrated forty-four of the best German divisions, including seven armored divisions, against the French Ninth and Second Armies, which were holding a front of over ninety miles with sixteen poorly equipped reserve divisions.

How this complete strategic surprise was achieved remains one of the mysteries of the war. It has generally been attributed to the blind faith of Gamelin and the French staff that the hilly forest country of the Ardennes was impassable to tanks, but the facts do not wholly support this interpretation. At an inter-Allied conference at his headquarters in October, 1939, Gamelin showed full awareness of the possibility of an attack through the Ardennes, though he believed that a sweep through northern Belgium was more likely. Ironside favored the Ardennes alternative; but both agreed that the way to meet it, if it came, was by a move forward into Belgium, which would enable the Allies to counterattack it from both north and south. Gamelin was a political general, and he was certainly subjected to political pressure, it being urged upon him that after the humiliation of Poland it would be politically impossible to surrender Holland and Belgium to the Germans without a fight. The British were acutely aware of the danger of allowing German air bases in the Low Countries, while the French

---

* The *Times* military correspondent in December, 1939, had described French armored tactics: "Tanks, it is enjoined, will not normally be used in attack except under the protection of very powerful artillery, and they will not attempt deep penetration until the hostile defensive system has been disorganised." Colonel Charles de Gaulle was ignored in France, as Liddell Hart had been in England.

were naturally anxious to keep the war off French soil and, if possible, to secure a base from which to attack the heart of German industry in the Ruhr.

For whatever reasons, so convinced had the French High Command become that the main German attack would be from the north that the French Seventh Army, originally held in reserve near Reims, where it would have been well placed to counterattack a German thrust through the Ardennes, had been committed to a long advance into Holland, on the extreme left of the Allied line. There it was severely mauled before the French added to the existing chaos by attempting to pass it behind the entire Allied front to plug the gap in the south.

The armored spearhead of Rundstedt's Army Group, advancing to the south of Liège, consisted of some twelve hundred tanks which, with lorries carrying the motorized infantry, formed a block a hundred miles deep from head to tail, and one may ask why there seems to have been no air reconnaissance report of this enormous mass, moving not only by day but by night with headlights burning. Rundstedt's Army Group initially had the support of only one air fleet, compared with two for Bock, but even this gave the Germans such an overwhelming command of the air that the French pilots, flying largely obsolete planes, may have been understandably reluctant to press reconnaissance too far. Nor was the German armor heavily bombed. The French began the campaign with fewer than a hundred bombers, of which only twenty-five were modern, but in any event it was May 13 before General Vuillemin, Commander-in-Chief of the French Air Force, gave orders for any bombing at all.

In addition to the French planes, there were available 256 light bombers, Battles, and Blenheims, of the British Advanced Air Striking Force. The A.A.S.F. was commanded by Air Marshal Arthur Barratt, who sent the British bombers into action on May 10. When he telephoned General Georges, commanding the North-East Theatre of Operations, to tell him that he had done so, Georges uttered a heartfelt *"Grâce à Dieu!"*

The British planes nominally had a sphere of operations north of Namur, but with the French Air Force inactive, Georges called upon Barratt for operations over the entire front, and Barratt did his utmost with the forces at his disposal. The British Battles were almost as obsolescent as the French Amiots; the German antiaircraft batteries put up a blanket of fire, and British losses in low-level daylight attacks were appalling: 50 per cent was a not abnormal rate of casualties.

The story may be read in the laconic, often stereotyped phrases of the Battle squadrons' operations record books. On May 9, life goes on: one squadron appoints a committee to organize a squadron sports day, to be held on May 28. Then: "10.5.40. State of readiness as from 0600 hrs. was 50 per cent available aircraft at 30 mins. notice and 50 per cent at two hours notice. 1200 hrs. 8 aircraft to bomb enemy columns on Luxembourg-Dippach road. 3 failed to return"; "F/O Vaughan of 'A' Flight did not return. P/O McElligott of 'A' Flight did dive bombing, dropping his bombs on the main road in the village of Givonne as no MET [mechanical transport] was observed; he also stated that he saw F/O Vaughan's bombs drop on the road in the same village. Intense light A.A. and machine-gun fire was encountered. Sgt. A. Winkler of 'A' Flight did not return, and was subsequently reported prisoner of war. Sgt. Johnson of 'B' Flight did not return. P/O McElligott after dropping bombs on the village of St. Fergeau was attacked by six M.E. 109's. The port tank of aircraft caught fire and the pilot was seriously wounded in the arm. Both the Air Observer Sgt. Long and W/T operator LAC Burgess replied to the fire. LAC Burgess is sure he shot down one enemy aircraft. Aircraft then lost height in a shallow dive and crashed in a wood. The crew managed to get clear, the pilot and air gunner were taken to hospital by the French where the pilot died of wounds. The French say two M.E.109's were shot down and located by them. Sgt. Long, the Air Observer, was uninjured and returned to the Squadron two days later to resume duty."

On May 15, after he had lost forty out of seventy-one bombers employed in operations the previous afternoon, Barratt had to withdraw the Battle squadrons from daylight attacks.

While this massacre was going on, the eighteen squadrons of Bomber Command—not Barratt's light Battles and Blenheims, but the "heavies" of their day, Wellingtons, Whitleys and Hampdens —were not committed. In *The Second World War,* Churchill has written that at the moment in the evening of May 10 when he became responsible, no fresh decision about meeting the German invasion of the Low Countries was required from him or his colleagues in the new and still unformed administration. This is not an exact appreciation. In prewar talks with the French, the British had been unwilling to commit themselves definitely on a number of points, but it was implied that the British would make up for their small army by providing air and naval forces; and one of the explicit commitments was that an attack on France through the Low Countries "would constitute a decisive situation and, in these circumstances, collaboration with the French Army and Air Force in stemming the invasion would become the primary commitment of the British Bomber Command."

Because of their comparative weakness in the air, as well as on moral grounds, both the British and French governments had been reluctant to begin bombing; but a conclusion had emerged that the most effective way of delaying the advance of the German armies in Holland and Belgium would be to bomb troop concentrations, marshaling yards, and oil plants in the Ruhr, with the principal weight directed against oil plants. Since this bombing was only to begin when the Germans attacked, the plan constituted a none too happy compromise between strategic and tactical objectives; but it has to be remembered that this was in effect the beginning of the first air war. In the disarming words of one of the participants, "We didn't really know what we were doing. We had to make it all up as we went along."

The French High Command was never happy with the Ruhr plan, believing that the heavy bombers should be used in a tactical role against German communications. Gamelin in particular retained an invincible faith in the power of a bomber to hit a crossroads or a railway bridge, while the British Air Staff were convinced that by night, which bitter experience had forced on them as the only possibility, a bomber with the rudimentary navigational and aiming equipment of the time would be lucky to hit the area of a big industrial installation.

In mid-April Barratt attended a session of the French War Committee, with instructions to join Gamelin and Georges in devising a plan for immediately bombing the Ruhr in the event of a German invasion of the Low Countries, without further reference to either the French or British governments. The French refused to agree, arguing that bombing the Ruhr would not delay the German armies, and might lay the almost undefended French armament factories open to devastating reprisals. Barratt, a forthright man, told Gamelin he must be mad if he believed the Germans would refrain from bombing French factories for a moment longer than suited them; and there, for the time being, the situation uneasily rested.

A meeting of the Supreme War Council on April 23 agreed to a compromise solution. A limited number of heavy bombers was to co-operate with Barratt's Battles and Blenheims in direct support of the Allied armies, but the main heavy-bomber force would operate against the Ruhr. The final decision on the start of this attack was left to the British government.

The French High Command, however, continued to press for tactical rather than strategic bombing, and on May 8, with the German attack expected within forty-eight hours, Ironside, who had once hailed the original plan as "decisive," executed one of his sharp turnabouts to Gamelin's side.

This was the complex situation which confronted the new British government on taking up office, and it seems possible that there was some substance in forebodings that a change of government at the moment of German attack might affect urgent decisions concerning the troops in the field, though there is no guarantee that the old government would have been more decisive than the new. The new Prime Minister himself, combining with his own the post of Minister of Defence, was engaged in Cabinet-making. The new Air Minister, Sinclair, can scarcely have been versed in the intricacies of this long-standing technical argument, and was certainly in no position to do more than echo the views of his Air Staff. The new War Minister, Eden, was quick to see the apparent advantages of bombing communications rather than industrial plants, and threw his weight behind Ironside and the French.*

Not until the crucial battle of the French campaign was already lost did the Cabinet unleash Bomber Command, and then against the Ruhr, which the French did not want, while temporarily with-

---

* In *The Reckoning*, Lord Avon (then Anthony Eden) writes that he did not take over at the War Office until the afternoon of Whit Sunday, May 12. He began arguing the War Office case over bombing on the following day. There was presumably a similar delay in Sinclair's take-over at the Air Ministry.

holding fighter squadrons, for which the French and Gort were urgently appealing, on the plea that the fighters must be retained in England to guard British industry against German reprisals. The Ruhr was attacked on the nights of May 15 and 16,* after which the combined pressure of Eden and the French forced a compromise, the effort of the comparatively few British bombers being dispersed over a wide range of targets.

Whether Bomber Command could have influenced the battle if it had been used earlier is obviously a matter of opinion, but one may look briefly at events from the German side. In January, when the Manstein plan was in process of evolution, Halder was grappling with a shortage of trucks. In February, he was officially informed that the state of the German railways was such that they would not be in any position to see the Army through a large-scale offensive, and Göring, in his role as economic overlord, had to be called upon to improve the situation. Almost as soon as the advance through southern Belgium and Luxembourg began, Rundstedt's Army Group was reporting difficulties from road demolitions, one of which, though undefended, held up movement at this point for twenty-four hours; and in their postwar accounts of the approach march to the Meuse, a number of German generals have expressed the apprehension they felt of the effect of concentrated Allied bombing on the masses of vehicles moving to an intricate timetable on steep, winding roads and tracks.

In the light of this background I have been given an informed British opinion that, allowing for Bomber Command's rudimentary techniques, a delay of two or three days might have been imposed on the Germans, if bombing had begun on the night of May 10, and had been concentrated on the masses of Rundstedt's army.**

There was no specific British undertaking to commit Fighter Command in France as there was with Bomber Command, but to the indecision over bombing the British added first a hesitancy, then a firm refusal, to send more fighter squadrons. Sir Hugh Dowding, the Commander-in-Chief of Fighter Command, was one of

---

* Little damage was done in spite of optimistic Royal Air Force claims. "Our people seem pretty well satisfied that they have done well in the Ruhr. I hope they are right." Halifax diary, May 17.

** For a contrary, and certainly authoritative view, see Slessor, *The Central Blue*.

the few senior Allied commanders at this time to be absolutely sure of his own mind, and his reiterated warnings that if further fighter squadrons were sent to France he could no longer hold himself responsible for the defense of Britain, influenced the British government to decide on May 20 to withhold its fighter planes. According to Cordell Hull, the American Secretary of State, this decision had considerable psychological effect on the French government.

The effect of Dowding's stand on the Battle of Britain in August and September has been much discussed and possibly overestimated; the effect on French morale in the earlier battle, coming as it did on top of the British performance in Norway, and the inbuilt French suspicion of British resolution in waging war, has possibly been given insufficient weight by British historians who, with the benefit of hindsight, have had no difficulty in proving to British satisfaction that the French were already beaten. The decision not to reinforce defeat is never an easy one to time correctly; but one cannot resist the conclusion that some members of the British government—Chamberlain, for instance, had never had much faith in Gamelin and did not share Churchill's admiration for the French army—had made up their minds that the French were beaten even before the campaign began. They certainly did not put up a great deal of resistance to Dowding's ultimatum.

Neither the French nor, more understandably, the British, realized the importance of Rundstedt's thrust until it was too late. If they had done so in time, and had concentrated all their efforts on an attempt to stop it, it is just conceivable that a delay of two days at this early stage might have given the French a chance to get their reserves into position and, by holding Rundstedt's armor on the Meuse, have altered the course of the war.

The German advance to the Meuse met with no resistance in Luxembourg, whose inhabitants behaved, by German standards, correctly; that is, the Luxembourg police helped regulate traffic for the German columns. The weak Belgian outposts behaved incorrectly, firing on these invaders of their country, and were rapidly forced into surrender. The French horsed cavalry proved no more successful against tanks than the Polish cavalry had been, and by May 12 advance units of the German armored divisions had reached the east bank of the Meuse.

The French had calculated that, if the Germans did attack through the Ardennes, it would take them several days of artillery preparation before they could attempt to cross the wide, steeply banked river, and during this time the French reserves could move into position. The Germans agreed with these calculations; and instead of waiting for five or six days to assemble guns and ammunition, they used bombers.

The Junkers 87 Stuka * had made its appearance in Spain and Poland, but both French and British troops had apparently had little warning of it. When resolutely attacked it could be brought down even by rifle fire as it dived, and in the Battle of Britain it was shot out of the air; but the British and French fighter strength was weak, the reserve French divisions on the Meuse were short of antiaircraft guns, and they quickly became too demoralized to be resolute.

French accounts speak of Stukas "bombing our troops with the tranquillity of hunters who expend their cartridges on surrounding game." One articulate observer, who had to face the Stukas, wrote afterward of their whistling scream, which conjured up terrifying images of death and destruction: "Strictly acoustic qualities worked upon the nerves so that they became wrought to the pitch of intolerable tension, whence it is a very short step to panic."

Supported by Stukas and heavier bombers, the German armored divisions began an immediate assault across the Meuse. In the north, French troops blew the bridges as the leading tanks of Rommel's Seventh Panzer Division began to cross. South of Dinant, two divisions of young French reservists, who had just arrived on the west bank, looked curiously across at the Germans moving on the steep slopes opposite, but the bridges were down, the river was wide, its banks steep and wooded. There seemed no urgent danger, the troops were exhausted after a long foot march, and they were ordered to settle into their billets instead of getting their guns into position.

By the early morning of May 13, Rommel's infantry had forced a toehold across the river, which they began to exploit with troops ferried across in rubber boats. Even so, the French brought the

* *Sturzkampflugzeug:* dive bomber.

crossings to a standstill, and Rommel's officers were badly shaken by heavy casualties among their men. Rommel, up with his forward troops, took personal command, crossing the river in a dinghy under heavy fire, and got the assault moving again. By daybreak on May 14, he had fifteen tanks across the river, with which he began to force a way into the French positions.

In the center of the German line, about Monthermé, Reinhardt's Forty-first Armored Corps also got troops across the Meuse on May 13, but like Rommel's they had a desperate fight to maintain their foothold and could make little progress out of their bridgehead. Higher up the river, to the north and south of Sedan, the most brilliant of the German tank generals, Guderian, made contact with French troops on the evening of May 12, at the boundary between the French Ninth and Second Armies. This French hinge was manned by three reserve divisions, lacking antiaircraft guns and antitank artillery. The troops were men of an age to have wives and children to think about. One of the divisions, the Seventy-first, was from the northeast suburbs of Paris, and was believed to be permeated by Communist propaganda. Its morale, like that of the neighboring Fifty-fifth Division, was certainly low. There is a legend that when the Germans put in their attack, French soldiers were seen to reverse helmets, the Communist sign, and run among their colleagues, shouting, "Here are the Germans. Bolt!" Gamelin afterward gave his opinion that Communist propaganda had played little part in the disaster, and that the defeatism of the French middle classes, and therefore of the officers of these divisions, had made a more important contribution. One may suspect that it was a matter of mutual distrust. There were cases of officers deserting their men under fire. There were also cases of officers and men seeking to make up for their lack of antitank artillery by attacking tanks with light machine guns and even pistols.

From the afternoon of May 13 until nightfall, these weak divisions were subjected to continuous and almost undisturbed bombing by twelve squadrons of Stukas. The Stuka usually carried one 550-pound bomb under the fuselage and four 110-pound bombs under the wings, but the pilots were ordered to continue circling and diving even after they had dropped their bombs, to bluff the French gunners into keeping their heads permanently down. The bluff succeeded and, under cover of the almost unopposed Stuka

THE GERMAN BREAKTHROUGH: In the early morning of May 13
Rommel's infantry crossed the Meuse River near Dinant and by
the dawn of May 14 fifteen of his tanks were on the west bank.
Farther south, at Sedan, Guderian's armor also broke through,
and the French began pivoting on the Maginot Line. By the following evening seven German armored divisions had driven
through a sixty-mile gap in the French front.

assault, Guderian got a single pontoon bridge across the river, over which he then passed one of his three armored divisions.

Throughout May 14, the Battles and Blenheims of the British Advanced Air Striking Force, and what there was of the French Air Force, pounded away at this bridge and at Guderian's debouching tanks. It was believed by the British squadrons that they had in fact knocked out the bridge, but that French resistance had virtually ceased, enabling the Germans to rebuild it. There is no confirmation of this, however, in Guderian's and other accounts of the battle. By the afternoon of May 14, Guderian had all his three divisions across the Meuse.

In front of the German armies, in some cases deliberately machine-gunned into motion by them, moved a steadily increasing flood of civilian refugees, a Sargasso Sea of woebegone humanity, in cars and farm carts, on bicycles or on foot, pushing perambulators and barrows loaded with possessions. By the end of the French campaign, there were some seven million of them on the move. Occasionally, through the terrible anonymity of war, one catches a glimpse of the individual suffering which this vast mass movement entailed: a Frenchman stopping a British general to ask how he might dispose of the body of his dead wife, in the van behind him; the corpses of sixty convent schoolgirls, laid out in four regular lines on the broad white pavement of a little French town; heaps of dead and dying men, women and children bombed while taking refuge in a gun pit. But for the most part they are faceless, a dead weight of disaster, clogging roads and railways, hindering the mobility of divisions and the movement forward of reserves, like a pestilence spreading stories of German invincibility, of parachutists dressed as Red Cross nurses and of boxes of mysterious white powder which they claimed to be a secret German explosive though in fact it was bicarbonate of soda.

General Corap, commanding the French Ninth Army, spent the greater part of May 11 and 12 in a car on roads jammed with these refugees, able neither to receive information nor to give orders. His reserves had been sited on the assumption that he would have several days in which to bring them into action. Like most of the French generals, he was a man no longer young, the high point of whose career had been reached when he received the surrender of the Moroccan guerrilla leader Abd-el-Krim fourteen years before,

Throughout May 14, Corap saw his front disintegrating under the desperate pressure of the German assaults. In the course of that evening Huntziger's Second Army on his right began to fall back, pivoting on the Maginot Line. In the early morning of May 15, Corap ordered Ninth Army units still holding the west bank of the Meuse to withdraw to new positions fifteen miles in their rear. The positions were unmanned, and before the retiring Ninth Army troops could reach them, Rommel's tanks were through and heading westward, shooting up French reserves moving toward what they believed to be the front.

Reinhardt's corps, which had been held, slipped through the gap opening between the Ninth and Second Armies, in turn releasing Guderian. What had begun as a French tactical withdrawal quickly became a rout. By the evening of May 15, seven German armored divisions had sped through a sixty-mile-wide gap in the French front, leaving themselves alternatives of either capturing a practically undefended Paris or making for the Channel Coast.

Chapter

7

THE SPIRIT OF DUNKIRK

At 1 P.M. on Friday, May 10, punctually according to plan, the armored cars of the Twelfth Royal Lancers, cavalry screen of the British Expeditionary Force, crossed the Franco-Belgian frontier. The advance was on the whole uneventful, such difficulties as the B.E.F. experienced being symptomatic of the relationship which was to exist between the British and their allies as the campaign progressed.

At one point, a unit of Major General B. L. Montgomery's Third Division was refused permission to enter Belgium by a zealous frontier guard, on the grounds that it did not possess the necessary permits. A fifteen-hundredweight truck charged the frontier barrier, and the advance continued. When Montgomery's division reached its allotted line east of Brussels, it found a Belgian division in possession which, taking the British for German parachutists, opened fire. While high-level negotiations were proceeding to induce the Belgian divisional commander to move, Montgomery made his own plan: to arrest the Belgian general when the Germans arrived, and take over command himself.

These slightly farcical proceedings were the surface manifestation of a deep-seated malaise. While the German armies moved as one, the French, British, Belgian, and Dutch armies, though on paper numerically superior, were divided in command and weak in co-ordination.

Gort's position as Commander-in-Chief of the British Expeditionary Force was riddled with anomalies. He was directly responsible to a British government at the head of which was now Churchill, whom Ironside had accused, during the Norwegian campaign, of trying to supervise military arrangements as if he were a company commander running a small operation to cross a bridge.

At the same time, the British Commander-in-Chief was under three tiers of French control. At the top was Gamelin. Responsible to Gamelin, and on bad terms with him, was Georges, commanding the North-East Front. Under Georges was General Billotte, commanding Army Group Number One, which included the collapsing Ninth and Second Armies, and to whom after May 12 both Gort and King Leopold, as Commander-in-Chief of the Belgian army, were subordinated.

To complicate matters further, Gamelin entered the campaign under suspended notice. At a stormy Cabinet meeting on May 9, Reynaud, the French Prime Minister, had tried to force Gamelin's dismissal, and when this move was resisted, resigned. He was persuaded to carry on in view of the crisis, and agreed "provisionally" to allow Gamelin to continue as Commander-in-Chief. Gamelin's interventions in the battle were tentative, almost apologetic, as befitted his position.

To the difficulties inherent in this situation was added a faulty system of communications. A week after the campaign began, Gort had no telephone link with Belgian headquarters on his left, the French First Army on his right, or Georges' headquarters behind him, the only liaison being by personal visit, along bombed and narrow roads crowded with refugees and military traffic moving at night without lights. At least twice, in a swiftly moving battle, a car crash at a vital moment left one or other of the Allies without important information or orders.

The army of nine divisions which Gort commanded entered the campaign with an admirable but unwarranted confidence. They were, Hore-Belisha had told them, as well, if not better, equipped than any similar army; and they were certainly the only army on either side which did not depend to some extent upon that unpredictable beast, the horse.* But they were inadequately equipped with antiaircraft guns, short of antitank ammunition, and inferior in the air. The only operational British armored division was in England when the battle began, undergoing one of its periodic reorganizations. It was shipped piecemeal to France, with tanks and weapons which in some cases the crews handled for the first time after they landed, and which were squandered in a series of abortive attempts to break through northward from the Somme.

The B.E.F. had trained hard throughout the winter and spring, but for the most part in such activities as trench-digging, trench reliefs, patroling, and bayonet-fighting. A student on one junior officers' course remembers the pride with which the chief instructor informed them that they were to be trained "actually on the site of some 1914-18 trenches."

In spite of the writings of Liddell Hart and Fuller, and the practical lessons of Spain and Poland, little attempt had been made to drive home the effects of armored warfare supported by fleets of dive bombers. On the contrary, there had been on the one hand a constant belittling of the German army, while on the other the size, strength, prowess, and potential achievement of the B.E.F. and the French army had been built up into almost a caricature of invincibility. When the B.E.F. did meet the German army, it met a stranger.

On May 10, the olive-and-black three-ton trucks chalked with the names of girls, the Scammell tank-recovery vehicles labeled Snow White, with Doc, Grumpy, Happy, Sneezy as their potential burdens, churned confidently forward into Belgium. It was brilliant summer weather, the men often in rolled-up shirtsleeves, arms and necks burned to a deep brick red. As well as other less printable songs, they sang:

> Run, Adolf, run, Adolf, run, run, run.
> Here comes a man with his gun, gun, gun.

To make up for its lack of numbers, the German attack in the north employed a series of shock devices calculated to confuse the

---

* Apart from its spearhead of armored and motorized divisions, the German army depended on horse transport. Its Seventy-eighth Division was immobilized for over a week during the campaign by equine flu. German machine-gunning and bombing of horses brought whole divisions of the French and Belgian armies to a halt.

opposing generals who were geared, however unconsciously, to the infantry pace and static front of the First World War.

The Dutch had changed their dispositions on the night of May 9, leaving a weak spot in front of the single armored division facing them. This division broke through, and, without waiting for the infantry to consolidate their position, and, in the midst of superior forces, raced ninety miles to Rotterdam, where it linked up with a drop of four thousand parachutists. Rotterdam itself was bombed, leading the Dutch Foreign Minister to claim that thirty thousand people had been killed in half an hour. In fact, the dead numbered fewer than a thousand; and constant exaggeration of this kind, emphasizing German invincibility, played its part in paralyzing Allied wills. The Dutch surrendered on May 14, with the greater part of their army intact.

In Belgium, two unblown bridges over the Albert Canal were captured by German parachutists dropped on the canal's western bank, while the fortress of Eben Emael, commanding the canal, was paralyzed for twenty-four hours by no more than eighty parachutists who, landing on the roof, dropped explosives into the fortress' gun muzzles and casemates.

The French had counted on several days' delay on this front while their main forces swung into position on a line from Antwerp along the river Dyle to Namur; but as early as May 11 the French General Prioux, whose Cavalry Corps of two light mechanized divisions was out in front of the advance, was warning that he could not hold on for long * and asking permission, which was refused, to withdraw to the frontier defenses. By May 13, when the Germans began their assault across the Meuse south of Namur, the right wing of the French First Army was beginning to buckle and was presently involved in the ruin of Corap's Ninth Army on its flank.

Marc Bloch has painted a terrible picture of Blanchard, the commander of the First Army, whose outstanding characteristic was good breeding, staring in tragic immobility at a map spread on the table before him, saying nothing, doing nothing, searching the map as if hoping to find on it the decisions he was no longer capable of taking, as the kind of world he understood collapsed about him.

---

* The French Light Mechanized Divisions had, in fact, a higher proportion of well-armed and well-armored medium tanks than had the two Panzer divisions opposing Prioux. See Liddell Hart, *The Tanks*, Vol. II, Chap. 1.

Anarchic bands of demoralized soldiers from Blanchard's and Corap's armies began to roam along the Allied lines of communication, looting and holding villages to ransom. Officers who tried to control them were shot, and the tales these men told, to justify their desertion, of thousands of German tanks, thousands of parachutists landing without warning everywhere, added to the demoralization which they themselves were spreading. There were not many of them in relation to the size of the French army, but reports of British installations in the back areas besieged and ransacked did nothing to strengthen already weakening British confidence in their allies.

In describing the later stages of the campaign in northern France and Flanders, one is trying to present a battle fought on three levels.

On the ground there are a young infantry subaltern and his driver sent out in a fifteen-hundredweight truck to ascertain whether a village has been evacuated of civilians. Nine months ago, both these amateur soldiers were civilians themselves. They have not yet physically seen a German, although they have met the Stuka. They have been on the move and have had little sleep for several days. Their division is in reserve, many miles south of what men are still calling "the front." As the truck turns into the village street, there is the sound of motorcycle exhausts and the sight of a column of German motorcyclists moving on the crossroads three hundred yards away. A frantic reversal of the truck out of sight, two frightened men flattening themselves behind a house wall, as the convoy passes, and is succeeded by the shattering roar of tanks. Then an apprehensive drive along crowded roads to headquarters to report. Headquarters has moved on, with no indication of where it has moved to. Dodging in and out of convoys of trucks and the forlorn columns of refugees, the subaltern at last finds his headquarters, more by luck than skill. His report is met with disbelief: how can Germans be there? How can one expect an accurate appreciation from amateur soldiers liable to panic? By the time headquarters is convinced, the German column has moved on, not at infantry pace of three miles an hour, but at ten or fifteen.

Formation headquarters is also on the move. A motorcycle dispatch rider, however he curbs his inclination to dive into the ditch whenever a plane comes over, may take several hours—perhaps twenty-four hours if he starts in darkness—to find it. The enemy, meanwhile, has moved on.

The information is combined with other, often conflicting, reports, and filters slowly upward from headquarters to headquarters until hours, possibly days, later it reaches a staff officer moving flags on a map in a gloomy château at Vincennes. Upon this movement of flags, the Allied Commander-in-Chief bases his plans, always days too late.

At an even more remote level, the French and British War Cabinets seek to bring their influence to bear on the battle. Twenty-five years later, trying to distinguish some pattern among the chaos, one puts a question to a politician: was there disagreement in Cabinet on this point or that? The answer carries conviction: "There couldn't have been disagreement. We didn't know enough about the situation to disagree over."

All this among the paralyzing insanity of war, the situations anxiously rehearsed in the mind but not until now experienced, the burning buildings, the whistle and roar of apparently unopposed Stukas, the friend suddenly dead in a ditch, shot through the head. At every level there are frightened men, men afraid in the most fundamental terms for their lives, or with more sophistication for their careers, their place in history, the future of their countries.

Through the nights between May 16 and 19, the Allied armies in the north withdrew by too-slow stages from the river Dyle to the Scheldt, pressed strongly enough by Bock's Army Group to keep them engaged while Rundstedt's armor, which had crossed the Meuse, raced to cut them off to the south.

Like Ironside, Gort had been a devoted—some would say a slavish—supporter of the French before the campaign began; but as days passed without orders from his French superiors, and as the demoralization of the right wing of the French First Army became apparent, his disillusionment had been correspondingly great.

At a midnight meeting with Billotte on the night of May 18, Gort became convinced that the French were no longer capable of closing the gap to the south, and that in consequence there would shortly be German armored columns behind the unprotected back of his nine divisions. He began to think of the future. Three plans, he wrote in his dispatch, occurred to him. The first was to stand on the Scheldt, or in the frontier defenses prepared during the winter; but this would only be possible if the gap on the French Ninth Army front could be closed. The second was to fall back on the Somme, which would mean either that the French and British must abandon the Belgians, or the Belgian army must be persuaded to abandon Belgium. The third was to withdraw to the Channel ports, and hold a defensive perimeter long enough for the British Expeditionary Force to embark, preferably in concert with the French and Belgians.

It is a valid criticism of Gort that he had not informed his own government of his growing doubts about the situation before this point; though it is another question whether he would have got much sympathy from a pugnacious Prime Minister given to military meddling, emotionally committed to the French, and, by his own confession, without understanding of the revolution in warfare effected by fast-moving armor.

The first representation of Gort's views came as a shock. It was May 19, a Sunday. There had been a morning Cabinet meeting, at which the Prime Minister had been sturdily optimistic about the French. Both Churchill and his most senior colleague, Chamberlain, had then left London. The War Minister, Eden, was just leaving the War Office for luncheon with Halifax when Ironside urgently sent for him to report a telephone talk with Gort's Chief of Staff, Pownall. Pownall had not spoken to Ironside himself, but to the Director of Military Operations, and telephone communications were bad. There were thus a dubious telephone line and three intermediaries between Gort and Eden; and Eden's contemporary diary note of the conversation was that the French First Army on Gort's right had faded away, and that he proposed to base himself on Dunkirk, hold a semicircular line through Saint-Omer, Aire Canal, and fight it out with his back to the sea.

There is a substantial difference between Dunkirk as a port of evacuation and Dunkirk as the supply port for a defensive position, and from this initial confusion a number of unhappy consequences were to flow. Nor had the French First Army "faded away," though it was certainly in serious difficulties.

A later message from Pownall explained that Gort only contemplated his move if the French failed to fill or hold the gap about Cambrai, Le Cateau, and Valenciennes, which now threatened the B.E.F.'s supply lines. But in any event Ironside would have none of it. He believed that Gort must try to fight his way south to Amiens.

The Cabinet could not be gathered together until half-past four in the afternoon, and the ministers took the view, on Ironside's advice, that Gort must try to keep in touch with the French. There was a later meeting of the Prime Minister with the service ministers and Chiefs of Staff, at which the Prime Minister's was the decisive, indeed almost the only voice; from this meeting Ironside was sent off to France with a firm order to Gort to fight his way south.

The order was so hastily conceived that it and a number of copies were written in longhand in the train to Dover by Air Commodore J. C. Slessor, who accompanied Ironside. Slessor formed the impression that the C.I.G.S., understandably, was under considerable strain.

Apart from their temporary alliance against Hore-Belisha, Gort and Ironside had rarely been on good personal terms. When Ironside produced the order at G.H.Q. at eight o'clock on the morning of May 20, it created a sensation. Gort was stolid and apparently unmoved, but his Chief of Staff, Pownall pointed out with some emphasis that it was impossible.

Gort, however, had already given orders for an attack in the neighborhood of Arras with his only two disengaged divisions, and he undertook to mount this assault if he could get some orders out of the French. There is a haziness about the development of this operation which is characteristic of the campaign. In its inception, at any rate, it seems to have meant no more to Gort than a limited counterattack to relieve increasing German pressure on Arras, but Ironside seems to have taken it as an indication that Gort, while emphasizing his serious difficulties, did not entirely reject the Cabinet plan for a breakout to the south, if he could get French co-operation.

Ironside sped to Billotte's headquarters to blast the French into activity. There he found Billotte and Blanchard in a state of complete depression. This huge Englishman, six feet four inches in height, a formidable figure, lost his temper, took Billotte by the button of his tunic, and shouted at him, "You must make a plan. Attack at once to the south with all your forces on Amiens."

Blanchard had already had an interview with Gort early that morning, in the course of which Gort had spread a map on his desk, and, tapping Cambrai with his pencil, said slowly and emphatically, looking straight at Blanchard, *"Il faut tuer les Boches et il faut les tuer ici."* A witness of this scene recorded that Gort's words seemed to have made a deep impression on the demoralized Blanchard; but Blanchard's reactions apparently did nothing to convince Gort that he would in fact *tuer les Boches*.

Under this shock treatment, however, the French generals began to make an effort to pull themselves together. Billotte, according to Ironside's account, drew himself to attention, saying that he would make an immediate plan to attack southward; and he undertook to put in an attack by two French divisions towards Cambrai on the same day as Gort's Arras operation.

Ironside returned to London, giving the War Cabinet what Halifax described in his diary as "a not too gloomy view of France, provided the French can be persuaded to act with vigour. He had himself done a great deal in this direction."

One would perhaps not be wrong in detecting here a more hopeful emphasis than Gort himself would have given. The Commander-in-Chief of the B.E.F. was going to take a great deal of convincing that the French were any longer capable of acting with vigor, no matter how firmly the C.I.G.S. grasped them by their tunic buttons. But on the following day, May 22, Churchill, at a meeting of the Supreme War Council in Paris, committed Gort to an agreement "that the British Army and the French First Army should attack south-west towards Bapaume and Cambrai at the earliest moment, certainly tomorrow, with about eight divisions, and with the Belgian Cavalry Corps on the right of the British."

These differences of emphasis were exaggerated by a failure of communications in the widest sense, not only by broken or faulty telephone lines, but by barriers of language and national temperament, and by complicated thoughts imperfectly expressed in the rush and confusion of events. An impression arose among the French, fostered by defeatists in the French government, that Churchill was playing a double game, assuring them of Gort's willingness to attack, while secretly encouraging him to withdraw on the Channel ports. The French could not understand that Gort, whom they had learned to regard as no more than a friendly and jovial battalion commander, was being driven into defiance of his own government; and Gort's defiance sprang from despair at his apparent failure to make his government understand the true situation as he saw it.

One must now deviate to trace two important series of events occurring at the same time as those already described.

On May 19, after long reflection in his headquarters at Vincennes, Gamelin issued a directive, prefaced by the apologetic phrase, "Without wishing to intervene in the conduct of the battle now in progress," but calling upon Georges to plan a counterattack from both north and south against the German armored thrust.*

That evening he was replaced as Commander-in-Chief by General Maxime Weygand, suddenly recalled from distant Syria, surrounded by the magic aura of having been Foch's Chief of Staff through the static warfare of the First World War, and seventy-three years old.

Weygand's first action was to place Gamelin's directive in abeyance. When Georges told him that night that he would like to explain the situation, Weygand said, "No. Tomorrow." When Georges did explain it next day, Weygand answered, "I must go and see on the spot what the situation is." On the following day he did so. At 3 P.M. on May 21, after a journey subject to all the hazards of bombed airfields and consequent changes in rendezvous, this elderly man drove into Ypres, where he hoped to meet the three northern commanders, Billotte, Gort, and King Leopold of the Belgians.

Gort had been informed that Weygand was coming, but had been given no time and place for the meeting. A second message went astray—communications were now such that Weygand could telephone Billotte only by way of London—and Gort waited all day at his headquarters for news of Weygand's arrival. It says much for the state of liaison between British and French that no one thought

* A belated application, it may be noted, of the countermove against an Ardennes thrust which Gamelin and Ironside had agreed to six months before.

of sending a messenger there for him; but some light may be thrown on this omission by the fact that at one stage First Army headquarters did not know where Gort's headquarters was. It had been properly notified, but such was the confusion that no one had read the appropriate signal before it was locked away among the security files.

Weygand left Ypres without having seen Gort, and convinced that the British Commander-in-Chief had deliberately avoided the meeting as a sign of his refusal to accept French orders. Gort eventually reached Ypres, to have Weygand's plans for a co-ordinated north-south counteroffensive explained to him by Billotte, whose capacities he had learned to distrust. That night Pownall gave orders for work to begin on evacuation plans.

Billotte, on his way back from the Ypres meeting, was fatally injured in a car crash. His successor was Blanchard, who did not know what, if anything, had been decided at the Ypres meeting, who was already demoralized by the collapse of his right flank, and whose appointment was not in any event confirmed for several days.

A short time before Weygand arrived at Ypres, a British counterattack consisting of two divisions took place southwest of Arras. Not entirely to Gort's surprise, the supporting attack by two French divisions promised by Billotte had not been ready in time, and was now promised for the following day. The effects of the British thrust were so extraordinary that one must be left wondering whether, if the British and French had been able to co-ordinate a north-south attack on the lines proposed by Gamelin and no later than this date, 1940 might not have had its battle of the Marne.

The attack, though nominally made by two divisions, was in fact carried out by the remainder of the First Army Tank Brigade, together with two Territorial battalions of the Durham Light Infantry. The tanks had gone 120 miles in five days, on their own tracks, mostly at three miles an hour along roads crowded with refugees. They did not receive their orders until midday on May 20, and the last tank did not reach the assembly point until five o'clock on the morning of May 21, a few hours before the attack was due to begin. The infantry had not yet arrived, the artillery support was delayed, and the promised air support never material-

ized. The brigade commander asked for a postponement, but was
told this was impossible, and the tanks went in without initial
infantry support. They caught the flank of the motorized infantry
regiments of Rommel's Seventh Division as it was moving into an
attack of its own, and the division was saved from a nasty mauling
by Rommel himself, who personally organized a screen of antitank
and antiaircraft guns, and ran from gun to gun, giving them their
targets and ordering rapid fire. An S.S. mechanized infantry division, already suspect under fire in Poland, panicked.

The effect on the British troops was heartening. For days they
had retreated without apparent reason. Now they were exhilarated
to find that even direct hits did not penetrate the heavy armor of
the British tanks, and that they were knocking out the German
tanks about which such wild rumors had been spread.

Inevitably, however, the few British tanks ground to a halt, and
whereas the British could summon air support only from England,
the targets having moved on by the time the Blenheims arrived, the
Germans were able to call up a hundred Stukas which bombed
tanks and infantry for twenty minutes, driving the infantry into
open country, where they were forced back by German tanks.

The corridor held by the Germans at this point was some twenty-
five miles wide, and it was not, as it was two days later, crammed
with troops. A flank attack against the quickly moving armor while
it was too far ahead of the marching infantry had been a constant
fear of the German High Command, and there had been a series of
halt orders to the armor, one of which had so infuriated Guderian
that he had asked to be relieved of his command. On May 17, and
again on the following day, Brauchitsch had had painful scenes
with Hitler, who raged and screamed that the generals were going
to ruin the campaign by their insistence on a speedy thrust westward.

This uneasiness at the top percolated downward, and Halder's
diary entries for May 21, 22, and 23 reflect German preoccupation
with what was happening on this vulnerable flank at Arras: "Only
when we have seized the high ground of Arras shall we have won
the battle"; "the armor drive on Calais, ordered by us, has been
temporarily halted by Army Group A on the line St. Pol-Étaples,
and will not be resumed until the situation at Arras is clear"; "von
Gyldenfeldt communicates Kleist's anxieties. He feels he cannot

tackle his task as long as the crisis at Arras remains unsolved. Tank losses are as high as 50 per cent. — I point out to him the crisis will be over within 48 hours. I am aware of the magnitude of his task. He will have to hold on until then.''

On May 21, on the left of the German corridor, Guderian's three armored divisions had halted, awaiting orders. According to Guderian's account, he had one division poised to advance on Boulogne, one on Calais, and one on Dunkirk. On May 22, the Boulogne and Calais divisions were given permission to advance. The Dunkirk division was withdrawn from Guderian's command by Kleist's order, and held back temporarily as Armored Group Reserve. On May 24, an order from Rundstedt to halt the armor again while the infantry closed up was converted by Hitler himself into a two-day standstill. Throughout this period, all that stood between the German spearhead and Dunkirk was a series of scratch forces hastily improvised from British line-of-communication troops and the not fully equipped divisions which had been serving as pioneers in the back areas. There were other causes, but there can be little doubt that this battle at Arras on May 21 by the First Army Tank Brigade and the Durhams was a major contribution to the survival of the British Expeditionary Force.

Gort, however, had now shot his bolt. On May 22, a single French motorized division attacked in the direction of Cambrai, but like the British attack it was stopped and withdrawn. On the morning of May 23, Gort had a conference with Blanchard about the Weygand plan. He suggested an attack southward with the two British divisions from Arras, one French division, and what remained of the French Cavalry Corps; but he emphasized that the main weight of the north-south assault would have to come from the south, and that the British divisions, having taken part in the Arras operation, could not be ready until May 26. Blanchard was not yet confirmed in his appointment and could do no more than undertake to submit these proposals to the French High Command. For the rest of the day Gort awaited an answer, but the only messages which reached him seemed to bear no relation to reality, while Rommel's armored division was offering an only too real threat to cut off Arras from the west.

At about six o'clock in the evening, Gort came into Pownall's room and said, "Henry, I've got a hunch. We've got to call off the

Fifth and Fiftieth Divisions from the attack to the south and send them over to Brookie * on the left." Pownall pointed out that this was against all orders, and that, without the British divisions, the French First Army would be unlikely to attack. "Yes, I know that quite well," Gort answered. "All the same it's got to be done."

He did not consult his government, and information did not reach Blanchard until after the order had been given. The order reached some British formations in an almost *sauve qui peut* form. During the afternoon, the First Army Tank Brigade had been told to hold ground to the last round and the last man. Shortly before midnight, an order reached brigade headquarters to retreat immediately northeastward, each unit to fend for itself, as the routes to the north had been cut. Brigadier Pratt refused to pass on the order to his regiments in this form, but issued a normal withdrawal order, and in fact the routes to the north had not been cut.

Gort may not have been the greatest of British generals, but there is an impressive single-mindedness about him in these later days of May. He meant to save the men for whose lives he was responsible from the trap into which he believed the politicians and the French had led them, and this he did, by grace of the Royal Navy. Nine months before, he had achieved the height of his ambition, to command an army in the field. He had left for France with the boyish exclamation, "Isn't it *grand* to be going to the war!" Perhaps he went to the wrong war. One meets him later in the year, unemployed, haunting the busy War Office like an unwelcome ghost from a past it preferred to forget, trying to get published the dispatches which would justify his actions, and complaining of criticism in a contemporary light novel by Dennis Wheatley. But he had now twice defied his political masters, and though he served with distinction in a number of high offices, he was never again entrusted with a field command.

The consequences of Gort's defection—as the French have always considered it—were far-reaching. When the Belgian army capitulated on May 28, the two divisions withdrawn by stages from Arras were already strengthening the British line toward the sea, and were therefore instrumental in enabling the gap left by the Belgians to be sealed. But after it, every point of contact between the Allies was the subject of bitter recrimination. They were now,

* Lieutenant General Alan Brooke, commanding the British II Corps.

in Spears' phrase, like rats thrown into the water, tearing at each other to save themselves from drowning.

Whether the British withdrawal contributed much to the final French collapse may be doubted—militarily, the decision to withhold fighter planes was more important. The chance of a breakout by the northern armies, which had existed when Gamelin issued his directive and which was still faintly there when Gort put in his Arras attack, had gone, and the alternatives existing for the Allied armies in the north were capitulation, a last-ditch stand, or evacuation.

What is certain is that those French politicians who had been talking more and more openly of an armistice since the Meuse break-through, found in Gort a convenient scapegoat. What reliance, they urged, could be placed on British promises of assistance? British generals always made for the sea. Look at Norway. Look at Gort. While the French army bled to death, the British ran away and kept back their air force to defend themselves. What was the use of continuing resistance in France itself, or in the colonies? Would it not be better to find out what terms Hitler would offer, while there was still an army to keep the Communists under control, and a navy as a bargaining counter?

Against this whispering, in which there was some truth, Churchill hurled his confident rhetoric in vain. Least of any British politician was it Churchill's fault, but there was bitter irony to patriotic Frenchmen in his offers of twenty to twenty-five British divisions if the French could hold out until 1941, of Franco-British union while Fighter Command was withheld for the defense of Britain. On May 25, the French War Committee began for the first time openly to discuss the possibility of armistice talks with Germany.

Now a British Expeditionary Force of more than two hundred thousand men and what remained of their tanks, guns, and lorries began to converge upon the harbor of Dunkirk and the wide sandy beaches stretching from it.

As early as May 20, rumors of evacuation had begun to reach even the lower ranks. They were incredulous. Many thousands at that date had not seen a German. They knew little of what had happened on the Meuse, or why it should affect them. As the rumor spread, some of them experienced a feeling of being trapped. Doubts entered their minds whether someone, somewhere, was not getting away, while they were being left behind. Where leadership was bad, this feeling grew, and men slipped away, retired in face of a bluff, or surrendered too easily. Along the lines of communication, stretching back toward Le Havre, there was some panic as German tanks appeared at the end of a street, across familiar fields; and as rumors of tanks, paratroops, Fifth Columnists passed from mouth to mouth, they sounded only more frightening.

The army was saved from disintegration, not for the first time in its history, by its warrant officers and noncommissioned officers, regular soldiers or time-expired men recalled from their civilian jobs, sometimes from unemployment, in one case from hawking fish from a barrow about the streets of a small Cumberland town. They were not all heroes or saints, but they knew their trade.

The action developed into a series of small, isolated, almost private wars. A party of infiltrating Germans has taken up position on the top floor of a house in the rear of a British post. A junior officer, a peaceful civilian nine months before, living with his family in the kind of house which is now the scene of his first face-to-face encounter with the enemy, is sent with half-a-dozen men to rout them out. The officer is armed with a forty-five pistol, with which he has fired six practice rounds on a course in England. He kicks open the house door. A German soldier, holding a light automatic gun, is halfway down the stairs immediately facing him. Englishman and German stare at each other for a moment in surprise, then the Englishman fires two shots, point-blank as he thinks, but in fact high above the German's head. The German bolts back upstairs. The Englishman throws a grenade up the stairs, and his men throw another through the bedroom window. When the explosions are over they wait, keeping stairway and window covered. A single dazed German comes to the window, ready to surrender. They shoot him.

At this level, life, or death, was direct, even simple. At higher levels, however, imprecision of thought and failure of communications continued to produce confusion and recrimination between the Allies.

On May 19, as a result of Pownall's telephone talks with the

War Office, there had been a conference between Admiralty and War Office representatives to consider plans for supplying the British Expeditionary Force through Dunkirk, Calais, and Boulogne. The evacuation of about forty-five thousand troops with their equipment was also envisaged, though thought to be unlikely. On the following day, Vice-Admiral Ramsay, Flag Officer at Dover, was put in command of this operation, and on Tuesday, May 21, another meeting was held "to consider the emergency evacuation of very large forces, the necessity of air protection, and the need of a large number of small boats to carry troops to the off-shore ships."

Independently, on the morning of May 19, Gamelin asked the French naval Commander-in-Chief, Darlan, to investigate the possibilities of evacuating French troops by sea. French and British naval planning, however, seems never to have been co-ordinated, and it became a French source of complaint that the plans for what was given the name of Operation Dynamo were not revealed to French naval representatives in London until May 27, with the result that, according to Weygand, "French improvization had to be superimposed on their unilateral and well-organized preparations."

When Weygand finally abandoned his plan for a north-south attack, his thoughts seem to have turned, not to evacuation, but to something resembling the version of Pownall's message which had reached Eden on May 19, a plan to use Dunkirk as supply port for a bridgehead to be held by the Allied armies. On the night of May 24, he sent Blanchard an order to organize as extensive a defensive perimeter as possible round Dunkirk, and Blanchard in his turn issued an order for withdrawal of the French and British forces to "a bridgehead covering Dunkirk in breadth" from which there would be "no thought of retreat."

On May 25, Eden sent Gort a signal telling him that the French offensive from the Somme offered little hope of success, and "should this prove to be the case you will be faced by a situation in which safety of B.E.F. will be predominant consideration. In such conditions only course open to you may be to fight your way back to west where all beaches and ports east of Gravelines will be used for embarkation."

There were thus two separate operations going on simultaneously, the French preparing Dunkirk as the base for a last-ditch defense, the British preparing it as a port of evacuation, which in fact began on the night of Sunday, May 26, with a lift of thirteen hundred men from base units and lines of communication.

Until May 28, no French ships co-operated, since the French Admiral Abrial was still under orders to organize Dunkirk as supply port for the bridgehead which was to be held with no thought of retreat. He was surprised by the British evacuation, of which he claimed not to have been informed, while the British for their part complained that Abrial, working from a concrete emplacement thirty feet underground, was inaccessible and largely unaware of what was going on.

The British Prime Minister gave orders that the French should have their share of British shipping, *bras-dessus, bras-dessous,** as he later put it, and eventually 123,000 French soldiers were evacuated. But Churchill's order took some time to penetrate, and in Dunkirk meanwhile Gort had given his own order that French troops were not to be embarked in British ships.

French soldiers from the First Army stood packed together on the bombed beaches, watching the British sail away. A kind of escape-hysteria seized them, and they tried to rush the boats, from which British sailors threw them back into the sea. The French interpreter who had been attached to a British brigade, who had shared billets with its officers and accompanied them into battle, stood disconsolately on the beach as the brigade sailed. The British had been very kind, very polite, but they could not take him with them, and what happened to him after they had gone was no responsibility of theirs.

Dunkirk had been frequently and heavily bombed since the start of the campaign. On the day evacuation began, German bombers set the harbor oil tanks on fire, and on the following morning they dropped thirty thousand incendiary bombs in and around the town itself, so that a first view across the flat countryside was of drifting clouds of black smoke through which, as men came closer, the shells of still-burning buildings were dimly visible.

The main basin of the harbor was blocked by sunken ships, and the docks could be used only by smaller vessels, suitable for embarking men, but not their guns and heavy equipment. This equipment lined either side of the roads which ran straight be-

* Arm-in-arm, like comrades and allies.

tween canals and drainage ditches: three-ton trucks with sugar in the fuel tanks, tires ripped, cylinder blocks smashed; guns splayed into chrysanthemums of twisted metal by shells exploded in the breeches with muzzles blocked; the product of three years of British rearmament.

The men marched in, unwashed, unshaved, and sometimes on the verge of exhaustion, having had little to eat but tea and biscuits for two days, no proper sleep since the campaign began. But still many of them had not seen a German, nor fired a shot in anger. When they reached their rendezvous points, waiting under the diving Stukas to move forward to the harbor, bloody bastard officers and N.C.O.'s gave them something to think about by making them wash themselves and clean their weapons.

At first it was not anticipated that more than a few could be taken off and, on the evening of May 27, the situation seemed so unpromising that Captain W. G. Tennant, the naval shore commander at Dunkirk, signaled a request for every available craft to be sent on the following day, since "evacuation tomorrow night is problematical."

Churchill, according to Spears, had become suspicious of Gort's belligerence, and on May 27 sent a message: "At this solemn moment I cannot help sending you my good wishes. No one can tell how it will go. But anything is better than being cooped up and starved out . . ."

In the early hours of the morning of May 28, the Belgian army capitulated, and Churchill warned the House of Commons to prepare itself for "hard and heavy tidings." In the afternoon he addressed a meeting of Cabinet ministers, telling them, according to Dalton's diary note, "I have thought carefully in these last days whether it was part of my duty to consider entering into negotiations with That Man. . . . I am convinced that every man of you would rise up and tear me down from my place if I were for one moment to contemplate parley or surrender. If this long island story of ours is to end at last, let it end only when each one of us lies choking in his own blood upon the ground." The ministers, according to Churchill's recollection, jumped up from the table and came running to his chair, shouting and patting him on the back.

The civilians, as is usually the way, were more militant than the military. "Horrible as it is," George Orwell noted in his diary on this desperate day, "I hope that the B.E.F. is cut to pieces sooner than capitulate."

On May 29, Gort received a further signal from Churchill: "If you are cut from all communications from us and all evacuation from Dunkirk and beaches had in your judgement been finally prevented after every attempt to re-open it had failed, you would become the sole judge of when it was impossible to inflict further damage upon the enemy. H.M. Government are sure that the repute of the British Army is safe in your hands."

This series of messages was not sent without opposition. Halifax's diary note of May 27 reads: "Winston and Greenwood talking bilge, told them our ways would separate." On May 29, his diary refers to much discussion about Gort's orders and adds, "I pleaded for giving him the greatest possible assurance of support in whatever he might think it right to do." On the following day, May 30, he noted: "Orders for Gort, great improvement on what Winston insisted on sending 36 hours earlier." The later orders formally instructed Gort to return to England when his command was so reduced that it could be handed over to a corps commander. His successor was to continue the defense of the beaches in conjunction with the French, and when in his judgment no further organized evacuation was possible and no further proportionate damage could be inflicted on the enemy, he was "in consultation with the senior French Commander to capitulate formally to avoid senseless slaughter."

When Tennant, the naval shore commander, sent his signal on the evening of May 27, it had seemed to him unlikely that any further evacuation could be made from Dunkirk harbor, and that future operations would have to be conducted entirely from the open beaches east of the town. If that appreciation had proved correct, Churchill's messages of May 27 and 29 would have left Gort little option but to fight it out to the last round, if not to the last man. Fortunately it was not.

On the north side of Dunkirk harbor, a wooden mole about five feet wide stretched some fourteen hundred yards out to sea. It was continually under heavy attack and had to be repaired with whatever could be found: ships' gangways, naval mess tables, any available fragments of timber. Along this narrow pathway, under bombing and later under shellfire, marched in the nine days of Operation Dynamo more than a quarter of a million men, to the comparative safety of ships berthed precariously alongside. Discipline improved as the fighting troops came in, and after the first few days the men moved in the orderly fashion of a Wembley football crowd going through the turnstiles.

One man described the experience: "We reached the East Jetty at 11 P.M. On one place there had been a direct hit on the mole. The gap had been patched with boards. A final halt was made 200 yards from the end, which was altogether about a mile long. Most of the men laid down on the jetty and went to sleep in spite of the cold. A German bomber flew over us at one o'clock, dropping bombs. The battalion just behind us was heavily shelled and machine-gunned and suffered severe casualties. Two ships had already been sunk at the end of the jetty. It was apparently impossible to embark till the tide rose. At five o'clock a destroyer drew alongside. It was daylight, but luckily there was a mist. We were conducted below and all were very soon asleep."

It was made to sound simple. Overwrought army officers complained that the promised timetable of two ships every four hours was not being kept, but forty-one destroyers of the Royal Navy, some of them making two trips a day, lifted nearly a hundred thousand men. By the end of the operation, six of the forty-one had been sunk, fourteen damaged by bombs, and twelve damaged by collisions.

The second biggest lift was made by Channel packets like "Princess Maud" and pleasure steamers like "Royal Daffodil," which had been in action on this coast once before when as a Mersey ferryboat she had taken part in the Zeebrugge naval action of St. George's Day, 1918. "Royal Daffodil" made seven trips and on the eighth was attacked by six German bombers. Five salvos missed her. A bomb from the sixth went through her decks into the engine room and out on the starboard side before bursting. She was then machine-gunned and set on fire. She was listing heavily to starboard, and her master had the port boats lowered into the sea and filled with water, which lifted the hole clear of the sea. Two engineers plugged the hole with beds, and one stood up to his neck in water, holding open a bilge valve, while the other kept the pumps going. In this way she returned to Ramsgate.

In one way or another, the inspired improvisations and discipline of Dunkirk enabled 338,226 men to be brought back to England.

On the night of June 3, twenty-four hours after the last British troops had left, the Allied rearguard came in, thirty thousand men of the supposedly broken and demoralized French First Army. To lift them, Ramsay called for a final effort from his almost exhausted crews; but the Germans were now within three miles of the harbor, and at half-past three on the morning of June 4, evacuation had to be abandoned, leaving several thousand French troops behind on the beaches. Their discipline and bearing, according to the official British naval historian, left a deep impression on all who had witnessed the final scene.

On June 14, German troops entered Paris, and the young officers of Rundstedt's headquarters were able to equip themselves with an artillery stereotelescope through which to spy on the girls using a nearby swimming pool.

On June 22, in the railway carriage at Compiègne in which German delegates in 1918 had acknowledged their defeat, General Huntziger of the French Second Army accepted the German armistice terms on behalf of a French government headed by Marshal Pétain, eighty-four-year-old ghost of the victor of Verdun.

Chapter

8

"ALONE"

From the beginning of the war, British strategy had had its roots in the belief that, if Germany obtained air bases in the Low Countries, the knockout blow from the air might well prove irresistible. Germany now held bases not only in the Low Countries, but across the narrow seas of the Channel, as well as naval and air bases in Norway and Denmark which put the industrial northeast within range of German bombers, and North Atlantic sea traffic within easier reach of German submarines. In a great arc from Alesund, overlapping the Shetland Isles, to the Breton Peninsula, facing Cornwall, stood an enemy ruthless and apparently invincible, whose future actions, judged by his past performance in Poland, Norway, and France, seemed certain to take the form of violent and direct assault.

With their backs to the wall and believing in the justice of their cause, a posture in which they have always delighted to see themselves and which indeed they have sometimes seemed to seek when they are not in it already, the islanders met the threat with what Hitler would certainly have described as frivolous dilettantism.

On May 24, while the B.E.F. was withdrawing upon Dunkirk, the *Times,* under a headline, "Are We Really at War?" drew attention to crowded hotels and cinemas with uniformed commissionaires standing outside; scores of young men with nothing to do but hang about amusement arcades; unemployed miners singing as usual for coppers in the streets of the West End of London. When De Gaulle came to London on June 9, fresh from the chaos of France, he detected a look of tranquillity, almost indifference, the streets and parks full of people peacefully out for a walk, long queues at the entrances to cinemas, many cars.

An elderly lady was much quoted: "Oh, well, if the Germans win, at any rate I have my pension, and they can't touch that." Later in the summer Mass Observation, whose observers tended to be young, earnest, and Left Wing, recorded with apparent dismay the refusal of West Country villagers to show any concern about the war—at any rate to Mass Observers.

One school of letter-writers to the *Times* urged Britain to wake up, while another school commented with mild acrimony on "a very prevalent feeling of resentment at being exhorted over and over again, by a miscellaneous collection of doubtless very brave people, to keep calm. It would be interesting to know on what grounds these eminent people base their assumption that the British man or woman is less imbued with courage and calmness, under any ordeal, than themselves."

The British had not, in the summer of 1940, acquired that habit of apologizing for their own existence which is perhaps their most striking legacy from the war. The security given by three centuries' immunity from warfare on their own soil, combined with the legend that the British army always loses every battle but the last, imbued them with an invincible sense of their own superiority which, however infuriating to foreigners, was a wonderfully powerful weapon. They simply could not conceive that they might be beaten.

The tone was set by that very typical Englishman, King George VI, who wrote to his mother after the fall of France, "Personally, I feel happier now that we have no allies to be polite to and to pamper."

Lord Baldwin, under whose government Germany had been allowed to attain the capacity to deliver the threatened blow, found in the French surrender a sign of the hand of God. At the time of Dunkirk, he wrote to Halifax, he had a vision in which a voice said to him, "Have you not thought there is a purpose in stripping you one by one of all the human props on which you depend, that you

are being left alone in the world? You have now one upon whom
to lean and I have chosen you as my instrument to work my will.
Why then are you afraid?"

Lady Baldwin, in a letter to the *Times*, asked that churches
should keep their flags flying, as a token that Britain was fighting
for Christianity against the powers of evil. "It is a daily inspiration
to myself," she declared, "to look out of my window and see that
our parish church is bearing the Red Cross of St. George on its
tower by night and day." Just over half the British people, according to a later Gallup Poll, would have agreed with her sentiments.
Kingsley Martin, in the *New Statesman*, drew an angry correspondence when he quoted a taxi-driver who, upon hearing of the
Belgian capitulation, had said "That's what comes of a day of
prayer."

Nor was Lord Baldwin's mystical experience unique. On two
occasions later in the year, a lady living in North London opened
the black-out curtains in her lightless bedroom to see what was
happening over the city. On both occasions she had the sensation
that someone had switched on a light in the room, but turning her
head, found the room still dark. She remembered the saying of a
clairvoyante fifty years before: "You will never come to any harm.
There is someone looking after you. I can see a light over your
right shoulder."

Another woman described to Mass Observation "an almost mystical feeling" that the Germans would not come. One wonders how
many Jews, Czechs, Poles, Norwegians, Belgians, Dutch, French,
had had a similar mystical feeling; but it is true that the Germans
did not come.

The British intelligentsia were on the whole deprived of these
comforting thoughts, but among them there was a great searching
of the heart. At the end of April, John Strachey and Victor Gollancz, founders of the Left Book Club and protagonists of the
Popular Front alliance with the Communists, dissociated themselves from the Communist line that there was little to choose
between the government of Hitler and the governments of Chamberlain and Reynaud. In June, Bertrand Russell wrote to Kingsley
Martin from America that he was no longer a pacifist and that, if
he were young enough to fight himself, he would do so, though he
found it more difficult to urge this course on others. The propor-

tion of conscientious objectors fell with each age group called up for the services, and by the autumn the pacifist *Peace News* was reporting that many former pacifists had discovered in Naziism something worse than war.

Unity was not quite complete. A former member of the International Brigade, which had fought on the Republican side in the Spanish Civil War, was asked to lend his experience to training the newly formed Local Defence Volunteers, afterward renamed the Home Guard, in guerrilla tactics.* He refused, on the grounds that "We don't support the war yet." The *New Statesman* reported a young Communist overheard as saying earnestly, "Yes, I'm beginning to realise how grave the position is. Arming the British Legion against the parachutists—it's nothing but the introduction of Fascism."

The Local Defence Volunteers, indeed, caused concern to a number of people. Motorists were shot dead at night by L.D.V. sentries, and others who escaped with nothing worse than wounds testified that they had heard no call to halt before they were fired on. In September it was announced that any "Local Defence Volunteer who shoots out of a personal grudge is liable to be suspended," but meanwhile the Chief Constable of Glasgow, proceeding on urgent duty with a police surgeon, had had a loaded, fully cocked rifle pushed into the pit of his stomach, his identification papers waved aside, and had formed the opinion that, in the neighborhood of Glasgow at any rate, criminals had taken the opportunity to enroll themselves, with possibilities which he found alarming.

Responsible for this trigger-happiness of the early Home Guard was an outbreak of spy mania, arising from reports from the Low Countries of thousands of parachutists dropped behind the Allied armies, and of a proliferation of Fifth Column saboteurs. The reports were exaggerated. The Germans used four thousand paratroopers in Holland, another five hundred in Belgium, although

---

* Local Defence Volunteers were called for in a broadcast by the War Minister, Eden, on May 14. The first recruit arrived within four minutes of the end of the broadcast. The force's name was changed in July to the Home Guard—Churchill's inspiration. There is an abyss of mentality and upbringing between Churchill's suggested title and Herbert Morrison's, the Civic Guard. I would like to make it clear that in spite of its somewhat frivolous early history, the Home Guard quickly settled down and did many years' invaluable if often dreary and unspectacular work.

as a *ruse de guerre* they dropped a number of empty parachutes, as they did later in Britain. They had infiltrated agents into some French factories; but these were less effective in sabotaging the French war effort than the mass callup of French workers and the mutual suspicion of French Left and Right.

Some of the British, neurotic as nesting blackbirds in the early summer of 1940, easily convinced themselves of the truth of the wildest rumor. Elderly ladies bravely followed trails of sky-blue wool which, they believed, had been laid to guide parachutists across country. The critic Cyril Connolly, sitting late at night in the lounge of an Oxford hotel, was arrested by a military police officer on the grounds that he "seemed very interested" in the conversation of a group of evacuated B.E.F. officers who were talking nearby. Connolly had the misfortune to possess a passport issued in Vienna, and this circumstance, allied to the fact that he revealed himself as the editor of a literary magazine, led to an inquisition by eight police officers which ended only when he was able to establish that he had been educated at Eton and Balliol.

In such an atmosphere, Ironside, newly installed as Commander-in-Chief Home Forces, came to his finest flowering, telling zone commanders of the Home Guard that "the people of this country have not yet realised what this war means, and it will be for you, the cream of the leading population, to make them understand what it is like"; proposing to turn a certain Captain Orde Wingate loose in Lincolnshire with a posse to hunt down Fifth Columnists; complaining that "it is extraordinary how we get circumstantial reports of Fifth Column and yet we have never been able to get anything worth having. One is persuaded that it hardly exists. And yet there is signalling going on all over the place and we cannot get any evidence."

In mid-June he confided to his diary, "Guts and discipline is what we want. We shall come to conscription of everything and a dictatorship in the end. Winston with a very small executive." One might hazard a guess who one member of that executive ought to have been; but the Commander-in-Chief's dispositions for home defense did not meet with approval, and in mid-July he was discreetly removed from his command and promoted Field-Marshal for his distinguished services. One sees his departure, a little sadly, as marking the end of an age of innocence. After Ironside, British generals may have been more efficient; they were certainly less colorful.

Ironside's preoccupation with the Fifth Column was shared by the British Left Wing. In July, the *New Statesman* criticized government measures: "Though a few more of the more prominent Nazi sympathisers of British extraction have been interned, there is no evidence that the Home Office is resolutely attacking the Fifth Column in this country. The British Union [of Fascists], we learn, has 'moved into smaller headquarters,' while 'The Link' [an association still defiantly advocating Anglo-German friendship] continues to hold private meetings. Part of the trouble may be undoubtedly the liberalism of Home Office officials; they do not want to destroy freedom or give offence to anyone who matters."

The problem of the Fifth Column, native or imported, did indeed present the authorities with a genuine dilemma. At the time of the German invasion of the Low Countries, the Dutch, Belgian, and French intelligence services, on the basis of what can be seen with the benefit of hindsight as somewhat panic-stricken experience, all advised the British government to take the most stringent precautions.

Thousands of enemy aliens, including of course Jews, Germans, Austrians, Czechs, who had sought refuge in Britain from the Nazis, were interned. There is no doubt that this was a popular measure. It had been advocated for some time by several mass-circulation newspapers, including the Labour *Daily Herald,* and a Gallup Poll published in July showed that 43 per cent of those questioned wanted all aliens interned, while another 48 per cent favored interning unfriendly or dangerous ones. Until the elaborate business of screening had been gone through, however, it was scarcely possible for the authorities to distinguish between friendly and dangerous aliens. In the meantime, husbands, wives, and children had been separated, men and women accustomed to academic or sedentary lives confined under primitive conditions in hastily built camps guarded and surrounded by barbed wire. At least one committed suicide rather than face even the comparatively mild British equivalent of what he had already undergone in Germany.

Upon those not interned, a curfew was imposed, which was sometimes administered with what can only be described as panic severity. A woman servant was summoned because she had left her place of residence during restricted hours to take shelter from an air raid. The police, it was reported, had told her that she ought not to leave the house but must shelter under the stairs, though they were able to agree that it would be permissible for her to leave the house during restricted hours if it were set on fire.

The internment of aliens was an unedifying episode, and one records with gratitude that liberal Britain was quick to rally to the defense of these defenseless and on the whole innocent people. But the difficulties confronting the authorities may be illustrated by two incidents, one comic, one of major seriousness.

When Italy entered the war on June 10, Italian citizens became subject to internment. The police, incidentally, took the opportunity to detain numbers of Italian criminals against whom they had insufficient evidence to bring formal charges: petty gangsters, pimps, racecourse razor slashers, and the like. Among the respectable Italians interned was a distinguished film producer, who at the time was working on a film about underground resistance to the Nazis. Influential people took up his case and urged the injustice of it on the highest levels. An order for his release was obtained, but when it reached his detention camp in the Isle of Man, the producer was found jubilantly and patriotically reading aloud to his fellow internees a report in the morning paper of an advance by the Italian army in Libya. The film industry continued to be deprived of his services.

The serious case concerned a young German scientist, Klaus Fuchs, deported to and interned in Canada, where he did not conceal the fact that he was a Communist, and indeed took an active part in the work of a strong Communist section in the camp where he was held. In 1942, when the Communist line had changed as a result of the German attack on Russia, he was allowed to return to Britain, given work under distinguished sponsorship on atomic research for the British government, and admitted to British citizenship. This took him, a year later, into the inner circle of research workers on the American atomic project, whose secrets he passed on to the Russian government over a period of years.

The detention of Sir Oswald Mosley, the leader of the British Union, and of Captain Archibald Ramsay, a member of Parliament, was hailed in 1940 as something which would "meet with the approval of all who cherish Liberal beliefs." But the *New States-*

man in January, 1941, protested mildly at the suppression of the Communist *Daily Worker,* which was certainly doing more damage to the British war effort at the time than Mosley ever did.

Nazi sympathizers among the British people themselves were few, and uniformly petty; though here one must make a careful distinction between Nazi sympathizers and those who, for one reason or another, would have collaborated, as some of the French did, in the event of defeat. A woman in the Isle of Wight was sentenced to death for cutting military telephone wires, though the conviction was reversed on appeal, and she was sentenced to fourteen years' imprisonment on other charges. Two men hung about the refreshment room at Preston railway station, telling soldiers that Hitler wouldn't be a bad boss. A woman was charged with trying to obtain official secrets from soldiers. She had told them, "When this country is invaded by the Germans, the Royal Family and members of the Cabinet will be publicly executed, and Sir Oswald Mosley will be made ruler of England."

This was the caliber of the dreaded Fifth Column. There is no evidence that it would have been more powerful if the Germans had attempted an invasion. A young officer serving on the south coast in the summer of 1940 was given a list of a dozen local residents whom he was to arrest if an invasion began. The only black mark against one of them was that his wife had been associated with Mosley's British Union.*

The German intelligence network in Britain was in fact extraordinarily ineffective. The Military Intelligence estimate, supplied to the German army as a basis for its invasion planning, put British strength at thirty-seven divisions, instead of twenty-nine, and for the most part located them in the wrong places. The assessment of British opinion which emerges from William Joyce's broadcasts and the published archives of the German Foreign Ministry, points clearly to the fact that no reliable information was coming from inside Britain.

It has been suggested to me that one reason for this ineffectiveness is that, in about 1935, the Nazis carried out a purge of German intelligence agents who were not considered ideologically sound,

---

* The officer, now middle-aged, has suffered the social embarrassment of having to sit down to dinner since the war with some of those whose names had been on his list.

and so lost the services of many of those mainstays of intelligence, the well-established professional man, or the news agent by the dock or barrack gate whose shop has been there for so long that nobody notices him. If this was indeed the case, no adequate replacements were found among British traitors.

One remembers long, hot summer days, the scent of crushed grass in the canteen tent, a honky-tonk piano battering out "Deep Purple" and "Somewhere Over the Rainbow."

A pink-cheeked subaltern, fresh back from a course, instructs us that in the event of invasion we are to lay soup plates upside down in the road, which German tank crews will mistake for mines. When they get out to remove them, we will machine-gun them. In that summer of our honeymoon with the army, most of us accepted anything we were told; but one of those professional nonconformists, who insists to the army's embarrassment that his civilian trade is Silk Stocking Smuggler, his religion Atheist, asks what happens if the German tank crews don't get out to remove the soup plates. The subaltern has not been given the answer to that one and, as his cheeks become pinker, can only reply huffily, "Oh, but they will."

There are in the country fewer than a thousand tanks, most of them obsolete or unserviceable. No division has anything like its full strength quota of field or antitank guns. At the current rate of production it will take two months to bring a single division up to strength in twenty-five-pounders; and there are twenty-nine divisions.

Instead of guns, containers of gasoline are mounted beside strategic roads. As the Germans approach, a heroic Home Guard will spray the road and lob a hand grenade into the gasoline. Hundreds of pillboxes are being built, many of them sited the wrong way round.

The weather suddenly becomes much more than a topic of polite conversation. "The weather still remains very fine, worse luck," Ironside notes in his diary at the beginning of July. "We could do with storms." And Halifax, hearing a rustle of trees in St. James's Park, looks up from his desk at the Foreign Office and says hopefully, "That sounds like a nice storm."

May and June, according to the Meteorological Office records, were warm, dry, and sunny, particularly June, when temperatures reached 90 degrees. July was cool and wet, August was dry, with average sunshine and temperature. September began warm and sunny, but turned cool after the first week. October was generally wet and dull. One does not remember it so, only the sun rising out of the calm sea at dawn, and sinking again at dusk. And one wonders, without apprehension but with idle curiosity, what the first sign of invasion will be. This was not because we were brave, but because we were innocent.

In May, 1940, while the French campaign continued, 3 per cent of the British people according to a Gallup Poll, believed that they might lose the war. By the end of the year, the percentage was so small that it could not be measured. Confidence in the Prime Minister stood at 88 per cent in July, rose to 89 in October, fell to 85 by the end of the year. The lowest level it ever touched was in July, 1942, when Tobruk and Singapore had fallen. It stood then at 78 per cent. The highest it had reached for Chamberlain was 68 per cent.

There is no doubt that the British were united, nor is there the least doubt that they found in Churchill an exact expression of their own obstinacy, courage, and refusal to recognize the apparent logic of facts.

Chapter

9

PEACE?

The difficulties of reading Hitler's mind are not lessened by the fact that, on a tactical level, he changed it frequently and had more than the normal human capacity for believing contradictory things at the same moment. He used words and thoughts as weapons, and before accepting any recorded utterance of his at its face value, one has to consider whom he was addressing and what effect he was trying to achieve.

His record until June, 1940, is like that of a financial gambler whose coups, made against all sound advice, have left him a millionaire. In seven years, by a series of brilliantly opportunist strokes, he had raised Germany—and through the medium of Germany, himself—from a position of humiliating weakness to that of conqueror of a great part of Europe. Before every step, his advisers had warned him that ruin would follow. Ignoring them, he achieved triumph after triumph, the most recent of which had been an annihilating victory over what had been regarded as the strongest military power in Europe.

In the face of his progress, the British had consistently run away, and there can have seemed no reason to the successful gambler why they should not continue to do so. He had not bothered to prepare for war with Britain. In September, 1939, Germany had only forty-three U-boats and an inferior fleet. The four-engined heavy bombers which might have pulverized Coventry in 1940 as the R.A.F. pulverized Hamburg in 1943 existed in prototype form in 1936, but were then scrapped, and the German air force, the Luftwaffe, had to a considerable extent been subordinated in design and training to the tactics of the land *Blitzkrieg*. The French army was the enemy, and it had been beaten. "The British won't come back in this war," Hitler told Kleist, when his armored-group commander ventured to reproach him for allowing the British Expeditionary Force to escape through Dunkirk.

As early as May 28, after Brauchitsch had seen Hitler in the morning, Halder's diary refers to the "projected peacetime army: 24 armored divisions, 12 motorized divisions, 30-40 other divisions," and after Halder's evening conference with Brauchitsch on that day there is a note on "Demobilization: Must be handled by a Special Commissar." On June 15, Halder's note of a directive from the Führer contains the passage: "Based on the assumption that with the now imminent final collapse of the enemy, the army will have fulfilled its mission and so, while still in enemy country, could comfortaby start on work to prepare the projected peacetime organization. Air force and navy alone would be carrying on the war against Britain."

At the beginning of June, General Milch, Secretary of State of the German Air Ministry and Inspector General of the Luftwaffe, put to Göring a proposal for a co-ordinated series of mass parachute landings on R.A.F. Fighter Stations which, in the state of British defenses at the time, could not have failed to create confusion, if nothing worse. Göring agreed to place the proposal before Hitler. It was discussed on June 18 and 27, but no more was heard of the plan, and indeed on June 18 Hitler told Göring, "The war's finished. I'll come to an understanding with England."

It has been argued that during the crucial weeks after Dunkirk, Hitler believed a naval blockade combined with air assault would be sufficient to convince the British they had had enough. Yet this does not seem the whole, or even a major part, of the explanation of why Hitler remained convinced that the British would come to terms. The conviction was certainly rooted in the inglorious British record over Czechoslovakia, Poland, Norway, France. It was strengthened by reports from a variety of sources.

On June 6, Stohrer, the German Ambassador in Spain, reported that at a meeting with the Spanish Foreign Minister Sir Samuel Hoare, the new British Ambassador in Madrid, Hoare had spoken quite openly about the possibility of the English government moving to Canada, and although Hoare had said the English were determined to continue the war even from there, the impression made on the Spanish Foreign Minister had been politically depressing.*

On June 7, Björn Prytz, the Swedish Minister in London, had an interview with R. A. Butler, the Under-Secretary of State for Foreign Affairs. According to Prytz's recollection of the meeting, which has been challenged, Butler said that the attitude of Churchill was not decisive, and that the war would not have to be fought until a decision was reached; indeed, that no occasion would be missed to reach a compromise peace if reasonable terms could be obtained. During the talk, Butler was called away to Halifax, and returned with a message that "common sense and not bravado" would govern British policy.

The significant point, however, is that whatever was said at this meeting reached Berlin—as might perhaps have been calculated—and emerged on June 19 as a memorandum by Baron Ernst Von Weizsäcker, the State Secretary of the German Foreign Ministry, noting that Prytz had given the impression of a return to "sound common sense in authoritative circles in London." Three days later another memorandum by Weizsäcker recorded reports of an invitation to Lloyd George to join the British government, take over the post of Prime Minister, and conclude a compromise peace. The Swedish Minister, consulted about this, said he could hardly believe it, but a peace trend was beginning to be perceptible in the English Cabinet which, he hinted, was represented by Halifax, and of which the Germans would hear more.

At the end of June, Ribbentrop began to evolve an elaborate—and rather farcical—plot to detain the Duke of Windsor in Spain, to which he had escaped when France fell, and pay him fifty mil-

---

* This report, like others in the following pages, is taken from the *Documents on German Foreign Policy* captured at the end of the war and since published under Anglo-American auspices. I must make it absolutely clear that I do not advance these documents as evidence of what was said or done by Hoare, the Duke of Windsor, or anyone else mentioned in them. The only evidence they provide, unless supported from other sources, is of the kind of information which was reaching the German Foreign Ministry, and to that extent influencing German policy.

lion Swiss francs to place himself at Germany's disposal for future use.

On July 8, Halder noted in his diary a report that Hitler had postponed the Reichstag session at which he was to speak, because of a probable reshuffle of the British Cabinet; but three days later there is a note of another briefing: "Internal situation of Britain. Discord between Churchill and Halifax. Churchill has prevailed: 'War to the finish.' " This, indeed, is the common explanation of these manifestations: a war party led by Churchill and a peace party led by Halifax, with Churchill emerging as victor. Life is rarely as simple as that.

No one who has read Churchill's own records of his early life can doubt that, while like the Duke of Wellington he shed genuine tears over the wounded and the slain, he actively enjoyed the waging of war. In Churchill's philosophy, he really was dead who would not fight.

This attitude was sometimes skeptically received even in Britain in May, 1940. A very junior minister, invited to join Churchill's government, recalls being treated, for no very apparent reason, to a half-hour harangue on the perils to be faced. With what appeared to be considerable relish, the Prime Minister fought graphically and dramatically beside his junior colleague until finally, their last rounds expended, they mingled their lifeblood in the gutters of a devastated Whitehall.

"Now," said the Prime Minister, scowling ferociously. "That is what I have to offer you if you join my government. Can you face it?"

"I don't know," said the junior minister rather coldly. "They are not circumstances to which I am accustomed."

Halifax certainly shared this skeptical attitude to Churchillian rhetoric and he was, as he noted of himself, not one to burn the house down, because he would continue to hope that he might later get it back again. He retained a civilized sense that a war in which some thirty million people were eventually killed ought to be stopped if possible, provided it could be guaranteed that war would not shortly break out again. This does not mean that he was prepared to negotiate with Hitler, except on the terms laid down under Chamberlain. These started with the demand that the German armies must withdraw from all conquered territories. Only then could there follow negotiations about German territorial claims in Europe and the return of German colonies.

Halifax's attitude, and that of the Chamberlain government, is concisely summed up in a letter Halifax wrote on July 24 to a ducal correspondent who was urging him to explore further Hitler's peace appeal of July 19: "You will, of course, have profoundly disagreed with it but I think that what I said in my broadcast speech on Monday is my answer to your letter. Everything that he has done and said shows that Hitler's picture of the world is utterly different from mine, and I do find it very difficult to see how, unless that diagnosis is completely wrong, any useful purpose is served by pretending that he can be persuaded at this moment to do something that all his actions and words belie.

"The most probable consequence, as I see it, would be that we should achieve no result with him but merely sow profound discouragement in all the quarters on which we have to rely for our strength (Roosevelt).

"We have said over and over again that we have no wish to destroy Germany and that we want a freely negotiated peace, and so on. Hitler of course also knows that Germany must retain a predominant place in Europe and therefore it is impossible to believe that he can be under any illusion as to the attitude of this country. But this, of course, does not get over the fundamental gulf between what I am bound to think is his picture of a Europe subordinate to a dominant Germany and our picture of a Europe in which Germany enjoys the position to which her greatness entitles her but in which other nations are not debarred from living in freedom."

There is of course no reason why a man should not write such a letter on July 24, when a few weeks earlier he had been urging negotiations for peace; one can only register a personal conviction that, in the context of Halifax's character, it seems unlikely.

The British situation in the early summer of 1940 was, however, a desperate one. The British Expeditionary Force had been saved, but without the bulk of its equipment, and with no reserves of guns, tanks, or lorries upon which to draw. Until the Germans launched their southward assault against the remaining French armies on June 3, the British government had no means of knowing whether the attack might not be directed instead across the Channel, leaving the French to be dealt with later. There were agonized meetings of ministers to decide on the division of inadequate resources between home defense and propping up the French for as long as possible, at which it is clear that a brake was being placed—certainly by Halifax, among others—on Churchill's instinct to keep the fighting front in being for as long as possible. "Normally," Churchill once told Eden of those desperate days, "I wake up buoyant to a new day. Then I awoke with dread in my heart."

On May 15, Churchill told Joseph Kennedy, the American Ambassador, that he expected Britain to be attacked within a month. July 9, according to Halifax's diary, was "from many quarters alleged to be the day of Hitler's invasion." * The days of British weakness between the beginning of June and the second week of July were therefore of crucial importance to the government's thinking.

Churchill was a fighter, prepared to use any weapon that came to hand to beat the Germans, including mustard gas on the invasion beaches and flaming gasoline to burn the invasion barges and their human loads. The evidence suggests that he was not averse from at any rate countenancing the use of more subtle weapons, which appear to have originated in the Foreign Office.

Dr. Fritz Hesse, a German journalist, had represented the official German news agency in London before the war, and had been involved in the last-minute attempt through Birger Dahlerus, a Swedish intermediary, to reach a settlement over Poland. On his return to Berlin, Hesse had joined the German Foreign Ministry as an adviser on British affairs. Although he had access to Ribbentrop, the German Foreign Minister, he was not at the center of events, and his book, *Hitler and the English,* is no more than the interpretation of a shrewd political journalist, based upon information much of which he claimed to have obtained from Walther Hewel, Ribbentrop's personal representative at Hitler's headquarters. He cannot therefore be cited as a firsthand authority, but neither need he be ignored.

In *Hitler and the English,* Hesse says that about a fortnight before the end of the French campaign—that is, in the first or second

* On July 9, Halder wrote in *his* diary of "work on draft operation plans for invasion of Britain." German planning of invasion had only just got under way.

weeks of June—the German Foreign Ministry and a number of secret organizations received a report about contacts which had been made with British agents. For some reason, this report gave Hitler and Ribbentrop the impression that it would be possible to take up conversations with the English.

The facts, according to Hesse, were that a British agent, evidently acting on instructions from the British Consul-General in Geneva, had approached Krauel, the German Consul-General in Zurich, inviting him to open a discussion about the possibilities of peace. The British Consul-General had also approached an agent of Admiral Canaris, the head of German Military Intelligence, who, it will be remembered, was in touch with the German opposition. Krauel, says Hesse, had thereupon been instructed to approach the English through the Papal Nuncio in Berne.

Asked by Ribbentrop his opinion of these approaches, Hesse expressed doubt about them. "They amounted to this—that one agent had expressed the wish to speak to other agents. Nothing was stated about any authorisation on the part of the British Government. I believed that hundreds of agents had received instructions to establish contact with their German counterparts to find out what the Germans were thinking on the subject of peace. The purpose of such attempts was information for the use of the British Government and no more. At least, it seemed to me that genuine peace-feelers would have quite a different character."

There is this much confirmation of Hesse's story: that at the end of June the Pope did sound the German, Italian, and British governments about their possible reactions to a peace appeal by him;* and the *Documents on German Foreign Policy* contain a note of two talks during the summer and autumn between H. B. Livingston, the British Consul-General in Geneva, and a Dr. Riesser, who was not an agent of the Foreign Ministry but is described as having "military employers." The record of the earlier talk, in fact, was not made available to the Foreign Ministry until it was asked for later in the year.

According to Riesser's account of this talk, dated July 18, Livingston asked to see him, having repeatedly tried to reach him by telephone during the day, and their conversation lasted for over an

---

* Churchill knocked this one on the head on June 28; Hitler, who had apparently inspired it, not till July 26.

hour. Livingston began by saying that information reaching him from Berlin suggested that Germany had nothing against England and the British Empire, and that there were reports from Italy that the Italians also were advocating peace. Livingston was in a position to inform Riesser that the British government also preferred peace to the total financial and economic destruction of Europe.

Riesser asked three questions: was that Livingston's own view, or that of his government?; if the latter, how was a recent speech of Churchill's to be explained?;* and on what basis did the British government envisage such a peace?

Livingston answered that what he had said was not his personal view; that Churchill's speech meant England would fight on to victory if she were attacked; and that the basis of peace would be the recognition of the British Empire by Germany and the recognition of Germany's economic, but not political, living space in Europe.

Livingston was reported as adding that the struggle against "Hitlerism" would have to stop, but this would be all the easier for England to do because it appeared certain that the influence of the army would be extremely great in Germany after the war—an obvious reference to the army's implication in anti-Hitler conspiracies. The era of "European guarantees" was over for England, which had to act "egotistically." The former German colonies would have to be returned to Germany.

Riesser, according to his account, said that he would have to think over whether, and in what form, he could inform old friends and former colleagues of the substance of this talk; and he did apparently make an immediate report, not to the Foreign Ministry, but to his "military employers," presumably Canaris.

Another contact which certainly took place was between the British Minister in Berne, later Sir David Kelly, and Prince Max of Hohenlohe-Langenberg, and there exist both Sir David's pub-

---

* In the course of a broadcast on July 14, Churchill said: "Should the invader come, there will be no placid lying down of the people in submission before him as we have seen—alas!—in other countries. We shall defend every village, every town, and every city. The vast mass of London itself, fought street by street, could easily devour an entire hostile army, and we would rather see London laid in ruins and ashes than that it should be tamely and abjectly enslaved." This passage seems to have caused considerable agitation in German ruling circles. See also page 168, below.

lished account of this episode and a report from Hohenlohe to Hewel.*

According to Sir David's account, before he left London to take up his appointment in Switzerland at the end of 1939, he had been given orally and secretly the names of two Germans to whom he might listen if they approached him. He had received these names from Sir Robert Vansittart, then adviser to Halifax, the Foreign Minister. One of them was that of Hohenlohe, whom the Foreign Office believed to be a less than wholehearted supporter of the Nazi regime.

In June 1940, Paravicini, the former Swiss Minister in London, suggested to Kelly a meeting with Hohenlohe, and Kelly agreed. He says that Hohenlohe visited Switzerland to see him three or four times during the summer, and his message, purporting to come from the German Foreign Ministry, was always the same. The message offered guarantees for the British Empire in return for giving Germany a free hand in Europe—an offer which had been consistently refused before the war by both Baldwin's and Chamberlain's governments.

At one meeting, Hohenlohe read Kelly a memorandum, said to have been shown to Hitler, which had a definite time limit expiring on a date which roughly corresponded with what proved to be the start of the big German air attacks on Britain.

Kelly says: "Knowing the vital importance of gaining time, I made a show of interest, while in fact of course merely reporting to Sir Robert Vansittart what he [Hohenlohe] said without comment. I never received from London any comment or acknowledgement of my unofficial reports, so there was never any question of discussion and still less of negotiation; but it was obvious that every day gained for the production of Spitfires and the training of crews was priceless." At a later stage of his account of his wartime service in Switzerland, Sir David Kelly records the receipt, on January 7, 1941, of a personal telegram from the Prime Minister: "All your work excellent and messages deeply informative."

Hohenlohe's account, which, like Riesser's, is dated July 18, mentions only one meeting, not four, and it was sent in answer to a

* Sir David Kelly's *The Ruling Few* was published in 1952; Volume X of the *Documents on German Foreign Policy*, which contains Hohenlohe's report, appeared five years later. Sir David was therefore unaware of Hohenlohe's report when he wrote.

letter from Hewel, dated June 30: "I would be interested in hearing from you, if you again hear of English attempts to approach
Germans for the purpose of orientation. While we will certainly
make no use of such channels, it is nevertheless interesting to observe exactly the tendency in England."

According to Hohenlohe—who, it must be remembered, was
writing "for the record"—he was pressed by Paravicini and by Professor Carl Burckhardt, former League of Nations High Commissioner for Danzig, to call on Kelly, but declined to do so until
Kelly sent Hohenlohe, through the Spanish Minister in Berne, an
express indication of his desire for a meeting. According to Kelly's
account, the second of his meetings with Hohenlohe took place at
the Spanish Legation.

"Immediately after my arrival," reported Hohenlohe, "Mrs.
Kelly, a native Belgian, took me aside and urged me to lose no time
and promptly to discuss peace possibilities with her husband. Kelly
asked me to go with him to an adjoining room. There he told me
after a few introductory remarks that he would very much like to
talk with me, as an old friend of his own friends in England, about
the situation and the future. He was, to be sure, only Minister to
Switzerland and therefore available only as a messenger. I stated
that if he was merely a messenger to Churchill it was meaningless
and the talk could be broken off at once. He replied that he was
aware that our common friends in England were Butler, Vansittart and also Halifax, with followers. . . ."

Kelly then seems to have sounded Hohenlohe as to where his
own sympathies lay, but Hohenlohe, at least according to his report
to Hewel, made it clear that his loyalty was to Hitler.

After an account of some flowery references alleged to have been
made by Kelly to the Führer and "the greatness of his conception,"
Kelly went on to say that it was difficult to arrive at a lasting settlement of questions, since experience had not facilitated reliance on
the Führer's word, and it was difficult to imagine what sort of definitive guarantees could be given for a general and lasting settlement.
There was some talk about the prospects of aid from the United
States, and "we then talked about the forces in English domestic
politics and I mentioned that he surely knew, as I did, how untrust-
worthy a person Churchill was, how he was often under the influence of alcohol (liquid courage) and that I could not believe that

*Above, the evacuation of London schoolchildren begins, June 1940.
Below, Londoners sleeping in an Underground station during the
Blitz.*

Above, American Ambassador Mr. Joseph Kennedy (right) and Lord Halifax, Foreign Secretary. Below, President Roosevelt broadcasting to the nation.

Above, London during the Blitz. Below, Coventry, November, 1940.

St. Paul's Cathedral, December 29, 1940.

this man was the embodiment of the English people. Kelly assented to my criticism of Churchill to the extent of saying that Churchill was a bull who was running his head against the wall, but that Butler's, Halifax's and also Vansittart's temperaments were different. I replied that this was what I imagined, for I could not see the English dying for the honour of their country among the ruins of the last house of London, if other solutions were available. . . .

"My general impression of the conversation, which was conducted by Kelly with great emotion and a good deal of temperament," Hohenlohe concluded, "was that he was engaging in it with frankness and a desire to develop these contacts further. I did not go along with him, however, for the suspicion that conversations are intended to gain time is an obvious one. . . ."

Hohenlohe's report was answered by another letter from Hewel, dated July 24: "As politics are at the moment, they do not permit in the Minister's view a continuation of such contacts, since thereby wrong impressions might be created on the other side. The Minister therefore requests you to do nothing more at the moment in that direction. The speech of Halifax has definitely destroyed our belief in a conciliation party over there and the Führer also does not wish that further attempts should be made to build bridges for the English. If the English want their own destruction, they can have it. Nor do I believe that we can achieve anything over there through unofficial channels at this time, for otherwise the English would at least have restrained themselves a bit in their official utterances."

In spite of this letter, a third meeting between Hohenlohe and Kelly did, according to Kelly, take place in Geneva, and there was a fourth in Paravicini's house, at which there was produced the memorandum said to have been shown by Ribbentrop to Hitler and offering Britain a time limit in which to accept German guarantees. According to Hohenlohe, Kelly again approached him in December, but this time met with a cold reception.

As a footnote to Hohenlohe's account, it may be added that he was believed by his friends in the British Foreign Office to be not only an unenthusiastic supporter of Hitler, but also to possess an almost English sense of humor. The late Aga Khan also had a sense of humor, robust rather than subtle. A week after the report of the meeting with Kelly, Hewel received Hohenlohe's account of a talk with the Aga Khan during which that potentate is alleged to have said: "The struggle against England was not a struggle against the English people, but against the Jews. Churchill had been for years in their pay and the King was too weak and limited. Lord Beaverbrook was the only man who had the courage, power and standing to bring about a change in England, even against Churchill, since the latter had for a long time been in his pay." His Highness also referred to the financial embarrassment he was suffering as a result of the war, and hinted none too delicately that he would welcome a small loan to tide him over. There is unfortunately no indication of how Hewel and Ribbentrop took this remarkable statement; though Hohenlohe had had the kindness to warn them that the Aga Khan did not strike him "as a particularly trustworthy person."

A figure upon whose pacifism the Germans built high hopes was Lloyd George. He had visited Hitler in 1936, had been civil to him —something so rare that it invariably seems to have registered in the Nazi mind as marking a friend for life—and on his return had written at least one article praising Hitler. In October, 1939, in a speech in the Commons, he urged the government not to reject out of hand the peace offer Hitler had made following the conquest of Poland, and his political reputation thereafter was that of a defeatist, though to put it in such black-and-white terms is an oversimplification of his attitude.

Lloyd George had been left out of the government formed by Churchill after May 10, but at the end of May the Prime Minister invited him to join, subject to Chamberlain's approval. According to the biography of Lloyd George by Frank Owen, Chamberlain did agree on June 16, "in scepticism and dismay." Lloyd George was pressed hard by Beaverbrook, among others, to accept the offer, but he constantly changed his mind, saying: "I am not going in with this gang. There will be a change. The country does not realise the peril it is in." He finally refused the offer because of the terms laid down.

Owen comments: "Did Lloyd George harbour another thought? Might not a day come when all the other great public figures had been discredited by personal failure, or by the general hopelessness of an apparently Endless War, and a call came for a statesman who had never wanted it, or waged it, but who was able and willing to wind it up?"

In such circumstances, and at this time, Churchill's offer to Lloyd George is a remarkable one. He had, it is true, a lasting veneration for Lloyd George, going back to their days as fellow members of the 1906 Liberal government. In the summer of 1940, Lloyd George was also the one formidable critic left outside the government, and it may well have been thought desirable to bring him inside and thus curb his always great capacity for mischief-making. But Halifax's diary of June 6 contains the note: "Winston exhorting Sinclair and Labour about heresy-hunting, especially Neville and Kingsley Wood. Ll G [Lloyd George] to join Government if Neville agrees. Winston told me that he meant to put him through an inquisition first as to whether he had the root of the matter in him. By this he means, so he explained to me, adopting a formula I suggested to him, that any Peace terms now, or hereafter, offered must not be destructive of our independence."

In this case Halifax, and Chamberlain, seem to have been more worried about Lloyd George's pacific reputation than Churchill was; and as has been seen, the offer to Lloyd George became known in Berlin and was noted as a hopeful indication of British willingness to make peace.

Finally one may cite the case of Sir Samuel Hoare, publicly known as a leading supporter of Chamberlain's appeasement policy. From May 12 onward, mounting pressure was put on Hoare, who hoped to become Viceroy of India, to go as Ambassador to Madrid. One can understand Churchill's reasons for wanting this able political opponent out of the country, but the world is a wide place, and one must ask, why Madrid, where Pétain had been French Ambassador? In the first place, the choice of Madrid probably arose from the fact that it was urgently necessary to keep Spain neutral, a task requiring greater weight than might have been applied by a career diplomat. But after Hoare had refused the office, he was pressed and pressed again; and after the collapse of France, the German impression that Britain might at some stage be ready to talk peace was strengthened by the presence of the appeaser Hoare in the capital through which the French had sought peace terms. The Germans, once again, heard what they expected to hear. A report, dated July 12, reached the German Foreign Minister of a talk between Hoare and the Spanish Foreign Minister, in which the latter, referring to Spain's role as mediator for France, said that she was ready to serve the English also, adding that in all likelihood Hoare would be the intermediary. Hoare answered, according to the report, "It is possible that it will sometime come to that."

The point has to be made that, if Hitler had invaded Britain at the end of May or in June, it might well have come to that. One reason he did not invade England was his belief that he could come to terms with Britain; and it seems clear that this belief had been deliberately nourished in a number of ways.

There were in fact several reasons for keeping open subterranean channels of communication between Britain and Germany during this period, all subtly shading into each other, and all detectable in Hohenlohe's account of his talk with Kelly. The first was that Britain might have had to make peace, and it was therefore prudent, in her precarious situation, to be prepared to "listen to"—not to discuss; there is a fine, but real, distinction—the kind of terms a victorious Germany might be prepared to offer.

It was certainly desirable to keep in touch with the German opposition, to ascertain its strength at any moment, because of its potential ability to sap and weaken German unity, and to explore the possibility of an alternative German government emerging. But it was not easy to ascertain who, at any given moment, was in opposition to Hitler. Until the Norway campaign, but not after, Brauchitsch and Halder had been halfheartedly in opposition. Weizsäcker and Canaris, equivocally, were. Göring had been prepared to take over from Hitler until the unexpected collapse of France made him execute a rapid turn-about. Diplomats like Kelly could never be sure whether they were talking to an agent of Canaris as a patriotic head of Military Intelligence or as an opposition intermediary.

And, as both Hohenlohe and Kelly noted in their various ways, keeping conversations going was a most useful delaying tactic for the British.

There can be no doubt that Churchill was aware of what was going on. Kelly and, as will be seen later, the British Ambassador in Washington, Lothian, reported their conversations, and Churchill saw the telegrams. He took strong enough action to stop any activities he disapproved of. Nor is it credible that he was so innocent as to be unaware of the impression likely to be created in Germany by the invitation to Lloyd George and the pressure on Hoare to go to Madrid.

The evidence, in fact, points to one conclusion: that for a limited period, until the intentions of the United States became clearer, and for a definite purpose, to prevent invasion during the crucial weeks of British disorganization, not only Halifax and the Foreign Office, but Churchill himself, were using every underground means at their disposal to foster Hitler's belief that the British were willing to think about peace. No one need doubt that Churchill would have fought with his bare hands in the last ditch. He would never have made peace. If it had come to that, he would have resigned, leaving some unfortunate to incur the lasting odium of picking up the pieces, and organized a resistance government in Canada or anywhere else that he could reach.

But it did not come to that. For six vital weeks Hitler did not even begin to contemplate invasion, and for the rest of the year he maintained the conviction that just one more blow might induce in the British a peaceful frame of mind.

Chapter

10

BIRTH OF A SEALION

Italy entered the war on June 10; and Mussolini almost immediately saw the rewards of his belated valor escaping him. The armistice terms offered to France were, in his view, absurdly light. There was alarming talk of peace with England. On June 26, he sternly drew Hitler's attention to the task ahead: "Führer: Now that the problem is to conquer Great Britain, I remind you of what I said to you at Munich [their previous meeting] about the direct participation of Italy in the assault on the island. I am ready to contribute ground forces and air forces, and you know how much I desire to do so." *

After Mussolini's letter had been received, a different note is apparent in German official circles. Weizsäcker circulated a memorandum to diplomatic representatives: "Germany is not considering peace. She is concerned exclusively with preparation for the destruction of England." He also briefed service chiefs, at a conference of which Halder noted: "Britain probably still needs one more demonstration of our military might before she gives in and leaves us a free hand in the east."

* Hitler's reply of July 13 is a nice example of how to decline with thanks. "However much, Duce, I appreciate your offer—of making a substantial number of Italian divisions available for the attack on England—as an act of comradeship and kindness, at the same time we must give consideration to everything that is likely to secure a successful outcome for this very bold decision . . ."

On the following day, July 1, Hitler had a long talk with Alfieri, the Italian Ambassador. Hitler began by saying that it was always a good tactic to make the enemy responsible in the eyes of public opinion in Germany and abroad for the future course of events. An operation such as Germany planned would be very bloody, therefore one must convince public opinion that everything had been done to avoid this horror. He went on to assure Alfieri that Germany was not really demobilizing, only regrouping her forces. The Germans were continuing to build bases on the coasts of France, Belgium, and the Netherlands, constructing positions for attack and organizing a flexible system for munitions, fuel, and aircraft requirements. "These preparations had been begun immediately after the French armistice . . . gigantic columns were rolling westward with the material for undertaking impending tasks. . . ."

Most of this was eyewash for Mussolini's benefit. No gigantic columns rolled westward, there were no tasks impending. On the same day, Halder for the first time got down to some planning for a cross-Channel invasion, although General Leeb, of the Ordnance Office, protested that "he was told all along that the invasion of England was not being considered." Commented Halder, "I tell him that the possibilities have to be examined, for, if the political command demands a landing, they will want everything done at top speed."

But toward the end of his talk with Alfieri, Hitler did at last come to what seems to have been genuinely occupying his thoughts. Having said that he could not conceive of anyone in England still believing in victory, he continued: "If England still entertained any thought of winning, they did so only because they counted on support from third countries, presumably mainly from the United States, but perhaps also with a secret hope as to Russia." This was the real worry. While German forces were still concentrated in the west, what were Russian intentions?

Hitler had signed the Nazi-Soviet Pact of August, 1939, in the expectation that this clever coup would call the bluff of the British and French governments over Poland, and end the possibility of that war before it had begun. This had not happened. Hitler respected Stalin as a hardheaded political realist like himself, and he had never had any illusions about the lasting reality of the pact. Why should Stalin?

As the magnitude of the French collapse became apparent, the Russian government did indeed show increasing apprehension that both Britain and France would make peace, leaving Hitler free to turn eastward. Stalin acted before the German forces could regroup, and on June 15, without consultation though within the letter of the 1939 pact, Russian troops advanced into the Baltic states of Lithuania, Latvia, and Estonia. Later in the month they occupied northern Rumania, approaching inconveniently close to the oil wells on which Germany heavily depended. According to Alexander Werth's *Russia at War,* Russian industry was put virtually on a war footing on June 26. Ribbentrop, in his evidence at the Nuremberg trial, referred to Hitler's anxiety over Russian troop concentrations near the East Prussian border, and of increasing Communist activity in German factories.

Then there was Sir Stafford Cripps, sent to Moscow in June as British Ambassador. What was he up to? Reports from Schulenburg, the German Ambassador in Moscow, were reassuring; but it was not Hitler's suspicious habit to place very much trust in the reports of ambassadors.

One need not doubt that Hitler would at some time have attacked Russia in any event. The question was, when? In July, Halder was instructed to start operational thinking about Russia, and for a brief period Hitler contemplated an attack that autumn, but was dissuaded by his military advisers Jodl and Keitel.

On July 13, there was a conference of which Halder noted: "The Führer is most strongly occupied by the question why England does not yet want to take the road to peace. Just as we do, he sees the solution of this question in the fact that England is still setting her hopes on Russia. Thus he too expects that England will have to be compelled by force to make peace. He does not like to do such a thing, however. Reason: If we smash England militarily, the British Empire will disintegrate. Germany, however, would not profit from this. With German blood we would achieve something from which only Japan, America and others will profit."

Three days later, on July 16, Hitler at long last issued his Directive Number 16 on the preparation of a landing operation against England. It is still phrased conditionally. "Since England," this document begins, "despite her militarily hopeless situation still shows no sign of willingness to come to terms, I have decided to prepare a landing operation against England, *and if necessary to carry it out."* *

Although the conqueror of Europe seems to have balked, according to Dr. Hesse, at "crawling up English backsides," he brought himself—or was brought—to make a final public bid to win his war without having to fight it; toward the end of a long speech to the Reichstag on July 19 he said: "In this hour I feel it to be my duty before my own conscience to appeal once more to reason and common sense in Great Britain as much as elsewhere. I consider myself in a position to make this appeal, since I am not a vanquished foe begging favours but the victor, speaking in the name of reason. I can see no reason why this war need go on. I am grieved to think of the sacrifices it must claim."

Ciano, in Berlin, noted in his diary: "I understand that, without their saying so, they are hoping and praying that this appeal will not be rejected." The B.B.C. reported the appeal with a note of mockery, and William L. Shirer observed the effects of the broadcast in Berlin: "Officers from the High Command and officials from various ministries, sitting round the room, could not believe their ears. One of them shouted at me: 'Can you make it out? Can you understand those British fools? To turn down peace now?' "

In London, Churchill was eager to answer the speech with a solemn, formal debate in both Houses of Parliament, and resolutions rejecting it from Lords and Commons. He was dissuaded, by Chamberlain and Attlee among others, on the grounds that this would give Hitler the important propaganda point that the British alone were responsible for continuing the war.

The reference to Hitler's speech in Halifax's diary occupies a few lines at the end of a long anecdote about the American Ambassador: "Hitler made a speech in the Reichstag in the evening, which appears to leave things very much where they were. He, of course, had never wanted the war, and it is everybody's fault but his!" On the following day there was another brief note: "Our impression—very little to be made of Hitler's speech." There was no official British reply to the appeal until Monday evening, July 22, when Halifax turned it down in the course of a routine ministerial broadcast already arranged.

An interesting sidelight is thrown on both sides at this period by

* The italics are mine.

some private negotiations which Malcolm R. Lovell, an American Quaker, had entered upon in Washington.* Mr. Lovell had had previous dealings with Dr. Hans Thomsen, the German chargé d'affaires in Washington, over the relief of Jews in Germany. Sometime in July, he made an approach to Sir Louis Beale, of the Anglo-French Purchasing Board in New York. According to Lovell's account, he told Sir Louis that he had access to Thomsen on peace matters, but not to the British Ambassador in Washington, Lord Lothian, and he asked Sir Louis to arrange a meeting with Lothian "to discuss the possibilities of peace." A few days later Sir Louis telephoned from Washington, asking Lovell to go to the British Embassy on Friday morning, July 19, which, apparently coincidentally, was the day of Hitler's Reichstag speech.

Lothian, like Halifax and Hoare, had been an "appeaser." He was a man of great personal charm, a gifted conversationalist, who delighted to range at large over the world stage. He received his visitor very graciously and listened to his pleading for peace with interest and courtesy. Lovell said that with the surrender of France there seemed no further reason for war, and that if Germany would agree to a generous and fair peace, which Britain could accept, he hoped the war could be ended.

Lothian replied, according to Lovell, that he knew there was some feeling in the British Cabinet that the war should be ended if a fair peace could be arranged. He did not know that the majority of the Cabinet felt that way, but he did know some members believed the war should end now. He himself, he said, longed for an end to the war and hoped that a way could be found.

Lovell said he had many times discussed possibilities of peace with Dr. Thomsen, and had always found him personally most sympathetic. He said he believed Dr. Thomsen would welcome any possibility of helping to bring together the governments of Germany and Britain to end the war.

Lothian made it clear that Lovell was not to approach Thomsen as a representative of the British Ambassador, but said he would be willing to listen if Lovell brought him any indication of a possible end to the war that "a proud and unconquered nation" could accept. He emphasized that the English had made definite commit-

* The interpretation I have placed at some points upon Mr. Lovell's account of this episode is of course my own.

ments to small European nations, and could not throw them callously aside. Unless a peace could be devised that would permit Englishmen to hold their heads up, he did not see how peace could come—death was truly preferable to a shameful and humiliating peace, even the deaths of a million innocent victims. The world would not condemn a bravely defeated England, conquered by superior force, after courageous defense, but it would properly condemn an England which accepted a shameful peace, before it had been conquered by a superior military force.

If England were conquered by force, Lothian said, according to Lovell's account, he felt the Empire would survive, that Canada and Australia would carry on, and that the fleet would find haven there. He believed that in due time the United States would enter the war, adding that America was much more powerful than its own people thought, and would be able to join the war by late autumn.

Lothian emphasized another point: that if peace terms were arranged, there must be some guarantee. Would Germany be willing to have the United States as a guarantor; and if the United States refused to act, what other method could be found that would assure England that the terms of peace would not later be changed and made humiliatingly harsh and dishonorable?

Lothian promised to send a full report of the talk to London. He hoped to have an answer by the following day and asked Lovell to remain available in Washington. Lovell then went over to the German Embassy, where Thomsen said he was sure his government would welcome any plan for peace, promised to communicate with Berlin, and like Lothian asked Lovell to stay in Washington.

Because of its coincidence with Hitler's appeal, Lovell's intermediation created some excitement both in London and Berlin. In London, Churchill, with his ideas for answering Hitler through Parliament, seems to have suspected the approach to Lothian had come from the German chargé d'affaires, and sent the Foreign Office a note: "I do not know whether Lord Halifax is in town today, but Lord Lothian should be told on no account to make any reply to the German Chargé d'Affaires' message."

In Berlin, Thomsen's telegram received a very different welcome. It is evident from Weizsäcker's memoirs that he at least believed the initiative had come from Lothian, and it must have been seen as a sign of the anxiously awaited British reaction to Hitler's appeal. Thomsen was authorized in a long telegram to continue the contact.

Thomsen sent for Lovell early on the morning of Monday, July 22, showed him the Berlin telegram which stated, according to Lovell, that the German government would welcome a fair peace and one that Britain could properly accept, and asked Lovell to put to Lothian one question which, if answered encouragingly, would lead to the next step. The question was: did Churchill speak rhetorically and for the benefit of home and colonial consumption when he said that England would be defended from house to house, and city to city? If Churchill meant it, the character of the war would be drastically changed from the usual offensive methods against military objectives, and it would mean the horrible and useless slaughter of noncombatants.

Lovell did put this question to Lothian, adding that Dr. Thomsen had said the Germans would not mind if the remarks were rhetorical, and would not change their military tactics; but unless Lovell could be given this assurance officially, the German government must presume Churchill's threat was actually meant, and act accordingly.

Lothian asked Lovell if the German peace terms were in Washington; Lovell replied that he did not know. He said he had been given the next step of procedure, but could not discuss it unless there was authority from London to proceed officially. Lothian said he would telephone London for authority; and Lovell gave Thomsen's assurance that any meeting between Thomsen and Lothian would not be publicized without Lothian's consent. There was some talk about Quaker ideals, and Lothian mentioned that he had once met Thomsen while he had been secretary to Lloyd George. Lovell assured him that Thomsen had a fine character and high ideals, to which Lothian answered that he understood Dr. Thomsen was a devoted Nazi. Lovell rebutted this comment. Lothian asked him to go back to his hotel and await developments.

At half-past one, Nevile Butler, the Counsellor at the British Embassy, telephoned the hotel to say that Lord Halifax's speech would go on the air as planned and that Lovell would hear later the decision of "the London officials" * on this whole matter. On

---

* Possibly a mishearing for "from London officially."

the following morning, Thomsen telephoned. He had received a message from Berlin, which Lovell copied: "Lord Halifax's yesterday speech is or amounts to, the definite rejection of the last offer of peace made by Mr. Hitler in his speech before the Reichstag. Germany was willing to come to an understanding with England. Now Lord Halifax has rejected such an understanding in most derogatory terms. In consequence of this speech the basis for confidential talk between Lord Lothian and Dr. Hans Thomsen has been destroyed."

Thomsen said he felt that the speech closed the door to peace and was violent in its terms toward Hitler. Lovell disagreed, and there was a discussion about the meaning of a paragraph at the bottom of a column in the *New York Times:*

TEXT OF SPEECH CHANGED

London, July 22 (UP)—The original text of the speech of Viscount Halifax, the Foreign Secretary, today was changed in many places only a few minutes before he stepped before the microphone, and various sentences that might have been interpreted in some quarters as a bid for Chancellor Hitler to make a new and more generous peace offer were stricken out.

As he spoke, Lord Halifax seemed to falter momentarily at these revised portions of his manuscript.*

Lovell suggested to Thomsen that this could mean certain violent sentences had been excised to leave the door open for further negotiations. Thomsen said he hoped Lovell was right, but did not feel that he was. He now asked Lovell to advise Lothian that the next stage in the plan of procedure—the meeting between Lothian and Thomsen—could not take place in view of Halifax's speech.

At the British Embassy, Lothian was not available, but Lovell

---

* In a letter to Mr. Lovell dated January 1, 1954, Halifax wrote: "About the other matter of the changes in my speech. I have no recollection at all of these being made or of any changes that were made being of substantial importance." What may have happened, however, is this: Halifax's rejection of Hitler's appeal was made in five paragraphs superimposed on the beginning of a script already written for his ministerial broadcast. It is possible that timing problems then caused cuts to be made, and that Halifax possibly read these opening paragraphs less fluently than the rest of the script. His letter, incidentally, confirms that the account Mr. Lovell had sent him of his Washington talks was "substantially the same" as Halifax's recollection of the account sent officially by Lothian.

saw Nevile Butler, who said the British felt it was possible Hitler was using Lovell to build up a future alibi to present to the world, and would use Lovell's meetings with Lothian as proof that the fault for the failure to make peace lay with the British. He went on, according to Lovell's notes, to make some sharp remarks about Quaker peace activities, which may have been designed to probe the extent to which Lovell was acting on his own and how much as an agent of Thomsen.

Lovell returned to the German Embassy without having delivered his message to Lothian. Thomsen, however, told him that if he were summoned to the British Embassy again, he should still deliver the message, but add that it was predicated on the understanding that Halifax had closed the door to peace.

The next day, July 24, Lovell spent shuttling between the British and German Embassies. At 9:45 A.M. (American time) he saw Butler at the British Embassy. Butler, according to Lovell, asked "if I would unofficially show him the message I had tried to give him yesterday. I agreed, but explained that the message was based on Berlin's belief that Halifax's speech had closed the door to peace. I then read it to him. I also told him that I had advised Dr. Thomsen that I did not agree with their German interpretation of Halifax's speech. I felt it was not closing of any door and that the speech had been purposely changed to permit of further negotiations. I told him I had had no word today from Dr. Thomsen. Butler said that they were expecting a message today from London regarding permission to negotiate for peace here with me as intermediary and he asked me to stay in Washington until I heard further from him."

It is possible that there were genuine misunderstandings at this meeting, with Lovell convinced of the importance of his mission and reluctant to accept defeat, reading into some polite and formal remarks more than was intended. He went from Butler to Thomsen, to whom he reported that he had given Butler the message from Berlin, but "unofficially." Thomsen said he had acted properly, but greatly feared that England's procrastination had made any further peace efforts useless. "He felt," Lovell noted, "it was distinctly possible that word now arriving from London approving peace negotiations would be too late. He did not know that Berlin would now agree to permit him to meet Lord Lothian. I said I felt we both had done everything possible and history could not find fault with our sincere efforts to bring peace."

At 3 P.M., apparently at his own request and no doubt inspired by a sense of urgency instilled by Thomsen's remarks, Lovell again saw Butler. "I told Butler what Dr. Thomsen had said about the impossibility of stopping a vast military machine once the real attack had started," Lovell recorded. "I explained that Dr. Thomsen had said it was a complicated synchronization and one event logically followed another. To stop the machine would divulge to the defence what the plan of attack was, and this the Germans would not do. Butler was this time very mild and kind to me at this meeting. His attitude seemed much more friendly. He asked me to stay in my hotel until I heard from him. I returned there at 4 P.M. At 8:35 P.M. Nevile Butler telephoned to me and told me that official word had just come from London and that it was negative."

One would perhaps not be wrong in detecting in Lovell's account that the Germans were more eager than the British to keep the talks going, an anxiety to be assured that Halifax's broadcast did not mean what it seemed to say. But in Britain the panic days of May and June were over, and on July 19 an event of profound importance took place: Roosevelt allowed himself to be nominated for a third term of office as President of the United States. Until the last moment, Roosevelt had appeared to hesitate over his decision to stand, and upon that decision depended much in the way of future American aid for Britain. While Roosevelt delayed making up his mind, Churchill had to fight a delaying action.

After Roosevelt's nomination, the British tone changed, even in private. Within a week or two of Lovell's talks with Lothian in Washington, and Kelly's with Hohenlohe in Switzerland, Churchill was rebuking the Foreign Office for its draft reply to an offer of mediation by the King of Sweden: "The ideas set forth in the Foreign Office memo. appear to me to err in trying to be too clever, and to enter into refinements of policy unsuited to the tragic simplicity and grandeur of the times and the issues at stake. At this moment, when we have had no sort of success, the slightest opening will be misjudged. Indeed, a firm reply of the kind I have outlined is the only chance of extorting from Germany any offers which are not fantastic."

Only just over the horizon lay the policy of unconditional surrender.

With the rejection of Hitler's appeal, the German press began to
utter bloodcurdling threats of the blows which would shortly fall
upon the British; but Halder's diary for July 22 sounds a rather
different note. Reporting a meeting between Hitler and Brauchitsch he records: "Crossing of the Channel appears very hazardous to the Führer. On that account invasion is to be undertaken
only if no other means is left to come to terms with Britain." Hope
was still to be found in letters alleged to have been sent by Lloyd
George to the King and Parliament, by the Duke of Windsor to
the King, and in the familiar dream of a Lloyd George-Chamber-
lain-Halifax Cabinet.* At the Hitler-Brauchitsch conference, Admiral Raeder, the German naval Commander-in-Chief, made it
clear that naval preparations could not be completed by August
13, the date requested by Hitler, and that no invasion date could
be fixed until air supremacy had been obtained over the Channel.

Between July 22 and the end of the month, there were further
conferences, at which Raeder dragged his feet. The pocket battleship "Lützow" and the battle cruisers "Scharnhorst" and "Gneis-
enau" had all been put temporarily out of action as a result of the
Norway operations. The only heavy ship Raeder had to use was
"Admiral Hipper," with "Prinz Eugen" expected to be available
in the autumn. His destroyer losses off Norway had been heavy,
and he could produce only four, with three motor torpedo boats
and forty-eight submarines. With such forces the naval staff repeatedly, and rightly, refused to guarantee protection from the Royal
Navy during the Channel crossing. All this Raeder knew perfectly
well, but he was inept in his personal dealings, subservient to Hitler, and he could never quite bring himself to pronounce the word
"impossible." He therefore made difficulties: the weather, the
tides, the problem of landing on an open coast, lack of information
about the position of British mines, above all air supremacy—once

* Chamberlain had been taken ill on June 16 with pain in the abdomen. On July
24, X-rays revealed a partial stricture of the bowel, and an exploratory operation
was ordered. It proved to be cancer. He returned to work for a brief period at the
beginning of September, but he was a dying man.

given air supremacy, *then* the navy would not be found wanting.

Memoranda flew between army and navy headquarters. The army had demanded transport for forty divisions, with equipment, to be landed on a wide front from Ramsgate to Lyme Bay. Raeder got the army's demands scaled down to thirteen divisions, though still on a wide front. He said he could not do it. On July 29, Brauchitsch and Halder agreed that "we cannot carry through our part in the operation on the basis of the resources furnished by the Navy," and on July 30, Halder recorded notes of a conference with the navy: "Navy Operations Staff can't be ready before 15 September. Earliest jump-off 20/26 September. If not then, next May. Operation can't be protected against British Navy . . . Effectiveness of Air Force said to be exaggerated." On this basis Brauchitsch and Halder agreed that the navy would be unlikely to provide them with the means of a successful invasion that autumn. They then discussed various possibilities in the Mediterranean, and "the question whether, if a decision cannot be forced against Britain, we should in the face of a threatening British-Russian alliance and the resulting two-front war turn first against Russia, must be answered to the effect that we should keep on friendly terms with Russia . . . This being so, we could deliver the British a decisive blow in the Mediterranean, shoulder them away from Asia, help the Italians in building their Mediterranean Empire and, with the aid of Russia, consolidate the Reich which we have created in Western and Northern Europe. That much accomplished, we could confidently face war with Britain for years."

Their master, however, had other ideas. On July 31 took place the definitive conference, under Hitler's direction, at which differences of opinion between the army and navy were to be thrashed out. Raeder again advanced all his difficulties: the weather, the call-up of people from inland waterways affecting the transport of coal, iron, and food, and "fishing boats must be requisitioned as tugs, thereby the supply of fish is endangered." He was nevertheless given an order to continue preparations for invasion and left the meeting. After he had gone, according to Halder's notes, Hitler *"emphasizes his scepticism concerning technical possibilities:** is satisfied with accomplishment of Navy. . . . U-boat and air war can decide the war; will last, however, 1-2 years."

---

* These italics are mine. All the following italicized passages are Halder's.

There followed a dissertation by Hitler which, as recorded in Halder's notes, must be given at length: *"England's hope is Russia and America. If hope on Russia is eliminated, America also is eliminated,* because enormous increase in the importance of *Japan* in the Far East will result from the elimination of Russia.

"Russia Far Eastern sword of England and America against Japan. An unpleasant wind here for England. Japanese like Russia have their program, which is to be realized before the end of the war. . . .

"Russia the factor on which England is mainly betting. Something has happened in London!* The English were entirely 'down,' now they are up again. Monitored conversations. Russia unpleasantly impressed by the quick development of the western European situation.

"Russia never need say more to England than that she does not want Germany to be great, then the English hope like a drowning man that things will be entirely different in 6-8 months.

"Should Russia, however, be smashed, then England's last hope is extinguished. Germany is then master of Europe and the Balkans.

"Decision: In the course of this contest Russia must be disposed of. Spring '41.

"The quicker we smash Russia the better. Operation only makes sense if we smash the state heavily in one blow. Winning a certain amount of territory only does not suffice. A standstill during the winter hazardous. Therefore better to wait, but decision definite to dispose of Russia. Necessary also because of situation on the Baltic. No use for a second Great Power on the Baltic: May '41. Five months' time for carrying out. Preferable still in this year. Can't be done, however, if it is to be carried out as a single operation . . ."

There followed allocation of an army to be built up to a hundred and eighty divisions: seven in Norway, fifty in France, three in Holland and Belgium, a hundred and twenty for the east. Then in Halder's notes comes the crucial paragraph: "Camouflage: Spain, North Africa, England. New formations in areas protected from the air." ** A footnote to the German edition of Halder's

* Wrong. It had happened at the Democratic Convention in Chicago on July 19.
** In the original, *"Tarnen: Spanien, Nordafrika, England. Neuaufstellung in luftgeschützten Räumen." Tarnen:* to mask, hide, camouflage, screen; or figuratively, to veil, to cover up.

diary, published in 1962, makes quite clear what was meant: "The preparations for the offensive should be so camouflaged as to appear as if enterprises against Gibraltar with Spain, against North Africa or Egypt with the Italians, and against England, are being prepared."

Events followed the pattern of these notes closely enough to convince one that, with certain deviations and changes of mind, this was the plan Hitler was following from now on. The invasion of Britain to him was at best a side show, no more than camouflage for his real intention to attack Russia.

The Army High Command, however, continued to be haunted by the fear of a war on two fronts, and did its best to make a reality of the cross-Channel invasion, given the code name of Operation Sealion, in order to finish with Britain before they had to launch their attack in the east. Under the circumstances, they had very little chance of success.

Chapter

11

"BUT WESTWARD, LOOK . . ."

Devoted adherent of the monarchy though he was, Churchill was unable to share King George VI's happiness at having no allies to be polite to and to pamper, and it did not need any very great prescience on Hitler's part to foresee that the British would make determined attempts to involve the two great uncommitted nations, Russia and the United States.

The Left Wing politician, Sir Stafford Cripps, was hurriedly sent in June as Ambassador to Moscow; according to some accounts, Cripps, a man with a strong sense of mission, practically sent himself. He had a long interview with Stalin on July 1 and, according to the report of the meeting which Molotov, the Russian Foreign Minister, afterward gave the German Ambassador, Cripps was apparently empowered to appease the Russians by offering British recognition of the Balkans as a Russian sphere of influence and acknowledging Russian aspirations in the Dardanelles at the expense of Turkey.* Stalin, however, preferred to continue trying to avoid conflict with Germany for as long as possible, and said frankly that he was prepared to run the risk, if Britain were beaten, of having to take on the Germans singlehanded.

---

* Molotov's account must obviously be suspect, since the Russians clearly tried to use the British approach as a bargaining counter in their future dealings with Germany.

176

The United States was a different matter. During the long drawn-out agony of the French collapse, the French and British governments addressed a series of appeals to President Roosevelt, which elicited much sympathy, some unavailing diplomatic pressure on Mussolini to stay out of the war, and a little practical help.

The United States, in truth, was in no position to help, being militarily weaker than Britain at the time of Munich, although Roosevelt had had nine months longer than Chamberlain in which to prepare. In particular, America was heavily dependent on the British and French navies for her Atlantic defense. A German assessment, made in June 1940, estimated that America could not be ready for war until 1941 at the earliest. Louis Johnson, the American Assistant Secretary of War, publicly asserted that "full defense" would not be possible for two years.

But:

> . . . While the tired waves, vainly breaking,
> Seem here no painful inch to gain,
> Far back, through creeks and inlets making,
> Comes silent, flooding in, the main.

> And not by eastern windows only,
> When daylight comes, comes in the light;
> In front the sun climbs slow, how slowly!
> But westward, look, the land is bright!*

That bright land, the vast hinterland of American industrial potential, beckoned the British Prime Minister as, from time to time, it worried the German Chancellor. If America could be given time to arm, if America could be brought in on the Allied side, the war was won and, for Germany, lost. But if, before that happened, Russia had been knocked out and Britain reduced to a helpless island off the European mainland, what challenge could America offer to German continental supremacy?

Hitler did not understand the workings of the American mind, any more than he understood the British, but some of his advisers did, and planned a holding operation against the United States until the Germans had dealt with Russia, the basis of which was a tripartite alliance between Germany, Italy, and Japan, designed to keep American strength concentrated in the Pacific against the

* Arthur Hugh Clough, "Say not the Struggle Naught availeth."

Japanese. To this was added the nuisance value of building up movements sympathetic to the Nazis in the South American republics, notably Argentina, where German commercial interests were strong. Finally, as a short-term measure, German subsidies were made available for isolationist propaganda and activities in the United States themselves. Eminent American authors, including Theodore Dreiser, were invited by apparently patriotic isolationist organizations to write books or pamphlets advocating that America should stay out of this European quarrel. They were not of course to know that their ultimate paymaster was to be Germany, but it was. German money was also spent to secure the adoption of an isolationist candidate for the presidency at the Republican Convention which was to meet at Philadelphia in June.*

American public opinion, in so far as it could be measured by Gallup Polls, was decisively against intervention. In May, 7 per cent favored going to war on the side of the Allies. This rose to a peak of 19 per cent in mid-June, but began to fall away again after the French armistice. At the beginning of the war, 82 per cent of the American public had expected a British victory; after the Norway campaign, 55 per cent; after the French capitulation only 32 per cent, with another 33 per cent uncertain. There was thus fertile soil for German propaganda designed to convince the American people, first that it was wiser to stay out of the war altogether, and second that aid sent to Britain after the fall of France, which America urgently needed, would only be wasted in a hopeless cause.

In such dangerous waters, an American president had to navigate with skill. Roosevelt's navigation was impeded by the fact that a presidential election was due in November and that, if he ran at all, he would be the first president in history to do so for a third term, and that he would be running in the face of the bitter hostility felt by some Democrats, as well as Republicans, for his domestic New Deal policies.

The British Prime Minister also had to navigate with skill. In the short term, there was the desperate British need for American

---

* Since the British Foreign Office archives happily remained uncaptured and unpublished, the extent of British subsidies to interventionist causes, if any, remains unknown.

arms now, this instant, to save Britain from going the way of France in face of a German invasion. But beyond the immediate need was that crock of gold under the rainbow, thousands of American planes, hundreds of ships, millions of men, which might never be attained if any too precipitate step frightened away the shy American leprechaun.

There was a further consideration. While there is no doubt that Roosevelt had a general broad sympathy with Britain, he was President of the United States, whose primary concern must be for the safety of his own country. Nor was he wholly sympathetic to the British, being temperamentally opposed to colonialism in any form which was not American, and having a supremely patrician contempt for the muddle Britain's upper-middle-class rulers like Chamberlain had made of things.

Beneath the surface of the famous Churchill-Roosevelt correspondence, the greatest part of which remains unpublished, there is thus a subtle struggle going on: Churchill pressing for action now which will not only give Britain immediate help but will also commit the United States for the future; Roosevelt maneuvering eel-like to evade the Churchillian bear hug, yet holding out enough hope that if only Britain would keep fighting, then in time . . . when he had had the chance to work upon American opinion . . . when Congress was not so hostile . . . when American rearmament was really under way . . . then, at last, the end of the rainbow might be reached, the crock of gold within Churchill's grasp. It could have been a situation leading to as much bitterness as had arisen between Britain and France. That it did not do so is a high tribute to the stature of both the American President and the British Prime Minister.

The direct correspondence between Roosevelt and Churchill had been suggested by Roosevelt himself and begun in September, 1939, when Churchill returned to the British government as First Lord of the Admiralty. This correspondence assumed a new importance during the summer of 1940 because of the attitude of Roosevelt's official representative in Britain, the American Ambassador Joseph Kennedy.

Kennedy took the hardheaded businessman's view that the waste of war is worth avoiding at almost any cost, and he was moreover doubtful from the first about Britain's chances of winning. Early in September, 1939, he voiced his opinions to King George VI, and drew from the King a reply which was friendly but blunt: "As I see it, the U.S.A., France and the British Empire are the three really free peoples in the World, and two of these great democracies are now fighting against all that we three countries hate and detest . . . Misery and suffering of War we know. But what of the future? The British Empire's mind is made up. I leave it at that."

In November, 1939, Kennedy was warning his fellow countrymen against intervention in a speech at Boston: "As you love America, don't let anything that comes out of any country in the world make you believe you can make the situation one whit better by getting into the war. There is no place in this fight for us."

In April, 1940, the American government was disturbed by the apparent inability of the Royal Navy, upon which American Atlantic security depended, to prevent the German landings in Norway. Doubts were not set at rest by a cable from Kennedy giving what was, according to the American Secretary of State Cordell Hull, a long, dismal picture of British government unpreparedness and inefficiency.

On May 15, when Churchill was urging Roosevelt to send the greatest possible immediate help, Kennedy was advising Hull not to send any. In July, immediately before the Democratic Convention, he was only dissuaded by Roosevelt's direct intervention from making a nationwide broadcast warning America that the President, if re-elected, would plunge the United States into war.[*] These activities did not endear him to the British governing classes who, more blunt than the King, coined a phrase: "I thought my daffodils were yellow until I met Joe Kennedy."

To Kennedy's advice, during late May and June, was added that of William C. Bullitt, the American Ambassador in Paris. Emotionally committed to France and the French people, Bullitt took the view that Britain had betrayed France by withholding the full strength of the Royal Air Force, and in early June was transmitting to the American State Department, with his own apparent approval, Pétain's opinion that Britain was conserving her fleet and air force in order to use them as bargaining counters in negotiations with Hitler.

It was thus a heavy barrage of hostile opinion that Churchill had

[*] Mr. Randolph Churchill in the *Sunday Times*, June 20, 1965.

to counter in his efforts to convince Roosevelt that Britain was an acceptable risk. In the early stages of his fight to do so, the secrecy of his correspondence with Roosevelt was compromised by a security leak inside the American Embassy in London. On May 20, police raided the Kensington bed-sitting room of a cipher clerk at the Embassy, Tyler Kent, and found there some hundreds of documents copied from Embassy files, which Kent had accumulated during his five years' service overseas. He had been associating in London with an extreme Right Wing M.P., Captain Ramsay, and with the émigré daughter of a former Admiral in the Imperial Russian navy, Anna Wolkoff, who was friendly with an assistant military attaché at the Italian Embassy in London. There is indirect evidence that an accurate transcript of at least one message in the Churchill-Roosevelt series reached the German Ambassador in Rome; but although the effect of the reception of these messages by the enemy would have been grave enough, even this might have been a lesser evil than the leakage of their contents to isolationist propagandists in the United States.

Kent himself claimed to be an American patriot, who had abstracted the documents in defense of the right of Congress and the American people to know about secret commitments made by the President. He had, however, shown some of his documents to Ramsay and Wolkoff, who were members of a Right Wing, anti-Semitic circle which British security services had under routine surveillance. But for this chance detection, it is conceivable that Kent's activities might have escaped discovery until later, with possibly momentous consequences for Anglo-American relations.

The theme which runs through the early exchanges between Churchill and Roosevelt—third parties frequently intervening—is American preoccupation with the future of the British and French fleets. An American Atlantic Fleet did not formally exist until February, 1941, and in 1940 it consisted of four elderly battleships, four heavy cruisers, one aircraft carrier, and a destroyer squadron. America depended heavily upon British and French naval protection in the Atlantic, with the natural corollary that if either or both the British and French navies were neutralized or fell into enemy hands, the balance of naval power would swing heavily against America. One would not like to suggest that Churchill was so unchivalrous as to set out to make American flesh creep about this situation; but one can perhaps say that he was determined his mother's country should not run into danger for want of a warning from him.

On May 24, with the French and British armies in the north collapsing, Roosevelt urgently sent for an emissary of the Canadian Prime Minister, Mackenzie King, and told him that he and Cordell Hull were not convinced the French would be able to hold out. This would leave the way open for the Germans to attack Britain with a five-to-one superiority in air power, and Roosevelt and Hull doubted if Britain could resist.

The President said he had it from what he believed to be a good authority in Germany that Hitler might make an offer of settlement to Britain, based on turning over the whole colonial Empire to Germany and the fleet as well. The President urged Mackenzie King to persuade his fellow Dominion Prime Ministers to bring concerted pressure to bear on Britain not to accept any soft peace, "even though it might mean the destruction of England comparable to that of Poland, Holland and Belgium, and the killing of those who had refused to make peace, but to have her fleet make its base at different outlying ports away from England and to send the King to Bermuda. The U.S. would open ports to the British fleet for repairs." *

Mackenzie King's reaction to this approach from Roosevelt was that America was seeking to save herself at the expense of Britain, and that he was being asked to make an appeal to the selfishness of the Dominions. He would rather die, he recorded, than do any such thing; and he sent his representative back to Washington with a message that the most effective way of avoiding the dire consequences foreseen by Roosevelt was to let Britain have immediately the planes for which she was appealing.

Roosevelt replied that no planes could be spared—America had

* Hon. J. W. Pickersgill: *The Mackenzie King Record*. King George VI being the kind of man he was, I doubt if anything much short of physical force could have got him to leave Britain for Bermuda or anywhere else even in the direst circumstances. One may note, however, that Churchill did take considerable pains in July to get a member of the royal family, the Duke of Windsor, to the Bahamas, of which Windsor reluctantly became Governor. On the basis of a prewar visit to Germany and some perhaps unguarded remarks, when he thought himself among friends, about his personal affairs, the Duke of Windsor, like others, has been smeared with the taint of having had Nazi sympathies. Lest it be thought I have been hinting at this, I would like to say quite categorically that I have heard no evidence to suggest that the Duke of Windsor behaved one whit less patriotically than his brothers.

only eight hundred military aircraft left in the country—and again urged Mackenzie King to put the American view about the fleet immediately to Churchill, though presenting it as if it were his own. If Churchill were not wholly opposed to the idea, Roosevelt said, he would follow Canada's initiative with a message in a few days' time.

Mackenzie King did send a telegram to Churchill, receiving a reply on June 5: ". . . We must be careful not to let Americans view too complacently prospect of a British collapse, out of which they would get the British Fleet and the guardianship of the British Empire, minus Great Britain. If United States were in the war and England conquered locally, it would be natural that events should follow above course. But if America continued neutral, and we were overpowered, I cannot tell what policy might be adopted by a pro-German administration such as would undoubtedly be set up. Although President is our best friend, no practical help has [reached us] from the United States as yet. We have not expected them to send military aid, but they have not even sent any worthy contribution in destroyers or planes, or by a visit of a squadron of their Fleet to Southern Irish ports. Any pressure which you can apply in this direction would be invaluable."

It is perhaps worth noting that at this time Churchill was negotiating with Lloyd George to join his government, and it is conceivable that the usefulness of having this defeatist bogeyman in his hand when dealing with Roosevelt as well as Hitler was a thought not absent from his agile mind.

At any rate the point about a pro-German administration was reinforced when Mackenzie King passed on to Washington the gist of Churchill's message, with an explanatory memorandum of his own: "To Mr. King's mind, it means that Mr. Churchill will never consider any terms of surrender on the part of Great Britain to the enemy. That he will not so much as discuss them, regardless of what the consequences of continuing the war by England alone, if need be, against the enemy, may be. The only way in which negotiations could ever take place with the enemy on behalf of the U.K. would be by such a division of opinion arising within Britain itself that there would grow up against the Government of the day, a demand for surrender on terms. Mr. Churchill himself, as Prime Minister, would never take the responsibility for such a step. If he saw British public opinion ever become so strong that he, Mr. Churchill, felt that he and his Government were in the minority, the only way in which he would bow to the will of the majority would be to go to the King, tender his resignation and ask the King to call on whoever was the leader of the surrender party, to form a Government to negotiate terms of surrender. To Mr. Churchill's way of thinking such a Government would be pro-German."

Roosevelt replied that he and Cordell Hull did not accept Mackenzie King's interpretation of Churchill's message but felt that, if it really did represent Churchill's attitude, it was "alarming and distressing." A few days afterward, Lothian, the British Ambassador in Washington, was talking gloomily about the possibility of a "Mosley or Communist type" British government, and in a later message, at the end of June, Mackenzie King took the opportunity to remark that "Churchill was under a terrific strain, that the possibility of his having a hemorrhage of the brain at some stage was not to be overlooked."

Perhaps this was overdoing it; in some American minds, if not in Roosevelt's, doubts were certainly sown about British ability to survive. But under this assault Roosevelt did in fact produce some planes and, scraping the bottom of the American barrel, a quantity of First World War guns, small arms, and ammunition which, arriving in July, was thankfully received.

Churchill, however, was after bigger game than this, and for a fleeting moment in the middle of June the eel seemed to be really within his grasp. On the night of June 13, he triumphantly produced at a War Cabinet meeting a message from Roosevelt to Reynaud, exclaiming, "If he will consent to have this published, it pretty well commits America to war." * The message, sent in answer to one of Reynaud's increasingly desperate appeals, promised to redouble American efforts to make material aid available to the Allies, and urged France to go on fighting, if necessary in North Africa.

But the eel wriggled and escaped. Although Churchill seems to have misunderstood, or to have placed too optimistic an interpretation upon,** a verbal message delivered by the American Ambassador, Roosevelt immediately made it clear that his telegram could

* Halifax diary, June 13.
** Perhaps deliberately. He had to keep up British and French spirits.

not bear the interpretation Churchill placed upon it—only Congress, he pointed out, could commit America to war—and he forbade its publication. Churchill tried again: ". . . Although the present Government and I personally would never fail to send the Fleet across the Atlantic if resistance was beaten down here, a point may be reached in the struggle where the present Ministers no longer have control of affairs and when very easy terms could be obtained for the British Island by their becoming a vassal state of the Hitler Empire . . . This revolution in sea-power might happen very quickly, and certainly long before the United States would have been able to prepare against it. If we go down you may have a United States of Europe under the Nazi command far more numerous, far stronger, far better armed than the New World."

But the eel still had all his wits about him; he expressed sympathy for the heart-rending plight of France, promised that supplies would be sent in ever increasing quantities, but reiterated that this did not imply any American military commitment.

There is no doubt at all that Roosevelt did have to overcome very strong opposition both inside and outside Congress; but the worse the situation in Europe became, the higher his personal support rose in the public opinion polls, and one cannot entirely resist the thought that from time to time Congress and Public Opinion performed the same useful function in Roosevelt's often devious diplomacy as marriage did in that of Queen Elizabeth I.

He was now, however, very anxious about the British fleet, and, with the collapse of France, Lothian sent a telegram, at the request of the United States naval authorities, asking whether ammunition for the fleet and material for its repair ought not to be sent across the Atlantic. This drew a sharp answer from Churchill: "There is no warrant for such precautions at the present time."

In June, Roosevelt had agreed to a suggestion by Lothian that conversations should be opened on naval and air subjects between British and American officers. Lothian rightly regarded this agreement as an important development; but on June 24, Churchill turned down the suggestion: the Americans would only want to talk about the fleet.

On June 22, the American Chiefs of Staff recommended that if the French fleet passed under German control, the major part of the American fleet should be transferred from the Pacific to the Atlantic, in spite of the risk from Japan, and that there should be no further commitments of arms to Britain, or acceptance of orders which would endanger American needs.

On June 26, Roosevelt received a report on British prospects which he had requested senior service advisers to give him. They thought it doubtful whether Britain, as distinct from the British Empire, would survive the autumn or winter. And on June 28, Congress passed a bill providing that no material belonging to the American government should be delivered to foreign forces unless the Army Chief of Staff, or the Chief of Naval Operations, certi-fied that it was surplus to requirements. This was probably the nadir of Anglo-American relations. One faint star, however, shone through the gloom. At the end of June, the Republican Conven-tion adopted a comparatively unknown representative of American big business, Wendell Willkie, as the party's presidential candidate in preference to the isolationist Robert A. Taft. It was a close race, Taft commanding 377 votes to Willkie's 429 on the fifth ballot, and Willkie not sweeping clear of the field until the sixth, with 633 votes to Taft's 310. Support for Taft came mainly from the Middle West—Ohio, Illinois, Iowa, Minnesota—where, according to reports from friendly Americans currently reaching Britain, they were so scared of Hitler that they were having antiparachute drills.

Willkie's adoption was quickly recognized by the German chargé d'affaires in Washington for what it was, a major defeat for German policy. Its importance was not so quickly recognized in Britain, which at the time had a perhaps more understandable preoccupa-tion with antiparachute drills than Illinois, and where a certain Churchillian impatience with American slowness was discernible.

At this juncture occurred an episode of the highest drama. Roosevelt's concern about the future of the British fleet was cer-tainly no greater than British concern about the future of the French navy. During the days before the French armistice, the British government had put the most urgent pressure on the French to secure binding assurances that the French fleet, the fourth larg-est in the world, should not fall into German or Italian hands. The attempt had apparently failed. A clause of the armistice agreement prescribed that the French fleet, except that part left free for safeguarding French colonial interests, should be collected in ports to be specified, and there demobilized and disarmed under German or Italian control.

Darlan, now Minister of Marine, had, however, given Churchill his word that the French fleet would not be allowed to fall to the enemy, and on June 24, apparently unknown to the British government, he send to all French admirals and prefects of maritime departments a code message: "I am taking advantage of the last messages that I can transmit in code in order to inform you of my thoughts on this subject: these orders remain valid, whatever contradictory orders you may receive hereafter, even if signed by me.

"1. The ships which have been demobilized must remain French and under the French flag, reduced crews must be French, and they must remain in either Metropolitan or Colonial French ports.

"2. Secret preparations for scuttling must be made so that, if the enemy or an ex-ally seize a ship by force, they will be unable to make use of it.

"3. If the Armistice Commission, whose duty it is to interpret the position, should decide otherwise than in paragraph 1, all warships, upon this decision being put into effect, will, without further orders, set sail for the United States or be scuttled, if there is no other means of denying them to the enemy. In no circumstances will they be left intact in enemy hands.

"4. Such ships as take refuge in foreign ports must not be used in warlike operations against Germany or Italy without orders from the Commanders-in-Chief.

"5. In no circumstances will the orders of any foreign admiralty be obeyed."

It may be doubted that British actions would have been different if the government had known of the existence of this order. The risk was too great, too much depended upon the resolution, or political sympathies, of individual French naval commanders.

At the end of June, powerful French units lay in the harbors of Portsmouth, Plymouth, and Alexandria, in effect under British control. Others lay at Toulon, where they could not be reached. The French Atlantic squadron, about a fifth of the French fleet, lay in the North African harbors of Mers-el-Kebir and the neighboring city of Oran. There were two modern battle cruisers, "Dunkerque" and "Strasbourg," the battleships "Bretagne" and "Provence," a seaplane carrier, thirteen destroyers, and four submarines.

On the morning of July 3, Vice Admiral Sir James Somerville lay off Oran with the British Force H, which included the battle cruiser "Hood," the battleships "Valiant" and "Resolution," the aircraft carrier "Ark Royal," two cruisers, and eleven destroyers. His orders—which he understandably detested—were to present the French Admiral Gensoul with a choice between four alternative proposals, and if one of these was not accepted, to destroy the French ships. Gensoul could choose between joining the British to continue the war against Germany and Italy; sailing under British control to a British port, from which his crews could be repatriated; sailing to a French port in the West Indies, where the ships would be demilitarized and perhaps handed over to American custody; or, if he refused all these, sinking his own ships within six hours. It will be seen that Darlan's secret orders prohibited Gensoul from taking the first two alternatives, and certainly prevented him from obeying British orders.

During the long day's negotiations, Gensoul did not submit to his own admiralty the full text of the British terms. When the French Council of Ministers met, they were informed only that Gensoul had been ordered to sink his ships within six hours or be fired on by the British. In those circumstances they signaled their support for Gensoul's expressed intention to resist.

In the afternoon, Gensoul showed Somerville's representative the June 24 order from Darlan, and gave his personal word that if any German threat to his ships developed, he would take them either to Martinique or to the United States, but he refused to do so now, under threat of force. This was not enough for the British government.

Demobilization of the crews of the French squadron had begun the day before, and some of the ships were anchored in such a position that they could not use their guns. The British had mined the only practicable channel between the French antisubmarine nets. Nevertheless, Gensoul gave the order to relight fires and clear for action, and his crews cheered, believing that they were sailing in support of the British.

Just before six o'clock, the time that his ultimatum expired, and under strong pressure from London, Somerville ordered the British ships to open fire on the almost helpless French. The action lasted thirteen minutes. "Bretagne" was blown up, "Dunkerque" and "Provence" seriously damaged, "Strasbourg" and five destroyers escaped, although they were bombed the following day. Twelve hundred and ninety-seven French sailors were killed or missing, three hundred and fifty-one wounded.

The action at Oran, said Admiral Somerville, was "the biggest political blunder of modern times and I imagine will rouse the whole world against us . . . We all feel thoroughly dirty and ashamed that the first time we should have been in action was an affair like this." General de Gaulle, struggling against almost overwhelming difficulties to draw patriotic Frenchmen into his incipient Free French liberation movement, regarded the operation with "pain and anger . . . The British gloried in it, and the British press announced it as if it were a victory." Hitler hailed it as justification of his prescience in not demanding that the French fleet should be handed over to Germany. England and France, he triumphantly told Ciano, were now made mutual enemies; and Pétain's government did indeed break off diplomatic relations, and for a time, under Laval's influence, seriously considered German urgings to declare war upon France's former ally.

But all this was to ignore the effect of Oran in America, where it mattered most. James B. Reston reported from London, "Great Britain won the biggest naval battle of the war last night." Senator Pittman, the chairman of the Senate Foreign Relations Committee, who had been telling Roosevelt that he must "order" the British fleet to cross the Atlantic, said it was "the fear that this step would not be taken that shook the confidence of some as to the power of the British defense."

And Roosevelt? He had already told the French government that if the French fleet surrendered to Germany, "the French Government will permanently lose the friendship and goodwill of the United States." He had given qualified approval to his Chiefs of Staffs' recommendation of June 22 that if the French fleet passed under German control, the greater part of the American fleet would leave the Pacific for the Atlantic. Robert Sherwood says that the action at Oran "served forcibly to underscore Churchill's defiant assurance that 'we will fight them in the streets' and 'never surrender.' It exerted a particular effect on Roosevelt, who, it is reasonable to assume, knew of the action well in advance."

One would give a great deal to know what the unpublished

Roosevelt-Churchill exchanges have to say about Oran. Roosevelt knew, but how strongly did he urge this action against the French fleet? To what extent, under the sharp spur of necessity, was the new ally bought with the blood of the old? What effect did Oran have on Roosevelt's long-delayed decision to run for a third term as President, about which he kept his own council until the last possible moment?

It would of course be wrong to suggest that Churchill acted at Oran wholly, or even principally, because of the possible effect on Roosevelt; Britain's own need was great enough. But Churchill told Cordell Hull later that he wanted to show that Britain still meant to fight, and he has written triumphantly that henceforth there was no more talk about Britain giving in.

This was the sensitive moment chosen for the efforts through Malcolm R. Lovell to arrange a meeting between the British Ambassador and the German chargé d'affaires in Washington, when the effects of a Berlin "leak" that Britain was listening to peace terms would have upset a great many applecarts. It is evident that Mr. Lovell's dove had no great chance of becoming airborne, and also evident that the Germans had pressing reasons for hoping that it would.

Churchill seized the opening offered by the impact of Oran to revive the question of the loan to Britain of fifty old American destroyers, which he had raised as long ago as May 15, in his first telegram to the President as Prime Minister. The request had been renewed in the desperate days of June, then shelved because it became ensnarled in American anxiety over guarantees about the future of the British fleet.

On July 5, fortified by a telegram from London asserting that Britain could not hold the Channel against invasion without more ships, Lothian took up the matter again. He was able to report that informed American opinion was at last beginning to realize that if America remained neutral and Britain went down, the British fleet might be lost altogether; but still there could be no destroyers without some assurance that, if the United States entered the war, the British fleet would cross the Atlantic in the event of Britain being overrun.

Negotiations became complicated by another issue, a proposal to meet the requirements of Congress' new bill by exchanging the destroyers for the lease to the United States of bases in Newfound-land and the West Indies. Churchill was opposed to the idea of linking destroyers and bases in an exchange, as were several members of his Cabinet, notably that devoted crusader of Empire, Beaverbrook, who commented with some asperity, and indeed justice, that if a bargain was to be struck it should not be a bad one, and this was a bad one.

What the deal symbolized, sensed by both sides, was more important than the deal itself. The loan or gift of destroyers to Britain would mark a major step forward in American commitment to eventual war with Germany; the sale or lease of British territory to the United States would be a tacit admission that Britain was no longer capable by herself of defending her imperial interests. The transaction did indeed mark the first step in the eventual transfer of world power from Britain to the United States.

Negotiations dragged on through July and August. Roosevelt's Cabinet reached agreement at the beginning of August, after long discussion, that they would let the destroyers go, but only in return for the right to use naval bases on the Atlantic coast, and an assurance that the British fleet would make for ports in America or the Empire if Britain were overrun.

Harold Ickes, Secretary of the Interior, suggested that the evacuation of British children to the United States should be encouraged, since the more there were in America, the more British hostages to fortune there would be, and the greater the disposition to send the fleet. The President thought this was a good point, and there was discussion about making transportation available for the children; but, perhaps wisely, the matter does not seem to have been pursued.*

The British government still resolutely refused to link the fleet with the destroyers. Eventually, an ingenious formula was worked out. Britain freely gave the United States a lease on bases in New-foundland and Bermuda, thus establishing that she was a great power making generous concessions to American needs; Congress was satisfied by the exchange of fifty old destroyers for a lease of bases in the Bahamas, Jamaica, Antigua, St. Lucia, Trinidad, and British Guiana; and a formal exchange of agreed telegrams be-

---

* *The Secret Diary of Harold L. Ickes.*

tween Churchill and Roosevelt gave the required assurances about the future of the fleet.

The agreement was announced on September 5. Asked at his press conference following the announcement whether the assurance about the fleet was part of the deal, Roosevelt was able to answer, "No, it happens to come along at the same time." Thus Roosevelt secured what he had so long wanted; and if America was not yet in the war, at least she had come a great way toward it.

In London also the action at Oran made its impact. In the House of Commons the animosities of the Norway debate had not died away, nor resentment that "appeasers" like Chamberlain and Halifax, and so many members of the Chamberlain government, continued to hold office, to the exclusion of those who had helped put Churchill in power.

It was not the least of Churchill's services to his country that he refused to countenance inquests, heresy-hunting, or anything which made for national disunity. At the beginning of June he rebuked the Labour and Liberal leaders for their followers' attitude toward Chamberlain and Kingsley Wood. On June 19, Halifax notes: "Neville concerned about intrigues in the House of Commons to get him out." There were rumors near the end of June of an "intrigue" by Chamberlain and Halifax to bring Churchill down.

When Churchill spoke in the Commons, he was cheered from the Labour benches. The Conservative benches, remembering the previous Labour record of hostility to Churchill, rightly or wrongly regarded these cheers as a demonstration against Chamberlain rather than a demonstration of regard for Churchill, and accordingly did not themselves cheer the Prime Minister.

In the atmosphere of May and June, with its rumors of surrender and its ugly suspicions of treachery in high places, this Conservative reserve toward Churchill led foreign correspondents, particularly pro-British American journalists, to suspect that his own backbenches were hostile to him. So in a limited sense they were. They still resented his having come to power, through Labour and dissident Conservative votes, as a result of a fiasco for which he bore much responsibility, and in particular they resented the Opposition attitude to their own leader, Chamberlain. Foreign correspondents, however, drew a much wider conclusion, that there must be fundamental differences between Churchill and Chamberlain over Britain's determination to carry on the war, and that these were reflected in the House of Commons attitudes.

Dr. Paul Einzig, then political correspondent of the *Financial News,* had a large acquaintance among foreign journalists. Alarmed by their impressions, he took it upon himself to write to Chamberlain at the end of June, pointing out the effect that was being created. Rather to his surprise, he received a reply from Chamberlain in what were, for that aloof and shy man, almost cordial terms, resisting Einzig's conclusions, but undertaking "to see that your impression is not confirmed by anything more serious."

On July 4, Churchill made a long and emotional report to the House of Commons on what had happened at Oran. There were tears in his eyes as he spoke of the British ships firing upon their former allies. When he sat down there was silence. The Labour benches began to cheer. The Conservative benches remained silent. Then, according to Einzig's account, Margesson, the Conservative Chief Whip, rose and, turning toward his backbenchers, waved his order paper. As if at a signal all the Conservative members behind the Treasury bench and below the gangway on both sides of the Chamber rose and burst into enthusiastic cheering.*

Churchill himself, in *The Second World War,* writes of "a scene unique in my experience" after he had made his statement on the French fleet. "Everybody seemed to stand up all around, cheering, for what seemed a long time. Up till this moment the Conservative Party had treated me with some reserve, and it was from the Labour benches that I received the warmest welcome when I entered the House or rose on serious occasions. But now all joined in solemn stentorian accord."

The unity did not last. In a democracy it would have been unhealthy if it had. But for perhaps three important months, from July until October, it was almost complete.

---

* The late Lord Margesson and others have been unable to confirm for me Dr. Einzig's impression. This is not necessarily conclusive. Memories may be faulty after twenty-five years, and Chief Whips are discreet men; but for what it is worth, I think some recollection of such an arrangement would have remained in Margesson's mind, and I don't think he was "holding out" on me. I conclude that Churchill's reception was not prearranged on the Conservative side in quite the sense suggested by Dr. Einzig, although Chamberlain may well have let it be known that a spontaneous expression of unity at the first suitable moment would not be amiss.

Chapter

12

DEATH OF A SEALION

But America was not yet in the war, and there was no sign of the German invasion of Britain which might force Roosevelt to intervene. Halifax noted in his diary on July 25 a "great deal of evidence the Germans are hesitating," and by the end of the month seems to have made up his mind that there would be no invasion, a view he confirmed to his diary even on September 8, after the great flap when church bells were rung in the West Country, road blocks closed, bridges demolished, and British soldiers blown up on their own mines. On September 4, he expressed surprise at German air tactics: "I cannot understand why Hitler, if he has the immense reserve Air strength that we are told, doesn't throw it in instead of going on with the present plan which, though it causes a certain amount of damage here, is taking more out of his Air Force than it is out of ours."

This skepticism cannot have been soothing to the Prime Minister, who was determined that an invasion there should be. One afternoon in August, De Gaulle, visiting Churchill at Chequers, saw the Prime Minister shake his clenched fist at the sky, exclaiming, "So they won't come!"

De Gaulle asked quizzically if Churchill were in such a hurry to see British towns smashed to bits.

Churchill answered, "The bombing of Oxford, Coventry, Canterbury, will cause such a wave of indignation in the United States that they'll come into the war."

"They didn't come for France," observed De Gaulle.

"Sooner or later the Americans will come," Churchill replied, "but on condition that we here don't flinch. That's why I can't think of anything but the fighter Air Force. You see I was right to refuse it to you at the end of the Battle of France. If today it was destroyed all would be lost for you, as well as for us."

Across the narrow seas, the invasion of Britain was also the subject of disagreement. On June 15, with the collapse of France imminent, Hitler had ruled that the air force and the navy alone would be carrying on the war against Britain. On June 30, this directive, so far as it concerned the Luftwaffe, was translated into a general order from its Commander-in-Chief, Göring, which in part laid down that the war against England was to be restricted to attacks on weakly defended industrial and air-force targets, making the fullest use of conditions of surprise. The priorities given were, first, the Royal Air Force, its ground organization, and supporting industry, "to provide the necessary conditions for a satisfactory over-all war against enemy imports, provisions and defense economy, and at the same time provide the necessary protection for those territories occupied by ourselves"; second, by attacking harbors and harbor installations, shipping and warships, to destroy the British system of replenishment. Both tasks were to be carried out separately, but "must be carried out in coordination with one another."

This order is in many ways an embodiment of the doctrine of air power as a new dimension able to overleap seas and frontiers, evade defenses, and deliver its blow not on the defending forces—which can hit back—but on the sources of their strength: the factories, supply lines and, in the case of an island heavily dependent on material and food from overseas, on its "importing harbours and their installations, importing transports and warships," as Göring put it.

From July 10—when by British reckoning the Battle of Britain began—until the beginning of August, the Luftwaffe did indeed concentrate the bulk of its forces against convoys and harbors, on mine-laying, and on nuisance raids which created the maximum disruption of industrial production with the minimum of forces employed.

The air-raid warning system which had originally been used in Britain meant that for long periods many parts of the country were under "red" alert, although only a few localities were threatened with immediate danger. Night workers obeyed the official instructions to take shelter, day workers lost their sleep and quit work when the sirens sounded, and there was a noticeable drop in production from its June peak.

At the beginning of July, official policy began to put emphasis on production rather than safety first. Roof watchers were introduced to give the alarm to factories when immediate danger threatened, but this system suffered a setback when seventy German bombers escaped the net and made a daylight attack on Swansea and Falmouth, killing thirty people. For some time afterward, workers preferred to take shelter when they heard the "prolonged banshee howlings" of the air-raid siren, as Churchill called it.

From the beginning of July, on the Prime Minister's orders, destroyers were withdrawn from escort duty with Atlantic convoys, and concentrated at ports around the coast to guard against invasion. This action, combined with a gap in prewar destroyer building and the destroyer losses suffered off Norway and France, left convoys almost without protection, merchant shipping losses rose substantially, and the months from July to October became known to German U-boat commanders as "the happy time."

If the general tenor of Göring's June 30 order had been followed with consistency and determination over a period of time, the British defenses of Fighter and Anti-Aircraft Commands would have been stretched to their limits to cover such centers of aircraft production as Coventry, Derby, Bristol, Southampton. With naval and economic blockade added to the attrition of night bombing and hit-and-run attacks, it is possible that Britain might have been brought to the verge of defeat, as in 1917. But this would have been a slow decline. As Hitler told his army chiefs on July 31, "U-boat war and air war can decide the war; will last, however, 1-2 years."

Meanwhile, however, Hitler had developed his interest in Russia, and the Army High Command had in consequence developed its interest in beating Britain before the Russian campaign began. There were not one or two years to spare; only a few weeks. Operation Sealion got under way, and the confusion which this under-privileged amphibian spread in its wake is illustrated by Hitler's Directive Number 17, dated August 1:

"In order to establish the conditions necessary for the final conquest of England, I intend to continue the air and naval war against the English homeland more intensively than heretofore. To this end I issue the following orders:

"1. The German air arm is to overcome the English Air Force with all means at its disposal and in the shortest possible time. Attacks will be made primarily against the planes themselves, their ground organization and supply installations, but also against the aircraft production industry and the industries engaged in the production of antiaircraft equipment.

"2. After gaining temporary or local air superiority, the air war should be continued against harbors, especially against establishments connected with food supply, and also against installations for food supplies in the heart of the country. Attacks on the harbors of the south coast are to be undertaken on the smallest possible scale, in view of our intended operation.

"3. The war against enemy warships and merchant ships must take second place from the air war point of view in so far as it does not present particularly attractive opportunity targets or is not an additional bonus to the attacks carried out under paragraph 2 above, or where it is used for training crews for specialized future tasks.

"4. The intensified air war is to be carried out so that the Air Force can support naval operations on satisfactory opportunity targets with sufficient forces as and when necessary. Additionally it must remain battleworthy for Operation Sealion.

"5. Terror raids as revenge I reserve the right to order myself.

"6. Intensified air war is to start on or after August 5. The starting date is to be decided by the Air Force itself after completion of preparations, and bearing in mind weather conditions. The Navy is to begin intensified naval warfare at the same time."

In this order, not only is the classic use of air power almost completely discarded, but in repeatedly tying the permitted use of the Luftwaffe to the needs of Operation Sealion, which could take place only if air supremacy were gained, it makes it as difficult as possible to gain air supremacy.

The order to overcome the Royal Air Force in the shortest possible time, for instance, meant a daylight, head-on clash with Fighter Command, and Göring committed himself to a timetable under which he undertook to gain air supremacy in four days, and complete the destruction of the Royal Air Force in a month. To achieve this feat, he had a numerical fighter supremacy of less than two to one—just over a thousand fighters against seven hundred British—the German fighters being additionally burdened with the necessity of protecting daylight bombers which were being used as bait to lure out the British fighters.

Paragraph two of Hitler's directive limits attacks on south-coast harbors which may be needed for Sealion. The principal German bomber forces consisted of the Heinkel 111 and the Dornier 17, which were slow and inadequately armed, and in daylight operations had to have a close fighter escort. The fighter mainly used, the Messerschmitt 109, was a match for the British Hurricanes and Spitfires, but the capacity of its fuel tanks limited its range to just beyond London. Almost the only daylight bombing of harbors which could be physically undertaken, therefore, was of those on the south coast, a number of which were needed for Sealion.

Paragraph four enjoins the Luftwaffe to remain battleworthy for Sealion. Some forty groups of bombers—between a thousand and twelve hundred planes—were available to Göring for the Battle of Britain, but Halder was told on July 29 that nine bomber groups on the Channel coast and nine in the Brest area would be available for direct support of the invasion forces. The Luftwaffe therefore had to operate with almost half its bomber force to some extent held back in readiness for Sealion.

With the rest it had to lure the British fighters into situations where they could be destroyed by the German fighters; knock out the Royal Air Force's supply and maintenance organizations and the aircraft production industry; and conduct what had now become subsidiary operations against harbors and food installations. When it was not doing anything else, it had to support naval operations with sufficient forces as and when necessary. Admiral Raeder, still lugubriously pointing out that an invasion was impossible unless the Luftwaffe could establish air supremacy "soon," had frequent cause for complaint over the next few weeks that the Luftwaffe was operating without any consideration for naval requirements.

The two German air-fleet commanders principally charged with carrying out this directive, Kesselring and Sperrle, appear to have received their orders with an understandable lack of enthusiasm and wasted several days in arguing about methods.

Kesselring has revealed that he thought Hitler's peace appeal of July 19 was seriously meant, and for some time he expected peace. It is possible that this expectation was shared by his Commander-in-Chief. On July 24, Göring accepted the proffered services as peace negotiator of the head of the Dutch KLM airline. By accident or design, this particular feeler reached Halifax at about the time when the Luftwaffe, according to Göring's timetable, should have attained air supremacy, and when the British should have been in a receptive frame of mind. It drew from Halifax a reflection which Göring would not have found particularly palatable: "The more I ponder it, the more convinced I feel that the Germans have got to be more knocked about before they will be in any mood to learn any lesson. If we can persuade them to get rid of Hitler, all the better, but at least we want them to learn that war does not pay them. And to stop on the sort of terms that Hitler would be likely to contemplate now would definitely look to them as if war did not pay too badly."

The Luftwaffe's grand assault began on August 13, Göring's Eagle Day. In spite of a favorable weather forecast, the morning dawned dull and cloudy, and Göring sent a signal postponing the start of operations until the afternoon. German formations were already in the air, and among the squadrons which picked up the recall signal were the fighter escort for two forces of Dornier bombers heading for the Isle of Sheppey.

The fighters returned to base, the Dorniers continued unescorted. They should have been slaughtered, but the German strengths and positions were inaccurately assessed, and insufficient fighters were put up to meet them, with the result that most of the bombers got through.

This error by the Royal Air Force seems to have fostered an unwarranted spirit of overconfidence in the Luftwaffe. On August 14, Halder was given a report on the air operations of the previous days, in which it was claimed that eight major British air bases had been virtually destroyed, and 15 per cent of British first-class bombers and fighters knocked out, against only a 3 per cent loss of

German planes. In fact no bases had been knocked out, and while the assessment of British losses was fairly accurate, that of the Germans was not.

A day or two later, a young German pilot was produced for interview by foreign correspondents in Germany. William L. Shirer reported him as saying: "In a fortnight the British won't have any more planes. At first, about ten days ago, they gave us plenty of trouble. But this week their resistance has been growing less and less. Yesterday, for example, I saw practically no British fighters in the air . . . The British, gentlemen, are through. I am already making plans to go to South America and get into the airplane business. It has been a pleasant war."

The Luftwaffe seems genuinely to have believed its own propaganda. Its Intelligence branch had overestimated the number of British fighters available, but underestimated their quality and rate of replacement. In particular, it failed to spot the significance of the British radar system, which enabled the Royal Air Force commanders to direct their resources quickly to the point of attack. On August 12, the eve of Eagle Day, six British radar stations were bombed, and one, at Ventnor, destroyed, severing a link in the chain which was not restored until August 23; but the importance of this event was not appreciated and, on August 15, Göring made a major error by calling off further attacks on radar sites, "in view of the fact that not one of those attacked has so far been put out of action."

On August 15, the Luftwaffe developed what looks curiously like a halfhearted attempt to imitate Manstein's plan for the French land campaign. Heavy attacks were made on southern airfields to engage and destroy the British fighters while Stumpff's Fifth Air Fleet based on Norway came in through the back door, so to speak, to attack a supposedly lightly defended Tyneside and Yorkshire. Unfortunately for Luftwaffe calculations, Dowding,*

* I cannot forebear, if only in a footnote, to contrast the treatment received by Dowding and his principal lieutenant in the Battle of Britain, Air Vice-Marshal Keith Park, with that enjoyed by Ironside. Dowding and Park were victorious commanders. Ironside had presided over a series of military disasters. After the Battle of Britain, in which their tactics were criticized, Dowding and Park were both transferred to inactive commands, though Park later returned to active warfare. Ironside was promoted Field-Marshal in 1940 and created a peer in the following year. Dowding was never promoted Marshal of the Royal Air Force, and had to wait nearly three years for a peerage. The Royal Air Force would no doubt claim that it sets higher standards than the army.

the Commander-in-Chief of Fighter Command, was not Gamelin. He had not committed the whole of his fighter strength in the south, and the Germans' Fifth Air Fleet, losing sixteen out of a hundred and twenty-three bombers and seven out of thirty-four fighters, was given a severe mauling. It did not again intervene in the battle from Norway.

The air attack was co-ordinated with a different kind of assault on British nerves. On the morning following Eagle Day, some forty-five empty parachutes were found in different parts of the country, principally the Midlands and the Scottish Lowlands, together with wireless transmitters, maps, and lists of addresses of prominent people.

The discovery created enough excitement for the Prime Minister, until discouraged, to want to offer a reward for the apprehension of the supposed parachutists; but a cooler examination of the finds revealed that some of the parachutes had been found in standing corn, with no footmarks leading away from them, and that in photographs of objectives for sabotage, conspicuously dated to indicate that they had been taken by German agents in February, 1940, German thoroughness had not gone so far as to observe that the trees were in full leaf.

German radio broadcasts in English announced that parachutists in civilian clothes or British uniforms had landed near Birmingham, Manchester, and Glasgow. When the British authorities denounced the whole thing as a hoax, the German radio suggested that the parachutists were being hidden by native Fifth Columnists, ready to act when the invasion began.

Operation Sealion had in fact made a slight advance. On August 16, Keitel issued an order resulting from a conference at Hitler's headquarters on the previous day. Preparations for the operation to take place on September 15 were to be continued, though final orders would not be given until the situation was clear. Preparations for landing in Lyme Bay were to be abandoned, on account of the inadequate protection available in that area, and shipping was to be held in readiness along the coast between Ostend and Le Havre, "thus avoiding congestion in ports nearest to the enemy coast, and confusing the enemy as to our exact intentions." Dispositions were to be made in such a way that the landings could take place either on a broad or a narrow front, and to leave open the possibility of a single landing in the Brighton area.

A further directive followed, ordering that the crossing was to be made on a narrow front, beginning with the simultaneous landing of between four and five thousand troops at Brighton by motor-boat, with the same number of airborne troops dropping between Deal and Ramsgate. In addition, on D-1 day, the Luftwaffe was to make a strong attack on London, which would cause the population to flee from the city and block the roads. The landing areas finally selected were between Folkestone and Selsey Bill, the first objective being to secure a line running from Southampton to the mouth of the Thames.

I do not believe that it is only the imaginative difficulty of envisaging Horsham, say, or Tunbridge Wells, as a mass of battered ruins like Benghazi or Caen which gives this order an air of unreality. When Halder, the German Army Chief of Staff, heard that the landing was to be made on a narrow front, he commented that he might as well put the troops through a sausage machine. On August 16, he inspected the invasion harbors from Ostend to Dunkirk. He found practically nothing done: "Sunk vessels are obstructing the harbor basins . . . As to loading, Navy believes that it could be done from the Quays only with cranes, and many of these have either been destroyed or temporarily put out of commission by the fleeing British. There is no evidence of any repair work going on . . ."

Between August 19 and 23, cloudy weather brought a lull in the air battle, during which both sides reconsidered their tactics. The Luftwaffe High Command at last grasped that it had been dispersing inadequate forces over too many targets, and Göring now ordered concentration on one main task, "to inflict the utmost damage possible on the enemy fighter forces," which Luftwaffe Intelligence estimated at three hundred planes. The estimate was wrong by 133 per cent. Hurricanes and Spitfires were now coming off the production lines at a rate of a hundred a week. Dowding's problem was not so much a shortage of planes as a shortage of pilots.

It took eleven months to train a fighter pilot, and Dowding's losses in July and August were 222 killed or missing, another 205 wounded—almost a third of his strength. The pilot strength of Fighter Command dropped from 1,434 on August 3 to 1,396 a week

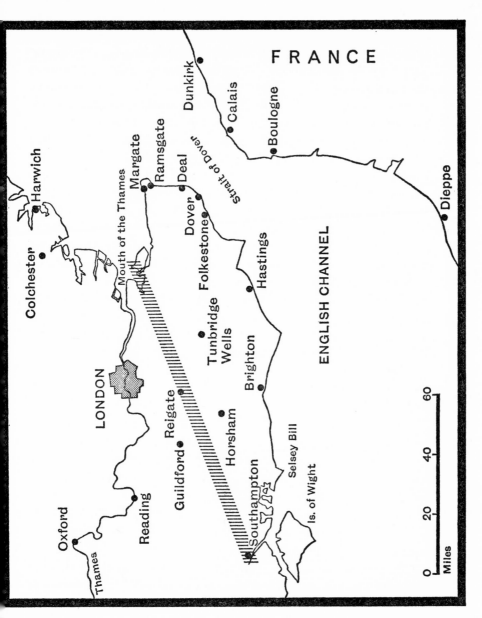

OPERATION SEALION: Keitel's order of August 16th laid down a narrow-front land-ng between Folkestone and Selsey Bill, with a paratroop drop between Deal and Ramsgate. The object was to secure a line running from Southampton to the mouth of the Thames, striated on the map.

later, and by August 17 decreased to 1,379. The fewness of The
Few is a literal, and still startling, fact.

To conserve pilots, orders were given not to engage over the sea,
in which a shot-down pilot might be lost, or to attack coat-trailing
German fighters which were not escorting bombers. Volunteer
pilots were recruited from the slow Battle and army co-operation
squadrons, given a brief course in Hurricanes and Spitfires, and
put into the firing line. But the drain continued as experienced
pilots tired, and learners died before they could learn. On August
28, 603 Squadron, whose Pilot Officer R. H. Hillary did what he
could in *The Last Enemy* to make his dead colleagues live for suc-
ceeding generations, went into battle for the first time. By September 6, it had lost sixteen aircraft and twelve pilots. The reason is
apparent in Hillary's description of his own downfall:

"Then, just below me and to my left, I saw what I had been
praying for—a Messerschmitt climbing and away from the sun. I
closed in to 200 yards, and from slightly to one side gave him a two-
second burst: fabric ripped off the wing and black smoke poured
from the engine, but he did not go down. *Like a fool, I did not
break away,** but put in another three-second burst. Red flames
shot upwards and he spiralled out of sight. At that moment, I felt
a terrific explosion which knocked the control stick from my hand,
and the whole machine quivered like a stricken animal. In a second, the cockpit was a mass of flames: instinctively, I reached up
to open the hood. It would not move. I tore off my straps and
managed to force it back; but this took time, and when I dropped
back into the seat and reached for the stick in an effort to turn the
plane on its back, the heat was so intense that I could feel myself
going. I remember a second of sharp agony, remember thinking
'So this is it!' and putting both hands to my eyes. Then I passed
out." **

Death or injury by burning was a major occupational hazard of
the British fighter pilot which he consciously faced every time he
went up. The Germans had self-sealing gasoline tanks. British de-
signers had spent time seeking the perfect tank, crash-proof as well
as bullet-proof, and a bullet through the tank of a Hurricane or

---

* My italics. Courage, alas, is not enough.
** Hillary got clear and was rescued from "the drink" by the Margate lifeboat. He
was killed in a later engagement.

Spitfire almost certainly meant a fire. Those pilots who, like Hillary, for the time being survived, spent painful months enduring skin-grafting operations, having their charred features reconstructed by the New Zealand surgeon, Archibald McIndoe, whose work won the lasting gratitude of the Royal Air Force. Meanwhile, however, they were lost to the battle.

In the last week of August, the Luftwaffe directed an all-out assault against the airfields and sector stations of Air Vice-Marshal Park's Number 11 Group. Park's forward airfields lay in an arc from Martlesham, northeast of Ipswich, in Suffolk, through Rochford, Manston, Hawkinge, Lympne. Behind them lay an inner arc of sector airfields: Debden, North Weald, Hornchurch, in Essex; Biggin Hill in Kent; Kenley in Surrey. These were the key centers through which the battle was controlled. On each sector operations room converged an elaborate system of communications through which orders and information were relayed forward from Group and Fighter Command, and other sectors and higher commands were kept informed of what was happening on each sector front.

These sector airfields had to be defended at almost any cost in planes and, more important, pilots. For ten days the airfields and sector stations were under almost continuous assault, and Park later revealed that for several days Manston and Lympne were unfit for fighters, that only one squadron, instead of three, could operate from Biggin Hill, and that six out of the seven sector stations had been extensively damaged.

The Luftwaffe announced at the end of August that the air situation was favorable in spite of the bad weather. On August 26, Brauchitsch, back from one of the Führer's conferences, reported that "Operation Sealion stands. Interest in this operation seems to have increased." But after the narrow front decision, Sealion had lost its only friends, the Army High Command. The conference, Brauchitsch told Halder, was "to all appearances the usual political potpourri. Pipedreams: Spain is to be brought into war (but the economic consequences for that country are ignored). North Africa is viewed as a theatre of operations against Britain (Egypt, Asia Minor, pushing Britain away from Cyprus and Haifa?!). Rumania is to be drawn into our orbit, but in a way that would not rouse Russia too much at this early date. We are going to be ready in the north (Petsamo) when Russia attacks Finland. And the

Army is supposed to have everything nice and ready without ever getting any straightforward instructions."

Nevertheless, on September 1, shipping began to move from German North Sea ports to the Channel coast, and on September 3 an order was issued from Hitler's headquarters:

"The following dates for the completion of preparations for Operation Sealion have been decided:

"1. The earliest date for the sailing of the invasion fleet has been fixed for September 20, and that of the landing for September 21.

"2. Orders for the launching of the attack will be given on D Day minus 10, presumably therefore on September 11.

"3. Final commands will be given at the latest on D Day minus 3 at midday.

"4. All preparations must remain liable to cancellation 24 hours before zero hour."

On the same day, the High Command of the Luftwaffe decided to switch the air attack from the battered sector stations to London. A number of reasons have been given for this dramatic change of target. According to the most popular version, a force of German bombers bound on the night of August 24 for Rochester and the Thameshaven oil tanks lost their way and bombed London instead. On the following night, the Royal Air Force began to bomb Berlin in retaliation and thus, it is said, caused Hitler and Göring to divert the Luftwaffe from the final destruction of Fighter Command into an all-out reprisal assault on London.

The bombing of Berlin was indeed inconvenient for politicians who had been publicly claiming that the R.A.F. was virtually finished. Göring himself had said that it could not happen, and William L. Shirer records that Berliners were stunned when it did, the ability of British bombers to evade the defenses being attributed to the fact that they were coated with invisible paint.

But at the Luftwaffe conference which decided the change, the lead was taken by Kesselring, who seems to have asserted without much evidence that the British fighter force was on the point of collapse. If this appreciation had been correct, an attack on London warehouses and docks would have been a logical next step to take in fulfilment of paragraph two of Hitler's Directive of August 1: "After gaining temporary or local air superiority, the air war should be continued against harbors, especially against establishments connected with food supply, and also against installations for food supplies in the heart of the country."

In the discussions preceding this directive, Kesselring himself had argued strongly in favor of London as a target which Fighter Command was bound to defend, and in defense of which it could be destroyed. He claimed after the war that the targets given in London were not the civilian population, but war factories and port installations, and the pattern of early attacks supports his claim.

At the Führer's conference of September 14, the Luftwaffe Chief of Staff, Jeschonnek, urged that London residential areas should be included among the Luftwaffe's targets, but Hitler, while not denying him, insisted that concentration on military objectives must have first priority. "Bombing calculated to increase mass panic," he said, "must be left to the last."

It seems most likely, therefore, that once again the Luftwaffe was betrayed by its Intelligence branch, and that the change of target was due, not to a political demand for reprisals, but again to an overestimation of British fighter casualties and the damage done to airfields and sector stations, and an underestimation of the replacement rate.

The attack on London, indeed, seems to have been seen, not even as the prelude to Operation Sealion, but as the final knockout blow. On September 4, following a day of raids on airfields, Hitler addressed a huge audience in the Sportspalast Berlin. He was in his most brilliant form, threatening retaliation for the raids on Berlin, and addressing his enemies almost jovially:

"When people are very curious in Great Britain, and ask, 'Yes, but why doesn't he come?' we reply: 'Calm yourselves! Calm yourselves! He is coming! He is coming!' " The British Prime Minister, who greatly hoped that he would come, was said to find the speech "very encouraging." But when Raeder saw Hitler on September 8, he found him inclined to regard Sealion as unnecessary. "He is finally convinced that Britain's defeat will be achieved, even without the landing."

On September 10, the day before Hitler was due to give the executive order for Sealion, the Naval War Staff met to consider the new situation. They concluded that the essential prerequisite for invasion, clear air supremacy over the Channel, had not been attained. The Luftwaffe, it was felt, should concentrate less on London, and more on Portsmouth and Dover, and on British naval forces in or near the operational area. But the navy did not consider it suitable to approach the Luftwaffe or the Führer at present with such demands, "because the Führer looked on a large-scale attack on London as possibly being decisive, and because a systematic and long-drawn out bombardment of London might produce an attitude in the enemy which will make the Sealion operation completely unnecessary. The Naval War Staff therefore does not consider it necessary to make such a demand."

The new bludgeon was complemented, as had become customary, by a new dove, which this time seems to have had an air of desperation about it. Dr. Karl Haushofer was an elderly retired general, President of the Society for Geopolitics, whose propagation of the concept of *lebensraum,* and of a German-controlled land empire stretching from the Atlantic to the Urals, had won him an understandable regard in Nazi ruling circles. His son, Albrecht, was Professor of Political Geography and Geopolitics at the University of Berlin. Albrecht Haushofer had some British connections, and even, it appears, a more accurate understanding of the British mind than was usual in the higher reaches of Nazi Germany.

On September 3—the day of the decision to switch the air attack to London—Karl Haushofer wrote to his son: "As you know, everything is so prepared for a very hard and severe attack on the island in question that the highest ranking person only had to press the button to set it off. But before this decision, which is perhaps inevitable, the thought once more occurs as to whether there is really no way of stopping something which would have such infinitely momentous consequences. There is a line of reasoning in connection with this which I must absolutely pass on to you because it was obviously communicated to me with this intention. Do you, too, see no way in which such possibilities could be discussed at a third place with a middle man?"

As a result of this letter, a meeting took place on September 8 between Albrecht Haushofer and Hitler's deputy as leader of the Nazi party, Rudolf Hess. There is some doubt as to whether Hitler himself was aware of the meeting, but Haushofer believed that he was, and that the subsequent instructions Hess gave bore the Führer's blessing.

According to Haushofer's account of the conversation, "I was immediately asked about the possibility of making known to persons of importance in England Hitler's serious desire for peace. It was quite clear that the continuance of the war was suicidal for the white race. Even with complete success in Europe, Germany was not in a position to take over inheritance of the Empire. The Führer had not wanted to see the Empire destroyed and did not want it even today. Was there not somebody in England who was ready for peace?"

Haushofer answered bluntly that practically all Englishmen who mattered regarded a treaty signed by Hitler as a worthless scrap of paper. "If the worst came to the worst, the English would rather transfer their whole Empire bit by bit to the Americans than sign a peace that left to National Socialist Germany the mastery of Europe."

Hess, apparently incredulous, interrupted to ask why the English were prepared for such a relationship with America, and not with Germany. Haushofer told him, "Because Roosevelt is a man, and represents a way of life, which the Englishman thinks he understands."

Hess than came to the point of the interview: didn't Haushofer think that feelers for an understanding with England had been unsuccessful because the right language hadn't been used? There followed an unflattering discussion about Ribbentrop, the Foreign Minister and former Ambassador in London, "but I again stressed," declared Haushofer, "the fact that the rejection of peace feelers by England was today due not so much to persons as to the fundamental outlook mentioned above."

Hess, however, was not to be put off. He asked Haushofer to name likely contacts, and Haushofer did so: Sir Owen O'Malley, British Minister to Hungary, Hoare in Madrid, Lothian in Washington. Lothian, he thought, was "perhaps best in a position to undertake a bold step—provided that he could be convinced that even a bad and uncertain peace would be better than the continuance of the war—a conviction at which he will only arrive if he convinces himself in Washington that English hopes of America are not realizable."

Since Lothian had just seen the conclusion of his long efforts to bring about the destroyers-bases exchange, this eventuality did not, perhaps, seem very likely; and the conversation returned to a name mentioned by the elder Haushofer in his letter, that of the Duke of Hamilton, "who has access at all times to important persons in London, even to Churchill, and the King."

Hess said he would consider the possibility of trying Hamilton, and the conversation ended. A few days later, on Hess's instructions, Albrecht Haushofer wrote to Hamilton through an intermediary, inviting him to Lisbon for a meeting.

With unerring skill, Haushofer and Hess picked the wrong duke. Scotland was not without ducal would-be peacemakers, but the Duke of Hamilton was not of that inclination; nor did he ever receive the invitation to Lisbon. His first knowledge of it came in the spring of the following year, when he was shown a copy by Intelligence officers, who asked him if he would be prepared to accept the invitation. He replied that he would, if it was an order; but Hess saved him further trouble by flying to see him in Scotland. By then the attack on Russia was almost ready to begin, the second front with Britain had not been liquidated, and the dove was very desperate indeed.

On September 11, Hitler postponed his decision on Sealion for three days. On September 13, R.A.F. bombers sank eighty invasion barges at Ostend, while the Royal Navy bombarded Calais, Boulogne, Ostend, and Cherbourg. On September 14, Hitler postponed his decision for another three days. On September 17, Operation Sealion was indefinitely postponed and, on October 12, called off until the spring, though with the proviso that an appearance of preparation was to be kept up "for the purpose of maintaining political and military pressure on England."

It passed unmourned, except perhaps by Winston Churchill and the Commander-in-Chief Home Forces, General Sir Alan Brooke, who said "I would actually welcome an invasion. I would welcome the opportunity of throwing them back into the sea. They have done it twice to us, and it's about time we got some of our own back."

Unlike Ironside in those now-remote days of early April, he was not called upon to justify his words.

Chapter

13

BLITZ

Twelve months after it had been expected, two years after Munich, and under a very different Prime Minister, the blow from the air fell on London.

"Sooner or later the Americans will come," Churchill had said, "but on condition that we here don't flinch." Sharp American eyes were watching: Edward Murrow, Quentin Reynolds, Drew Middleton, and other journalists, some of whom were less friendly; the American Assistant Chief of Naval Operations, Rear Admiral Robert L. Ghormley, the Assistant Chief of Army Staff, Major General George V. Strong, Major General D. C. Emmons of the Army Air Corps, who had been sent to Britain to assess the country's ability to put American aid to good use. Much depended on what these official and unofficial observers were able to report.

On Saturday, September 7, Göring himself had gone to Cape Gris-Nez to watch Kesselring's air armada, three hundred bombers escorted by six hundred fighters, pass overhead on its way to deliver "this stroke right into the enemy's heart."

The bombers came in from the east at about five o'clock on the evening of what one remembers as a hot, sunny day. They flew low enough for one observer to see the bomb doors open and note the slow, staggered fall of the bombs.

The attack achieved surprise. On the morning of September 7,

Fighter Command had no reason to suppose that the Luftwaffe was changing its tactics, and Park's forces were disposed to guard against another blow at his battered sector stations and at the aircraft factories which had been attacked in the previous few days. London's antiaircraft defenses, already weak, had been further depleted in an attempt to guard these other targets. As a result, the routes to London were only lightly protected and many of the German bombers were not attacked until after they had delivered their bombs.

The assault was aimed at the docks and warehouses of London's East End,* and by six o'clock pillars of smoke and flame rose from a number of points along the river Thames, which served as markers for another two hundred and fifty bombers continuing the attack after dark. In peaceful circumstances, the London Fire Brigade regarded a thirty-pump fire as a serious affair. By midnight they were trying to control nine hundred-pump fires in or around the docks, at Woolwich Arsenal, and Bishopsgate Goods Yard. Not only the buildings were ablaze, but the merchant wealth of London. Torrents of burning spirits poured from warehouses into the river Lea. Molten sugar coated dockland basins with fire. The wooden blocks of the roadways, along which fire engines and ambulances had to maneuver, were alight. An exploding ammunition ship added to the chaos and the fear.

This was the situation confronting a largely inexperienced fire brigade, whose wartime recruits had been accused not long before of finding themselves cushy billets. They worked through Saturday night among the exploding bombs, through the next day, and through Sunday night, when bombing began again. Some worked for forty hours without relief. "Most of us had the wind up to start with," one of them noted afterward, "but we were all unwilling to show fear. You looked around and saw the rest doing their job."

"Turn on the lights and turn out the A.R.P. workers," had been a popular newspaper slogan of the previous winter. Now, in the streets beside the docks, rescue workers had their first experience

---

* "It isn't possible to aim exactly in bad weather, or know where the bombs fall," Hitler was later to tell Mussolini. Smoke and flame of course had the same effect as bad weather, and some bomber pilots, on both sides, were naturally more anxious than others to drop their bombs and get away before they were hit. In October, the Royal Air Force formally abandoned the polite fiction that, in bombing a town or city, they could accurately concentrate on military targets only.

of tunneling through rubble, in an acrid fog of fumes and dust, for what might be a parrot, or a still living child, or only a handful of grubby offal.

The children, of course, should not have been there. Since the outbreak of war, repeated attempts had been made to evacuate them, together with pregnant and nursing mothers. When the blow did not fall, and in face of the hostility they had met in some reception areas, thousands of women and children had drifted back to the familiar streets. Some of the wives knew very well that, if they stayed away, they would lose husbands and homes as surely as if they had been hit by German bombs. But it is a mistake to think of the prewar East End as one pestiferous slum inhabited by problem families. Slums there were, but also thousands of rows of terraced cottages, their lace curtains and holystoned doorsteps indicating an intense pride, a tenacious clinging to respectability, sometimes in circumstances which would have defeated any but the strongest character.

There are many accounts, written during the summer of 1940, of the England for which people fought and were prepared to die. It often took the form of the English countryside, which was indeed particularly beautiful during those months of brilliant weather, when one looked at many things in the expectation that the chance would not come again. Newspapers published pictures of the kind which have an appeal for an essentially urban and industrial people: cricket on the green, old churches, splendidly muscled farm horses pulling harvest carts among the bomb craters in Kent and Sussex fields. This was not the England of Stepney, Poplar, and West Ham. All the evidence points to the fact that the people of those gray, respectable streets actively disliked and distrusted the dark disorder of the countryside. Since they were largely inarticulate, there is no easy explanation of why they clung so fiercely to their cottages and tenements, refusing to move when all the buildings about them were in ruin and decorating the bombed rubble with Union Jacks and banners proclaiming "God Save the King." That they were prepared to do so is as essential a part of the Battle of Britain as the numbers and dispositions of Park's fighters or of General Pile's antiaircraft guns.

On the nights of September 7 and 8, there was something which an eyewitness, choosing the words with care, has described to me as near-panic, not on a large scale, nor lasting beyond that short time, but watched with anxiety because of prewar anticipations and the contagious quality of the terror which had been so recently seen in France and Belgium.*

Toward the end of August, the German New British Broadcasting Station, which purported to be run by British personnel on British soil, had begun a virulent campaign against Churchill, urging its listeners to horsewhip him and his underlings, and burn their property. Fortuitously or not, this campaign followed the lines of advice which Dr. Fritz Hesse claimed to have given Ribbentrop, that the way to peace with Britain lay through Churchill's overthrow, and that this could be achieved by making him appear personally responsible in British eyes for their blood and tears. To this Nazi propaganda was added that of British Communists, who made much of the fact that the first blows fell only on the poor, with the implication that by some sinister arrangement the Germans were letting their rich friends in the West End escape.

When Churchill visited the East End on the evening of September 8, he was greeted with cheers and cries of "Hit 'em back hard," but among some people at any rate his pugnacity was not well received, and there were also shouts of "You've got to make them stop it."

During the week-end there was a voluntary evacuation of London on what was described in the *New Statesman* ** as "an unprecedented scale." Some people drifted vaguely west. Others took blankets and mattresses to Greenwich Park and Hampstead Heath. Yet others took trains from the main-line stations to wherever they could get to, and a resident of a West Country town was quoted as complaining that it was like Bordeaux during the collapse of France, with queues of women and children, their possessions done up in pillowcases.

Not all of this evacuation was from the East End, but much of it was. One of the worst-hit districts was Silvertown, which lies like

---

* My informant has to remain anonymous, but since the point may be controversial I should say that I did not accept the words without cross-examination. In any event, I should qualify them by the assessment of Sir Harold Scott, Chief Administrative Officer of the London Civil Defence Region, who was frequently in the East End and was one of the Prime Minister's party on the evening of September 8. He assures me he is "certain there was no panic of any importance."

** The *New Statesman's* reports on the blitz, especially by Ritchie Calder, were outstanding.

an island between the Thames in the south and a line of dock basins on the north. Here, on the night of September 7, an area of houses and cottages a mile and a half long was surrounded by fire, and its population could be rescued only by water. The local authority, whose prewar enthusiasm for Air Raid Precautions had been notably tepid, demanded the complete evacuation of Silvertown. Malcolm Macdonald, the Minister of Health, made a personal visit and with great psychological insight promised that transport would be provided for everyone from Silvertown who wanted to leave.

Fewer than three thousand, of a total population of thirteen thousand, chose to take advantage of the offer. It has been estimated that during September between twenty and twenty-five thousand people, from a total population of some three hundred thousand, moved out of West Ham, Stepney, and Bermondsey. In so far as it can be measured by figures, this was the East End's near-panic.

By September 11, the antiaircraft defenses had been more than doubled—at the expense, it must be pointed out, of Coventry, Birmingham, Plymouth, Southampton, Derby, and the Humber, among other places—and every gun blazed every round it could fire. There is no evidence that they hit anything, but the noise was comforting. On the same day, to the relief of the authorities, the West End of London was bombed as well as the East End, and Buckingham Palace was among the buildings hit.

"After the severe attacks of the last two weeks on London," the Spanish Ambassador reported to his government later in the month, "morale is still reasonably good. The danger in this connection arose during the first air attacks, since these were directed against the districts occupied by the workers. Later bombing also of the aristocratic and commercial quarters likewise aroused hatred of the enemy in people who had previously been unaffected and strengthened the single-minded determination to carry on the war to the limit. . . . Public opinion has displayed many variations, and will possibly fluctuate more, but up to now there is no weakening of the conviction that the war will continue for a long time."

By September 12, Sir Philip Game, the Commissioner of Police of the Metropolis, was able to record that there was no sign of panic anywhere in the East End, though some of its inhabitants were shaken by continued lack of sleep. There was, he also noted, no defeatist talk.

On Sunday, September 15, the Luftwaffe mounted a major attack which almost, but not quite, swamped Fighter Command with heavy raids on London, Portland, and the Spitfire works near Southampton. The raiders heading for London on this Sunday morning found themselves running the gauntlet of fourteen fighter squadrons, and those German pilots who returned were loud in their complaints that they had been under attack from British planes which, according to German radio and Intelligence reports, had long since ceased to exist.

It was a clear, bright day, and the British fighters could be distinctly seen as they engaged, breaking up the bomber formations and forcing them to scatter their bombs almost at random over the South London suburbs. In London the Law Courts were hit, and again Buckingham Palace.

Sergeant R. T. Holmes, of 504 Hurricane Squadron based on Hendon, who shot down a Dornier which landed on Victoria Station, was allowed to give an anonymous account to the press of this, his first battle, which so exactly catches the air of jaunty nonchalance the public had come to expect from the Royal Air Force that I asked him whether it really did represent the truth. His answer seems worth quoting in full:

"Jaunty? I suppose so. Why not! I think we all had a sort of hit-or-miss attitude to life then—perhaps today, too, some of us! We took our flying, and our training, and our fighter tactics very seriously, but not the possible consequences.

"We went through cumulus cloud at eight thousand feet. This was quite dicey, for we had only practiced formation flying in cloud in pairs, and to suddenly find twelve of us climbing through this bumpy stuff was quite a rare experience. Before we reached twelve thousand feet over base, we'd been vectored off to rendez-vous with another Hurricane squadron from North Weald at seventeen thousand feet, but we met the Dorniers first and we went straight in on a starboard quarter-attack.

"Pausing here, I personally think far too little has been said about the part our radar played in winning the Battle of Britain. We were given a perfect interception of these Dorniers at exactly their height, which must have shaken the Hun no end and made him wonder just how many squadrons we had on patrol. Without our ground control, interceptions would have been very few and far between, and the Hun would have been through time and again.

"We had devised our own formation (which we called our Hendon formaggers) because we thought it made us more maneuverable as a squadron . . . I was tail-end Charlie, weaving above, and consequently the last to attack.

"By then the Dornier formation had become ragged and was turning for home, and 504 had broken away to reform and I spotted three Dorniers blazing a lone trail toward London. No one seemed to have noticed them, so I decided to give them a little attention. I made quarter-attacks separately on the two outside men first, attacking from the flank and breaking away to come up on the other flank. The first man belched oil all over my windscreen, blotting my vision entirely; but when the oil cleared, due to my overtaking speed, I saw his tail very close to my nose, and one of his airscrews stopped and I just grazed under his belly as I went past below him.

"It was the second plane which caught fire at his wing root and from which came a parachutist who draped himself so artistically over my wing. I didn't give much for the chances of either of these machines getting home, but could not claim them destroyed as I had not seen them crash. I was officially credited with two probables for them.

"The leader still pressed on. One stern attack, without much apparent effect, left me low in ammo for we only had a total of fifteen secs' firing. I thought a head-on attack might cool his ardor, and climbed up and past him to his left from my last breakaway. It was then my engine sounded rough and I saw my oil pressure had dropped and that there was oil bubbling up the inside of my windscreen—my own oil. I made the head-on attack but during it actually ran out of ammo. I knew the engine had had it anyway, so more in frustration than in hate I kept on and clipped one side of his fragile-looking twin tail with my port wing. There was only a slight bump, and I thought his tail had snapped off without harming my wing, but my port wing started slowly to dip, and the nose to drop, and I looked out and saw the end of my wing had torn away. There was no answer to the controls; they were heavy and soggy. The spiral steepened until quite soon I was vertical and spinning. There was no choice but to try to bail out. Sliding back the hood was fairly easy, but trying to get out into that slip stream made me feel I was putting my head in the airscrew blades themselves. At this point I entered the cloud, and knew I was halfway down already. My R.T. headphones, oxygen mask, and goggles were blown off my helmet, and it was quite impossible to open my eyes. I worked my feet onto the seat to push my body out, but the parachute pack caught under the hood. Finally my feet found the control column and I kicked that forward, and the negative G spewed me free. Unfortunately, I hit the tail with my shoulder as I left the machine, so that my right arm was useless for pulling the rip cord. Precious seconds were lost while I worked my left hand under my left armpit and pulled the ring. There was a jerk so sickening that both my boots flew off my feet, and then complete silence, and I said to myself in awe: 'It worked.'

"Whether I was giddy, or spinning, I am not sure, but I reached up and gripped the lines, and tugged them, and my vision cleared for me to see a cobweb of railway lines three hundred feet below converging onto Victoria Station, and just above the station the front half of the Dornier floating lazily like an autumn leaf onto the station roof. Ten seconds after seeing this, I hit a Chelsea rooftop myself, missed my grip, and rolled off into the dustbin.

"I slipped out of the harness into a deserted garden, and shouted: 'Is anyone home?' Two girls popped their heads out of a next-door basement window where they had been sheltering during the air raid; so I jumped over the fence into their garden, and they came up to me and I kissed them both.

"Then I phoned my squadron. When I told the operator I was a fighter pilot who wished to contact his base at Hendon, my phone call, which would have taken anything up to two hours with delays in those days, was through in seconds. Then I had to persuade a husky Home Guard, who came rushing into the room with a length of lead piping in his hand, that I was on his side and was not a German parachutist; and he proudly walked me along Ebury Bridge Road followed by a crowd of curious Londoners to some crossroads where a fifteen-foot-deep crater marked the grave of my little Hurricane. I brought away a fragment of the valve cover from the Merlin engine, which had the S of Rolls and the R of Royce on it—all I could identify as having been my airplane—and wondered how I'd have gone on if we'd delayed parting company another couple of seconds.

"The Home Guard also took me to Chelsea Barracks, where I asked the medical officer to check if the harness had yanked out all of my guts when the canopy caught on the downspout.

"We'd had one panic that morning before breakfast, and word had come through that the Hun had packed it in, and that this had been his last attack. The squadron had been put on 'thirty minutes available' and I had brekker [breakfast] and took my mail to read in the bath. I had been hauled out of this onto readiness, in slacks and open-necked sports shirt and flying boots with no socks, and by the time the squadron brake arrived at dispersal the tannoys were blaring to scramble and orbit at angels twelve.

"At Chelsea Barracks the Commanding Officer asked, looking at my bare feet, sports shirt, and flannel bags, whether the R.A.F. always dressed like that. But he opened the mess bar at eleven o'clock on a Sunday morning, all the same. There was a call for me while I was there. A lady was asking for me from the road. I went outside, and through the railings she passed me a box of fifty cigarettes. 'Thank you,' she said, 'for missing our flats with your airplane. My baby was asleep under the stairs, and she might have been killed.'

"I didn't tell her I hadn't a clue where my airplane was going, and I didn't tell her I didn't smoke. She could not afford those cigarettes. I was so touched I couldn't tell her anything, except 'Thank you.'"

By the end of Sunday, September 15, the British radio was announcing that 185 German planes had been brought down. The claim was wildly exaggerated—the actual loss was less than a third of that number—but the defeat of the Luftwaffe by a supposedly broken Royal Air Force was nevertheless decisive.

At about this time, according to Dr. Hesse, there was a violent disagreement between Hitler and Göring: "The forces directed against Great Britain were practically used up. But Göring and the General Staff of the Luftwaffe were not willing to give in. They demanded that Hitler authorise the transfer of German squadrons stationed in Poland so that they might deliver the final blow against Great Britain. The orders for the transfer, which might have meant the defeat of Great Britain, were ready—and then Hitler intervened. He raged 'like a madman' (as Hewel put it) on the telephone and forbade all interference with his military dispositions. He yelled at Göring, saying that he would not allow air squadrons which were being kept in readiness for the Russian campaign to be wasted on a senseless enterprise. When Göring objected that this measure was, after all, necessary to win a victory over the British, Hitler replied that he knew these things much better than Göring and would not tolerate any interference with his political decisions."

The account is perhaps exaggerated, as political gossip tends to be, but at a conference with his commanders on September 16, Göring did order yet another change in Luftwaffe tactics, and after this date an increasing reluctance to risk bombers in daylight raids over London became apparent.

The knockout blow had fallen, and it had failed. The horse-whipping of the Prime Minister, like Operation Sealion, was indefinitely postponed.

Throughout September, Ambassador Kennedy had been telegraphing to Washington his doubts about British ability to survive, and at the end of the month the American military observers, Strong and Emmons, made their reports. Emmons was almost as gloomy as Kennedy about British prospects, but drew the very different conclusion that Britain must not be allowed to go under and that the United States must therefore enter the war. Strong was more optimistic, appreciating that if there had been no invasion by October 15, Britain was probably safe. More important, however, was a memorandum drawn up by Strong and Emmons which had considerable influence on American official and unofficial thinking. Its principal recommendations were that in spite of the threat from Japan, the greatest danger to the United States came from Germany, and that American industry must be virtually put on a war footing. The memorandum recommended that British arms orders already placed should not be disturbed, and American industrial expansion paid for by the British should be reserved for their use, although American capacity beyond those commitments must be primarily reserved for the rearmament of America itself.

On September 27, the Tripartite Pact was signed in Berlin between Germany, Italy, and Japan. In Berlin, Ciano noted, "even the Berlin street crowd, a comparatively small one, composed mostly of school children, cheers with regularity but without conviction . . . One thing alone is certain: that the war will be long. This does not please the Germans, who had come to believe that with the end of summer the end of the war would also come."

Though the Pact was aimed at neutralizing the United States, it created scarcely a ripple there. This fact, more important even than the defeat of the Luftwaffe, was the victory won for Britain by the Royal Air Force, Anti-Aircraft Command and the people of London.

After September 15, London settled down to the slow attrition of what its people chose to diminish, with subtle but unconscious irony, as The Blitz, their own abbreviation of *Blitzkrieg*, lightning war.

It has been rightly pointed out that Londoners stood up to nothing like the holocausts which later consumed Hamburg and Dresden, to say nothing of Hiroshima.* Sixty thousand people were killed by bombing in Britain during six years of war. The official estimate of deaths in Hamburg on three nights in 1943 was forty-three thousand, and this is almost certainly too low. But London endured bombing for seventy-six nights on end. What its citizens had to do was in a sense simple: to get to their work as punctually as possible, after a mad obstacle race in which trains ceased to run, familiar stations were reduced to a chaos of rubble, buses suddenly disappeared down chasms in the roadway. They had to concentrate on their work, and their wives queued for rations, while above the clouds, like a nagging wasp, droned something which might or might not be a Dornier.

After work there was another obstacle race, at the end of it perhaps an "incident"—that dry, remote and colorless word, as John Strachey pointed out—in which wife and children had been killed or injured, or home destroyed. At night disturbed or interrupted

* The seed of Hiroshima, and all that has flowed from it, was sown in the weakness and panic of 1940. On June 15, 1940, Roosevelt gave the executive order which led to the atomic bomb.

sleep, under the stairs or in the damp discomfort of an Anderson shelter in the garden.

Many of the people who faced these things were middle-aged, sedentary, cast in no heroic mold. They became—they are still, given the opportunity—great bores with their bomb stories. "During these trying days and nights," a correspondent wrote to the *Times* shortly after the blitz began, "it is quite natural that people should wish to compare their experiences on arriving at their work each morning. To continue doing so is not only wearisome, but is very likely to make us less able to meet in good heart any further trials which may come our way. At first to desist may be a little difficult, but with the loyal cooperation of all members of the staff, it will soon become a good habit, and will be a valuable contribution to the nation's war effort." By November, even the Foreign Secretary was referring to "the proprietary interest that everyone takes in his own bomb. If you let me tell you about my bomb, I will listen to yours."

But there is considerable truth, though also some lamentably un-British rhetoric, in the words of a refugee Hungarian doctor after he had treated casualties from a bomb disaster at Barking Underground station in the following January: "You English cannot appreciate the discipline of your own people. I want to tell you, I have not found one hysterical shouting patient. I think this is very important—that you should not take such things as given; it does not happen in other countries. If Hitler could have been there for five minutes with me, he would have finished this war. He would have realized that he has got to take every Englishman and twist him by the neck—otherwise he cannot win this war."

As it turned out, in spite of their elaborate plans, the authorities were ill-prepared for the blitz. They had an amplitude of shrouds and papier-mâché coffins, a million burial forms, thousands of hospital beds. For the obstinately unwounded living they had not planned so well.

A report had been available since 1936 in the Air Raid Precautions Department of the Home Office which gave a remarkably precise estimate of the damage which high-explosive bombs would do to bricks and mortar, but such was the fascination understandably exercised by the myth of the knockout blow that this document had been largely overlooked. The result was that, by the end of September, thousands of Londoners were homeless, forced to live and sleep in rest centers which had been set up and equipped on the assumption that they would be needed for, at most, an overnight stay.

Partly because people had no homes in which to sleep, partly because of the psychological need for companionship, the habit of communal sleeping became widespread for a time. Some of the London Underground stations had been considered unsafe as air-raid shelters because of the danger from flooding if they suffered a direct hit. The Underground was spontaneously and irresistibly taken over, along with even less safe shelters like a railway-goods depot under the Tilbury Arches off the Commercial Road. Here eight thousand people spent their nights on piles of rubbish or cartons of margarine and rolls of newsprint, among horse-drop-pings and the rising tide of overflow from two buckets which served the sanitary needs of either sex. Race feeling, an observer noted, was marked between black and white, with Cockneys, Jews, and Indians keeping strictly to their self-segregated enclaves.

Before the war it had been officially anticipated that regular troops would be needed to preserve order and prevent panic, but at Tilbury Arches a single policeman was enough to control the long queue which formed every evening: Indians with huge bun-dles on their backs; fat, blowzy women shouting to grubby children in the gutter; a thick-lipped Negro with a tart; youths in tight-waisted jackets of blue- and-green check with padded shoulders, split and down-at-heel shoes, wide flannel trousers. As the evening siren sounded, the policeman stepped aside, and there was a rush, not of panic, but of eagerness to secure a favored place. A rug or blanket was laid among the stacked goods or on the floor, and then, by unwritten law, the place was safe. There was no claim-jumping.

The discipline was impressive, the sanitation of such shelters, and of the underground stations, was not; and in such conditions the authorities began to fear that a winter of disease would accom-plish what the Luftwaffe had failed to do. Gradually, with much makeshift and improvization, the shelters were organized, sanitary facilities of a kind provided, homes found for the homeless. The twilight alert and the dawn all-clear became as accepted as sunset and sunrise. A census taken in early November, 1940, showed that only 13 per cent of London residents were still using public shelters of one kind or another. The rest stayed at home, most of them not bothering to leave their beds. Although ministers talked gloomily of the expectation that London, apart from its public buildings, would be gradually pulverized to rubble, 80 per cent of the British people, according to a Gallup Poll, believed that it would be impossible for Germany to win the war by bombing.

After October 5, daylight bombing of London virtually ceased, and the Luftwaffe, having wasted since Eagle Day two months, a thousand aircraft, and a high proportion of its experienced bomber and fighter crews, returned to its original plan of eroding the R.A.F.'s and the country's sources of supply.

During October there were night raids on Liverpool, Manchester, Tyneside, Bristol, Wolverhampton, Glasgow, Southampton, and, in particular, seven raids each on Coventry and Birmingham. On November 14, the Luftwaffe attempted a knockout blow at the comparatively small and concentrated city of Coventry, known to the Germans as the British "little Essen." Kesselring has claimed—and there is no reason to doubt him—that the targets in Coventry were the armament factories, but "fire and smoke clouds make it impossible to aim accurately. The dispersion inevitable in any bombing is thus considerably increased and punishes adjacent areas in no wise intended as objectives."

The German attack on Coventry has been described as probably the most concentrated and destructive on any British objective outside London throughout the war. Between four and five hundred bombers were used, flying in relays for eleven hours between dusk and dawn in ideal conditions on a clear, moonlit night, preceded by a marker raid with incendiary bombs to light their targets.

Coventry was one of the cities whose wisdom in pruning the strength of its Air Raid Precautions services had won the applause of the *Daily Express* during the previous winter. The number of its antiaircraft guns had been reduced in the recent attempt to protect London, and there were later allegations that the commercial center of the city was left with insufficient wardens and firewatchers after shop-closing hours. One clergyman wrote to the *Midland Daily Telegraph:* "More than half the fires could have been extinguished, without any help from the [fire] brigade itself, had men and stirrup-pumps been available. The truth is that we were not ready, nor organised, for anything so terrific as this."

In any event, the Luftwaffe had one enormous piece of luck which could not have been counted on. Early in the raid the main water supply was cut, and firemen often had to stand helplessly by as showers of incendiary bombs, mixed with high explosives to induce them to keep their heads down, started fire after fire. When the Cathedral caught alight, no help could be given, and by morning only its fifteenth-century spire and some ruined walls remained standing.*

A hundred acres of the center of the city were devastated, nearly a thousand houses totally demolished, another 32,000 damaged. Ritchie Calder described the damage, in the *New Statesman,* as looking as if the rubble of London dockland streets had been added to the wreckage of the tall buildings of Holborn and Oxford Circus, and these had been placed in the center of the last-war ruins of the Cloth Hall at Ypres.

An official visitor to the city in the early hours of November 15 found a daunting scene. Gas and electricity had been cut off as well as water, and in the candlelit cellar of the Council House sat a group of distraught councilors and officials, incapable of further effort after the strain of the night.

Outside, in the rubble-blocked streets, people with no water to drink were using any sort of liquid, including spirits, with which to quench their thirst. As day went on, crowds collected in the city center, with little to do but exchange stories of the horrors of the night. The police feared a panic, but there was no one to give them orders, and a government representative in the city took the responsibility of ordering a curfew.

The situation seemed to justify German claims that Coventry had been knocked out of the war. It had not been. Within twenty-four hours the local authority was functioning again, a fact of im-

---

* I have been told that when army demolition squads were brought in after the raid to knock down buildings considered unsafe, there was some anxiety that the Cathedral spire might be condemned with the rest. The then Parliamentary Secretary to the Minister of Health, Miss Florence (now Lady) Horsbrugh, pointed out to the army how impressed everyone had been by the symbolic significance of the survival of the spire in the shattered center of the city. The spire was left standing, to be embodied in Sir Basil Spence's new Cathedral.

mense importance if people were to go on believing that this was "their" war, not something forced upon them by a pugnacious Prime Minister. Armament production was down to a third of its normal volume on the day following the raid, but the damage to the factories themselves was small compared with that in the city center, and the fall in production was almost entirely due to the dislocation of services, and to workers staying away to look after their shattered homes or to find country billets for their wives and families.

Dislocation continued for some time, and there was continuing local acrimony about armament workers "hurrying away before darkness descends," although what they had very sensibly done was to evacuate themselves to areas in which they could count on a good night's sleep, after which they could work better by day. Within two months, arms production was back to normal; and the final lesson of Coventry was learned, not by the Luftwaffe, but by a British observer, the Deputy Chief of Air Staff, Air Vice-Marshal A. T. Harris, who as Commander-in-Chief of Bomber Command did to Hamburg nearly three years later what the Luftwaffe had tried to do to Coventry. The dead in Hamburg numbered forty-three thousand, in Coventry five hundred and fifty-four; but not even Hamburg was completely destroyed. Within a few months of the raids, production in its factories and shipyards was back to 80 per cent normal.

One further point about Coventry may be noted. "The bombing of Oxford, Coventry, Canterbury," Churchill had told De Gaulle, "will cause such a wave of indignation in the United States that they'll come into the war." The names of other cities raided later were withheld for several days. The name of Coventry was released almost immediately.

The veneer of civilization is at best a thin one, and one ugly minor aspect of the blitz was an outbreak of looting which occurred in the devastated cities. Most of it was on a small scale, but some sufficiently organized to made one wonder whether this activity did not form the basis of one or two wartime fortunes. In Coventry there had been a great deal of feeling because, while women and girls helped to fight fires and rescue the dead and injured, locally billeted troops were under orders to take shelter. It was alleged that at the height of the raid, two soldiers were seen helping themselves to jewelry and cigarettes from bombed shops, and others brought in after the raid to clear up the debris were found robbing the gas meters of bombed houses. Sight-seers who poured into the city after the raid helped themselves to what they could find; a sixteen-year-old boy who had traveled from London by car with two men was charged with stealing over sixty pounds' worth of goods.

In London, gangs were said to employ "spotters" to warn them of likely property and the situation became bad enough for special plain-clothes, antilooting police squads to be set up. People returning to a block of shops and houses from which they had been evacuated found everything gone—razor blades and lighters from the shops, clothes, tea and sugar rations from the houses, even live chickens from the backyards. One man charged with taking two lighters and a pipe from another bombed shop exclaimed with mild indignation, "I am unlucky. They are all doing it."

This was nasty; but of more fundamental importance was the demand for reprisals against German towns, which led General Sir Ian Hamilton, the veteran commander of Gallipoli, to write to the *Times* in September: "As president of the British Legion in Scotland and patron of the British Legion in the Metropolitan Area, I am brought into touch with many of the young generation who are about to join one of the Services, and I am sure that there are many of our airmen who would jib at an order to bomb women and children."

The British Air Staff did indeed jib for some months at a policy of retaliation, not on moral grounds, but because like Hitler at this time they regarded it as more important to concentrate on industrial targets. Sir Charles Portal, the Commander-in-Chief of Bomber Command, advocated retaliation, proposing that twenty German towns should be warned by radio that one of them would be indiscriminately bombed in retaliation for each indiscriminate attack on a British town. In October, Portal became Chief of Air Staff and, with the Prime Minister's approval, "retaliation" was adopted as official policy. So far as is known, no airman on either side fulfilled Sir Ian Hamilton's hopes by jibbing at the order to bomb women and children. In practical terms, the distinction was meaningless, bombing on both sides being so inaccurate that civilians suffered almost more than industrial and military targets, but in moral terms it was not. In spite of newspaper attempts to whip up popular feeling on the subject, there remained a strong segment of British opinion against retaliation, led by Dr. G. K. A. Bell, the Bishop of Chichester. In October, according to a Gallup Poll, those who opposed retaliatory bombing numbered as many as 46 per cent. In January, after the winter's blitz, only 22 per cent of those asked expressed strong feelings in favor of retaliation against German civilians.

On the night of November 20, a twenty-three-year-old Beaufighter pilot shot down a Junkers 88. The feat was considered so extraordinary that steps had to be taken to conceal the means by which he had achieved it, and it was given out that he had the unusual power of seeing in the dark, like a cat. In this way, to his lasting embarrassment, the future Chief Test Pilot of the de Haviland Aircraft Company received his nickname of Catseyes Cunningham.

A number of helpful suggestions had been made to deal with the night bomber: airborne searchlights, showers of magnesium flares, mines dangling from parachutes, antiaircraft guns mounted on balloons, a proposal that British bombers should fly above the raiders and drop sand into their engines. The moonlit Thames provided an admirable flare path for bombers approaching London, and attempts had been made to obscure the shining surface by launching quantities of coal dust downstream.

None of these things was quite as wildly visionary as Air Interception, a development of radar for night-fighting use with which the Royal Air Force had been experimenting since July, but which, until John Cunningham's success in November, had produced disappointing results. Air Interception, however, did not get into its real stride until the following year, and meanwhile the Luftwaffe made night attacks on city after city almost at will: Birmingham on November 18, Bristol on November 24, Southampton on November 23 and 30, and December 1, Liverpool on November 28 and again shortly before Christmas, Sheffield on December 12 and 15, Manchester on December 22. In each of these raids the story of Coventry was repeated with variations: much courage, some cowardice, the inevitable old lady grubbing among the ruins for a favorite tea service, telling would-be helpers that "Of course I don't expect to find any bits of it unbroken, but I would just like to save *one little piece*." In each of them there was temporary dislocation followed by eventual recovery.

The dislocation, however, had a cumulative effect, to which was added the policy of dispersal adopted in the early autumn by the Ministry of Aircraft Production under the energetic direction of Lord Beaverbrook. One big single aircraft factory was broken up between forty-eight different premises, another between thirty-eight, another between thirty. A state of perpetual war existed between Beaverbrook's Ministry and the Ministry of Labour over the supply of workers, and the air at Whitehall was blue with acrimonious minutes from ministries whose requisitioned properties, unwisely left empty, had been illicitly commandeered for aircraft production. "We are anxious to co-operate with you . . . but if you want us to continue you must stop your people from behaving like pirates," was one minute to the Ministry of Aircraft Production which would scarcely have been conceivable in a pre-Beaverbrook Whitehall.

The dispersal was invaluable in the long run, but for the time being the monthly output of new aircraft fell, and in December reached its lowest total since the early summer. War production in general had more than doubled between December 1939 and May 1940. It reached a peak in June, then fell as the impact of bombing combined with exhaustion among the workers, and by October the government was being advised to discontinue the overtime and week-end work which had been introduced during the summer.

Food supplies began to cause concern. Like Beaverbrook, the Minister of Food, Lord Woolton, tried to disperse his stores away from the bombed ports; cinemas, ice rinks, and disused racing stables were taken over, but the raids continued to take their toll, and to them was added a mounting tide of convoy sinkings. During the course of two hours one Friday afternoon, Woolton received five separate signals from the Admiralty reporting that food ships had been sunk on the Atlantic route. In November, for the first time since the outbreak of war, food imports fell below a million tons.

This situation was created by the accumulation of a number of deficiencies. Naval bases in Eire were not available. No new destroyers had been laid down in 1938, destroyer losses off Norway and France had been heavy, and of those that remained a high proportion had been taken off convoy escort duties to guard against invasion. Coastal Command of the Royal Air Force had been weakened by concentration during the summer on the production of fighters for the Battle of Britain.

In December, the Admiralty put to the Prime Minister proposals which have a somewhat desperate air about them, for laying an underwater carpet of contact mines, anchored to the bottom of the sea and reaching to within thirty-five feet of its surface. The mine field was to be three miles broad, sixty miles long, and would insulate the approaches to the Clyde and Mersey against U-boats. According to Churchill, the Admiralty urged that the laying of this carpet of mines must be given priority over all other operations as well as arms production.

Hitler had told his service chiefs in July that it would take one to two years to reduce Britain by air and sea blockade; but by December, despite the wasted months of the Battle of Britain, he had already induced in the British Prime Minister black memories of 1917. And still the United States was not in the war.

Chapter
14

BERLIN QUADRILLE

At the beginning of October, Hitler and Mussolini met on the Brenner Pass for one of their periodic reviews of the war situation. It was a meeting not without interest, since Hitler had to explain why he had not yet invaded Britain, and Mussolini had to explain why the Italian army in Libya, having rolled ponderously forward across the Egyptian frontier with a numerical superiority over the British of five to one, had then come to a stop at Sidi Barrani.

Ciano nevertheless described it as "cordial," with Hitler putting at least some of his cards on the table. The cards he did not put on the table proved in this case to be more important than those that he did.

The meeting began with a piece of news which seems to have made a great impression on the Italians: the resignation of Chamberlain which, said Mussolini, was an indication of a domestic crisis and an outgrowth of difficulties which the English government had to overcome. It was in fact a sign that Chamberlain was dying of cancer, but Mussolini's diagnosis, though for the wrong reasons, was not entirely wide of the mark.

Hitler then gave a long explanation of the delays in launching Operation Sealion. "It was clear," he declared, "that with the defeat of France the war had been won for the Axis powers, and that the rest was merely a question of time. However, for various reasons, especially with a view to economic reconstruction, Germany and Italy had an interest in bringing about the end of the war as soon as possible. It was for this purpose that preparations for a landing in England had already been instituted last summer, and this on a broad front from Normandy to Brest." The difficulties, however, had been enormous: railway bridges destroyed in France, French harbors full of sunken ships, above all the weather. Only five days of good weather had been needed to gain air supremacy, then eight to ten days of calm weather to permit a crossing by sea. The Wehrmacht had been waiting every day for the last four weeks, but hopes had been disappointed time and again.

The waiting period, however, said Hitler, had not been allowed to pass unused. Despite unfavorable weather the English were under attack day and night. Signs of disintegration were becoming visible. It was not possible to aim exactly in bad weather or know where bombs fell, but in the long run it was impossible to stand the strain of these constant attacks.

As soon as better weather came, Hitler added, there would be systematic attacks on airfields, engine and airplane factories, waterworks, canal installations, antiaircraft factories, gasoline and oil dumps, power plants, and so on. Owing to the constant attacks on London, the English had been forced to concentrate defenses there, so that it was easier for low-flying formations to carry out attacks to destroy key industries.

This explanation concealed a great many cards, including the information that Operation Sealion had been postponed indefinitely and was only kept in being, according to Halder's diary note of September 14, because "cancellation of our plans would not remain a secret. It would ease the strain on the enemy's nerves, and consequently must not be ordered now."

Having thus dealt with Sealion and given a more optimistic assessment of the air war than the facts warranted, Hitler came to the point: why did Britain hold out? Because of hopes from Russia and America.

America had been warned off by the Tripartite Pact. And Russia? "A year ago," the Führer said, "Stalin had certainly believed there would be a long European war accompanied by a general attrition of Europe. He had certainly expected this to result in a relief for Russia and new perspectives in a Europe which had been bled white, and now he was doubtless disappointed at the quick conclusion of the war. The Kremlin had calculated wrong this time. Germany was not afraid of Russia, and had prepared everything for defense. To be sure, seventeen divisions of older age groups had been demobilized, but forty new divisions had been organized, so that after March [1941] a total of a hundred first-class divisions, twenty-four of them armored, would be available."

Hitler said he considered it out of the question that Russia would undertake anything, but an attempt would be made to direct the Russians toward India. He thought they would not go, "but in any case it was no problem for Germany if the worst came to the worst."

In September, there had been rumors in German official circles of some German diplomatic initiative to reassure the Russians. On September 30, Halder recorded: "Reports are increasing that Russia expects an armed conflict with us in 1941. Preparations for this eventuality are quite manifest in the training of Russian troops; particular emphasis is placed on utilization of wooded terrain." Later that day he referred to talks with Brauchitsch after the latter's return from Berlin: "The Führer notified Stalin of the conclusion of the pact with Japan twenty-four hours before it was signed. Now a letter has gone out designed to get him interested in dividing up the estate of defunct Britain, and to induce him to join up with us. If the plan succeeds it is believed we could go all out against Britain."

Brauchitsch and Halder naturally welcomed any postponement of the eastern offensive until Britain had been dealt with; but there cannot be much doubt that the attempted *rapprochement* with Russia was no more than Hitler's equivocal fulfillment of his promise to Japan to obtain Russia's signature to the Tripartite Pact if at all possible. Nor is there much doubt that the Russians were not taken in by the attempt.

After the reference to Russia, the discussion between Hitler and Mussolini—perhaps monologue is a more exact description—ranged over the rest of Europe, with references to France and Spain which were intended, unsuccessfully, to assure Mussolini that those countries were not being courted at the expense of Italy.

Mussolini offered to begin an advance from Sidi Barrani to the

Nile in the middle of November. Hitler drew a graphic picture of forty divisions lying in readiness for the invasion of Britain, "practicing day and night the loading, unloading, landing, and every other kind of special operation."

Two days later German troops entered Rumania.

This was another card which had not been laid on the table. Throughout the summer the Italians had been warned off adventures in Yugoslavia and Greece, and Mussolini's fury at this double cross was recorded in Ciano's diary: "October 8: Telephone call from the Duce, requesting that we take action in Rumania to elicit request for Italian troops. He is very angry because only German forces are present in the Rumanian oil regions"; "October 12: Duce indignant at German occupation of Rumania . . . 'Hitler always faces me with a fait accompli. This time I am going to pay him back in his own coin. He will find out from the newspapers that I have occupied Greece.'"

On October 14, Mussolini fixed the date for an Italian invasion of Greece as October 26. A week before that date, knowing that Hitler was preoccupied with visits to Franco and Pétain, he sent his ally a warning of his intention in a letter which, according to Ciano, "does not make clear either the form or the date." Hitler hurried to Florence in an attempt to head Mussolini off, but was met on the railway platform by Mussolini himself, who, smirking with self-satisfaction, announced that Italian troops had that morning crossed the Greek frontier.

Retribution for this act of vanity and wounded pride was swift and terrible. On November 11, a strike by carrier-borne British aircraft crippled the Italian fleet at Taranto. By December 4, the Greek army had pushed the Italians back so fast and so far that Mussolini was telling Ciano, "There is nothing else to do. This is grotesque and absurd, but it is a fact. We have to ask for a truce through Hitler." On December 10, a small Commonwealth force of two divisions under General Sir Richard O'Connor struck at Graziani's army in Egypt and chased it back into Libya, capturing 70,000 prisoners on the way—almost twice its own number.

Hitler's plans lay in ruins. He now had three choices. He could maliciously watch his ridiculous ally's downfall in Greece and Libya. If he did, he would have to surrender the Mediterranean and allow Britain access to bases in Greece which would bring their bombers within range of the Rumanian oil fields. He could postpone the planned attack on Russia and turn his "camouflage" projects in the Mediterranean and North Africa into the real war. Or he could do what he did, prop up Italy just strongly enough to keep her in the war, but leaving the Balkans, North Africa, and finally Italy itself, as running sores which more and more drained away German resources urgently needed for the Russian and British fronts.

Hitler's whole temperament and mental outlook suggest that the choice was apparent rather than real. His mind was fixed on Russia as the enemy. The Mediterranean would have faced him with a sea war, which he did not understand and therefore distrusted. He could not allow the British a toehold in the Balkans. It is possible to see October 28, 1940, the day of the Italian attack on Greece, as the day on which the gambler's luck decisively deserted him.

The Italian invasion of Greece, following so closely upon German action in Rumania, added to Moscow's always present distrust of German and Italian intentions. On November 12, Molotov, the Russian Foreign Minister, arrived in Berlin for discussions about joining the Tripartite Pact. Evidence of the insincerity of Hitler's approach may be found in a directive issued on the same day from his headquarters: "Political discussions have been initiated with the aim of clarifying Russia's attitude for the coming period. Regardless of what results these discussions will have, all preparations for the East which have already been orally ordered are to be continued. Directives on this will follow as soon as the outline of the Army's plan of operations is submitted to and approved by me."

In any event, Molotov was not interested in the spoils of the British Empire laid so enticingly at his feet. He would talk only about the Balkans, and the Baltic. Cloudy plans for a division of the world between Germany, Italy, Russia, and Japan were pierced by sharp questions: What were the Germans doing in Finland, which under the Nazi-Soviet Pact belonged to the Russian sphere of influence? What was the significance of the Tripartite Pact? What was the meaning of the German guarantee to Rumania, "aimed against the interests of Soviet Russia, if one might express oneself so bluntly"?

Hitler, according to his interpreter, had never been spoken to like this by a foreign visitor. With difficulty he kept his temper, and it was left to Ribbentrop to place before Molotov the draft of a new agreement bringing Russia into the Tripartite Pact with a sphere of influence "south of the national territory of the U.S.S.R. in the direction of the Indian Ocean." *

On November 25, after Molotov had reported on his talks, Stalin sent Berlin an official intimation that Russia would join the Tripartite Pact if given a sphere of influence in the Middle East south of a line from Batum to Baku. But in addition Russia would want a free hand in Finland and Bulgaria, and the lease from Turkey of bases on the Bosporus. Hitler made no official reply to an offer as patently insincere as his own. On December 18, in spite of urgent advice from his service chiefs to concentrate first on eliminating the front with Britain, he issued his directive for Operation Barbarossa: "The German Armed Forces must be prepared to crush Soviet Russia in a quick campaign even before the end of the war against England . . . Preparations requiring more time to start are to be begun now—if this has not yet been done—and are to be completed by 15 May 1941."

---

* The proposal was presented by Ribbentrop while the two foreign ministers were sheltered from a not entirely fortuitous British air raid. I have the greatest doubts about Stalin's famous story of Molotov's retort to Ribbentrop: "If Britain is really finished, why are we in this air-raid shelter, and whose are the bombs falling outside?" It sounds to me like something Molotov afterwards wished he had said.

Chapter

15

"...THE LAND IS BRIGHT"

In September, Neville Chamberlain had presided over his last meeting as a Cabinet minister. An air raid was in progress, and behind him a big bow window. His private secretary drew his attention to the danger. Chamberlain thanked him, and continued with the meeting. The secretary became agitated and asked if they should not all adjourn downstairs. No, said Chamberlain, not unless the others wished to do so. The secretary took the only step remaining to him to preserve his master from the danger of flying glass. He began to draw the window curtains. Chamberlain stopped him, saying, "Let's have the daylight while it's there." On October 3, he resigned from the government and, asking his doctor on the following day how long he had to live, was told that it could be only a few weeks. He died on November 9.

Harold Laski noted with some perception that Chamberlain's loyalty to the Churchill Cabinet was largely responsible for its survival. Although the threat of invasion had held it together, there had indeed been signs of strain throughout the summer. The British government could not afford to antagonize Japan without American support, which was not forthcoming. In July, therefore, they closed the Burma Road over which supplies reached China for her war against Japan. The decision was widely seen as an example of Halifax' continuing policy of "appeasement," his presence at the Foreign Office was regarded as an obstacle to improved relations with Russia and, in August, Churchill told Eden that many people would like to see Halifax go. At the end of the year he in fact went, after Lothian's death, as British Ambassador to Washington, where he was a triumphant success.

There were disputes between Beaverbrook and Ernest Bevin, the Minister of Labor, and Morrison, Minister of Supply, over Beaverbrook's highhanded methods of taking whatever he wanted in the way of men or materials to produce his Spitfires and Hurricanes. While Churchill grappled desperately with problems of survival, Labour ministers pressed him to think about postwar planning. Churchill was still doubtful whether it would be a British government doing the planning; but he placated the Labour men by appointing a committee, Chamberlain, Attlee, Halifax, Bevin, Sinclair, and Duff Cooper, of which Reith commented wryly that "I never heard of it producing anything."

When Chamberlain resigned the Leadership of the Conservative party in October, Churchill was unanimously elected in his place. Churchill's election set up new strains, and an acrimonious note was again heard in the Commons. Aneurin Bevan fired a warning shot. "Henceforth," Bevan declared, "it will be necessary to watch Mr. Churchill from two aspects: as a national leader in an unprecedented situation, and as the spokesman of the Tory Party." A curious but effectively critical partnership emerged between the Left Wing Emanuel Shinwell and the High Tory Lord Winterton.

Outside the House, as the threat of invasion receded and tempers became frayed under the bombing, criticism reached almost the peak of the previous winter. In October, there was a long Cabinet discussion about suspending the *Daily Mirror*. Churchill became "frightfully excited," seeing in its tone "clear evidence of Fifth Column activity." *

Churchill had been as unsuccessful as Chamberlain in waving a magic wand over production and, in November, Mr. T. Balogh was writing to the *Times:* "Our war effort will not begin to be effective

---

* Halifax's diary for October 7. The offender on this occasion seems to have been, not the cartoonist Zec, but a front-page story by Bill Greig, headlined "He refused to funk—fired by Government," about an elderly government trainee who refused to take shelter during an air raid when ordered to do so. It certainly was not Jane, who was patriotically allowing herself to be kissed by an entire bomber crew before takeoff, to the grave discomposure of her dress.

until rationing is introduced to regulate consumption, until training is not organised by committees representing vested interests but consisting of production experts, and until production is not organised by financial and technical pooling." Drew Middleton, an American correspondent friendly but sometimes frank, reported that British industry had started the war on an eight-hour day, and still was not going all out. Britain, he commented, was passing through her darkest days since Dunkirk.

On November 5, came the long-awaited moment of Roosevelt's re-election as President of the United States. Churchill's message of congratulation went unanswered. Nothing seemed to change. Britain's dollar reserves were almost exhausted, she could pay for arms already ordered, but after that—bankruptcy. Lothian, returning to the United States after consultations in Britain, tried shock tactics, greeting reporters with the words, "Well, boys, Britain's broke. It's your money we want." The American Treasury was sympathetic, but the President seemed to pay no attention.

There is an air of desperation about Churchill as the year drew toward its end, as the bomb damage and the U-boat sinkings mounted, as parliament bickered and production fell. Minutes and memoranda flew: "Former Naval Person to President. I am sure you will have been pleased about Taranto . . ."; prodding on Wavell in the Middle East; driving Dill, the C.I.G.S., to declare, "I can't tell you how angry the P.M. has made me. What he said about the Army tonight I can never forgive. He complained he could get nothing done by the Army. Then he wished he had Papagos [the Greek commander-in-chief] to run it." When O'Connor struck in Egypt, Churchill rang Eden up in the early morning to complain that O'Connor was not pursuing the enemy and "had much to say about missed opportunities. After an angry riposte from me, it emerged that he had not seen telegram that appeared during night giving details of further plans . . ."

A week later the Prime Minister favored the House of Commons with a picturesque description of O'Connor's Australian cavalry charging, sword in hand, as if the Western Desert in 1940 had been Omdurman in 1898.*

* The Australians who attacked an Italian convoy near Jarabub Oasis on December 16 were indeed cavalry, of the Sixth Divisional Cavalry Regiment, but they were mounted in trucks, and what they had in their hands were machine guns. The

Offensive plans proliferated: plans to capture the Mediterranean island of Pantelleria, to invade Abyssinia from Kenya, to assail the Canary Islands, fight in Albania and Salonika, occupy North Africa, and descend on Normandy in 1941. But, the Prime Minister admitted in a sad moment of truth, there weren't enough teats on the old sow.

On December 2, Roosevelt left Washington for a Caribbean cruise. He fished, he played poker, he watched movies: Alice Faye and Betty Grable in *Tin Pan Alley;* Jean Arthur and William Holden in *Arizona;* Charles Laughton and Carole Lombard in *They Knew What They Wanted.* On December 9, a long memorandum from Churchill reached him, "one of the most important I ever wrote," Churchill recorded afterward.

It was a document of some prescience; Churchill was always a better strategist than tactician. He foresaw a long war: "It takes between three and four years to convert the industries of a modern state to war purposes . . . Germany certainly reached this point by the end of 1939. We in the British Empire are now only about halfway through the second year. The United States, I should suppose, is by no means so far advanced as we . . . It is our British duty in the common interest, as also for our own survival, to hold the front and grapple with the Nazi power until the preparations of the United States are complete."

The greatest immediate threat to Britain's continuance in the war, Churchill argued, lay on the sea, particularly in the heavy sinkings of merchant shipping, and he urged Roosevelt either to use American sea power to protect neutral shipping supplying Britain, or to make over to the British American ships for this purpose.

He urged that American industrial capacity should be expanded to reinforce British supplies of aircraft and munitions, but, "Last of all I come to the question of Finance. The more rapid and abundant the flow of munitions and ships which you are able to send us, the sooner will our dollar credits be exhausted . . . The mo-

---

Prime Minister may be forgiven, however: the Western Desert was still largely terra incognita in Britain, and the *Times* had recently referred to Tobruk in peacetime as "a pleasant little station."

ment approaches when we shall no longer be able to pay cash for shipping and other supplies. While we will do our utmost, and shrink from no proper sacrifice to make payment across the Exchange, I believe you will agree that it would be wrong in principle and mutually disadvantageous in effect if at the height of this struggle Great Britain were to be divested of all saleable assets, so that after the victory was won with our blood, civilisation saved, and the time gained for the United States to be fully armed against all eventualities, we should stand stripped to the bone . . ."

Roosevelt read and reread this document, sitting alone on his deck chair. He said little about it to his close associates.

In Washington, on his return, he began a press conference with the words, "I don't think there's any particular news . . ." Then, cigarette in holder tilted upward and waved to emphasize a point, he went on, "There's absolutely no doubt in the mind of a very overwhelming number of Americans that the best immediate defense of the United States is the success of Britain in defending herself." But the British, he pointed out, were short of arms, and lacked enough dollars to buy them. "Suppose my neighbor's house catches fire, and I have a length of garden hose, four or five hundred feet. If I can take the hose and connect it to my neighbor's hydrant, he may be able to put out the fire. I don't say the hose cost fifteen dollars, pay me fifteen dollars. I don't want fifteen dollars, but my hose back when the fire's over. The neighbor gives back the hose and pays me for the use of it. If it gets damaged in the fire, I'd say I was glad to lend it. The neighbor says he'll replace the part destroyed. If I've got back my hose, I've done a pretty good job."

A reporter asked if this kind of thinking would not take America into war. "Not a bit of it," said the President. "I don't think you'll get into war for legalistic reasons."

On Sunday evening, December 29, the President broadcast one of his fireside chats. It was not, perhaps, a particularly appropriate moment for folksy similes about lending a garden hose. As he went on the air, London was still burning. The German bombers had come in at 7 P.M., London time, scattering incendiary bombs. The raid lasted only two hours, but the level of the Thames was so low that fireboats could not be used, and many of the fires had to be left to burn themselves out. Wren's City churches, which were already old when the United States was new, crashed in ruin. A gas main flaring outside the National Gallery lit Trafalgar Square, and the dome and cross of St. Paul's appeared brilliantly illuminated in the midst of a sea of fire.

For those awake and not fighting fires, the President's voice came across the Atlantic as sometimes a reedy whisper, sometimes a blare of atmospherics. Did anyone seriously believe, he asked, that there need be fear of an attack anywhere in the Americas while a free Britain remained their most powerful naval neighbor in the Atlantic? And did anyone seriously believe that America could rest easy if the Axis powers were her neighbors there? "If Britain goes down the Axis powers will control the Continents of Europe, Asia, Africa, Australasia and the high seas and they will be in a position to bring enormous military and naval resources against this hemisphere. It is no exaggeration to say that all of us in all the Americas would be living at the point of a gun—a gun loaded with explosive bullets, economic as well as military."

What, then, was America going to do about it? On November 12, Admiral Stark, Roosevelt's Chief of Naval Operations, had come to the conclusion that the United States would have to send land and air forces to Europe because Britain had not the manpower to launch an invasion of an Axis-held Continent. Churchill in his memorandum had been carefully moderate: "Even if the United States were our ally, instead of our friend and indispensable partner, we should not ask for a large American expeditionary army." Roosevelt whittled this down to a reassuring, "There is no demand for sending an American expeditionary force outside our own borders. There is no intention by any member of your government to send such a force. You can, therefore, nail—nail—any talk about sending armies to Europe as deliberate untruth."

Instead, America must be the great arsenal of democracy. "As planes, ships and guns and shells are produced," Roosevelt declared, "your government, with its defense experts, can then determine how best to use them to defend this hemisphere. The decision as to how much shall be sent abroad and how much shall remain at home must be made on the basis of our over-all military necessities."

It had come at last—or had it? The eel had been so very slippery that the Prime Minister seemed far from sure. His message of thanks revealed almost as much disappointment as gratitude: ". . . Remember, Mr. President, we do not know what you have in mind, or exactly what the United States is going to do, and we are fighting for our lives. What would be the effect upon the world situation if we had to default in payments to your contractors, who have their workmen to pay? Would not this be exploited by the enemy as a complete breakdown in Anglo-American cooperation? Yet a few weeks' delay might well bring this upon us."

But in any event, the future was out of the hands of both the American President and the British Prime Minister. It was decided for them, as for many millions of others, by Hitler, who early in the New Year addressed a staff conference.

Russia, he said, sustained England's hopes, therefore Russia must now be smashed. Either the British would then yield or Germany would continue the war against England in the most favorable circumstances. The smashing of Russia would also enable Japan to turn against the United States with all her forces. This would prevent America from entering the war.

"The gigantic territory of Russia," Hitler went on, "conceals immeasurable riches. Germany must dominate it economically and politically, although not annex it. Thereby Germany will have all the means possible for waging war, even against continents, at some future date. Nobody will then be able to defeat her any more. If this operation is carried through, Europe will hold its breath."

EPILOGUE

From the safe advantage of twenty-five years later, one can see 1940 as a series of ifs.

If the Norwegian campaign had not been such a fiasco that it precipitated the fall of Chamberlain . . . If Hitler's timing of his western offensive had not influenced the succession in favor of Churchill rather than Halifax . . . If the Germans had been held on the Meuse . . . If Tyler Kent had been able to reveal the full Churchill-Roosevelt correspondence and influence the presidential nominations . . . If Gensoul had meekly surrendered at Oran, instead of fighting . . . how different would the history of the world have been? Of course quite different. But each event is shaped by what has gone before, and in turn shapes what comes after.

A wise American, who disguised his wisdom under a mask of folly, has reduced historical iffing to its proper absurdity by describing the scene if Grant had been drinking at Appomattox. But even if Grant with a hangover had succeeded in surrendering his sword to an astonished Lee, the Southern Confederacy would have stayed beaten; it was industry and manpower, not Grant's sword, that mattered.

What one can say with certainty is that there are not many people in the world today whose lives have not been influenced in some way by events in one small corner of Europe in this year of 1940. Not only Hiroshima and Nagasaki, but Korea, Suez, the Congo, and Vietnam are implicit in it. A vacuum is created; in one way or another it has to be filled.

By his victories over France and Britain, Hitler secured the freedom of maneuver to strike at Russia, and on June 22, 1941, he did so. By December of that year, German forces had reached the suburbs of Moscow, and with Russia apparently on the point of defeat, the Japanese prepared to take over the British Empire in Asia, first aiming what was intended to be a neutralising blow at the United States. Whether America would have entered the war on the British side if the Japanese had not attacked the American Pacific Fleet at Pearl Harbor is another fascinating historical if; it was not seen in Britain as inevitable. But on that night, Churchill has recorded, he went to bed saturated and satiated with emotion and sensation, and slept the sleep of the saved and thankful. The United States, like it or not, had been goaded into taking the place left vacant on the world stage by a declining Britain.

By the end of 1941, Hitler had raised up against himself a coalition which, if it had existed in 1939, would have made war unthinkable. In 1941 it could do no more than ensure the defeat of Italy, Germany, and Japan, at a cost of some thirty million lives and the temporary destruction of European civilization. It could not have done even as much as that if an unsinkable aircraft carrier had not existed off the coast of Europe, stoutly manned and resolutely commanded.

Principal Published Sources Consulted

(The editions used were published in London unless otherwise stated.)

Amery, L. S., *My Political Life*. Vol. III, *The Unforgiving Years*. McGraw, 1955.

Aron, Robert, and Elgey, Georgette, *The Vichy Regime*. Macmillan, 1958.

Attlee, Earl, *A Prime Minister Remembers*. Heinemann, 1961.

———— *As It Happened*. Viking, 1954.

Avon, Earl of, *The Eden Memoirs: The Reckoning*. Houghton, 1965.

Beauman, Brigadier General A. B., *Then a Soldier*. P. R. Macmillan, London, Geneva, 1960.

Bell, Reginald, *The Bull's Eye*. Cassell, 1943.

Benoist-Méchin, Jacques, *60 Days That Shook the West*. Putnam, 1963.

Birkenhead, Earl of, *Halifax*. Hamish Hamilton, 1965.

Bloch, Marc, *Strange Defeat*. Oxford University Press, 1949.

Blumentritt, General Guenther, *Von Rundstedt*. Odhams, 1952.

Boothby, Lord, *I Fight to Live*. Gollancz, 1947.

Bryans, J. Lonsdale, *Blind Victory*. Skeffington, 1951.

Bryant, Sir Arthur, *The Turn of the Tide*. Doubleday, 1957.

Bullock, Alan, *Hitler: A Study in Tyranny*. Odhams, 1952.

Butler, J. R. M., *Lord Lothian*. Macmillan, 1960.

———— *Problems of Grand Strategy*. H.M.S.O., 1957.

Carton de Wiart, Lieutenant General Sir Adrian, *Happy Odyssey*. Clarke, Irwin, 1950.

Chatfield, Admiral of the Fleet Lord, *The Navy and Defence*. Ryerson Press, 1947.

Chalmers, Rear Admiral W. S., *Full Cycle*. Hodder & Stoughton, 1957.

Churchill, Sir Winston S., *The Second World War*. Houghton, 1948.

Ciano, Count Galeazzo, *The Ciano Diaries, 1939-1943*. Doubleday, 1947.

Collier, Basil, *The Defence of the United Kingdom*. H.M.S.O., 1957.

Cooke, Colin, *The Life of Richard Stafford Cripps*. Hodder & Stoughton, 1957.

Cooper, A. Duff, *Old Men Forget*. Dutton, 1954.

Dalton, Hugh, *Memoirs, 1931-1945: The Fateful Years*. Saunders, 1957.

De Gaule, General Charles, *War Memoirs: The Call to Honour*. Viking, 1955.

De Guingand, Major General Sir Francis, *Operation Victory*. Scribner's, 1957.

Derry, T. K., *The Campaign in Norway*. H.M.S.O., 1952.

Divine, David, *The Nine Days of Dunkirk*. Norton, 1959.

Documents on German Foreign Policy, 1918-1945, Series D., Vols. X and XI. H.M.S.O., 1949.

Dulles, Allen Welsh, *Germany's Underground*. New York, Macmillan, 1947.

Einzig, Paul, *In The Centre of Things*. Hutchinson, 1960.

Ellis, Major L. F., *The War in France and Flanders, 1939-1940*. H.M.S.O., 1953.

Farrer, David, *The Sky's The Limit*. Ryerson, 1943.

Feiling, Sir Keith, *The Life of Neville Chamberlain*. Macmillan, 1946.

Fleming, Peter, *Operation Sea Lion*, Simon and Schuster, 1957.

Frankland, Noble, *The Bombing Offensive Against Germany*. Faber, 1965.

Front Line, 1940-41. H.M.S.O., 1942.

Führer Conferences on Naval Affairs. Brassey's Naval Annual, 1948.

Goodhart, Philip, *Fifty Ships That Saved The World*. Doubleday, 1965.

Graves, Charles, *The Home Guard of Britain*. Hutchinson, 1943.

Guderian, General Heinz, *Panzer Leader*. Dutton, 1952.

"Gun Buster," *Return Via Dunkirk*. Hodder & Stoughton, 1940.

Halder, General Franz, *Kriegstagebuch*. Kohlhammer, Stuttgart, 1962.

—— *The Halder Diaries*. Infantry Journal, Washington, 1950.

Halifax, Earl of, *Fulness of Days*. Dodd, 1957.

Hambro, Carl J., *I Saw It Happen in Norway*. Appleton-Century, 1940.

Hammond, R. J., *History of The Second World War, U.K. Civil Series: Food*. H.M.S.O., 1951.

Hankey, Lord, *Politics, Trials and Errors*. Regnery, Oxford, 1950.

Hansard. H.M.S.O., 1940.

Harris, Marshal of the Royal Air Force Sir Arthur T., *Bomber Offensive*. Macmillan, 1947.

Hassell, Ulrich von, *The Von Hassell Diaries, 1938-1944*. Hamish Hamilton, 1948.

Hesse, Fritz, *Hitler and the English*. Smithers, 1954.

Hillary, Richard, *Falling Through Space*. Reynal, 1942.

Hingston, Lieutenant Colonel Walter, *Never Give Up*, Vol. V of the *History of The King's Own Yorkshire Light Infantry*. Lund Humphries, 1950.

Hitler, Adolf, *Hitler's Secret Conversations*. Farrar, Straus, 1953.

Hull, Cordell, *Memoirs*. Macmillan, 1948.

Ickes, Harold L., *The Secret Diary of Harold L. Ickes*. Simon and Schuster, 1955.

Ironside, Field-Marshal Lord, *The Ironside Diaries, 1937-1940*. Constable, 1962.

Jones, Thomas, *A Diary With Letters*. Oxford University Press, 1954.

Jowitt, Earl, *The Strange Case of Alger Hiss*, Doubleday, 1954.

Kelly, Sir David, *The Ruling Few*. Hollis & Carter, 1952.

Kennedy, Major General Sir John, *The Business of War*. Morrow, 1958.

Kesselring, Field-Marshal Albert, *Kesselring: A Soldier's Record*, Morrow, 1954.

Koht, Halvdan, *Norway Neutral and Invaded*. Macmillan, 1941.

Langer, William L., and Gleason, S. Everett, *The World Crisis and America: Vol. I, The Challenge to Isolation; Vol. II, The Undeclared War*. Harpers, 1952, 1953.

Leasor, James, *The Uninvited Envoy*, McGraw, 1962.

Liddell Hart, Sir Basil, *Memoirs*, Vol. II. Cassell, 1965.

────── *German Generals Talk*, Morrow, 1948.

────── (Edited) *The Rommel Papers*. Harcourt, 1953.

────── *The Tanks*. Cassell, 1959.

Macleod, Iain, *Neville Chamberlain*. Antheneum, 1961.

Manstein, Field-Marshal Erich von, *Lost Victories*. Regnery, 1958.

Manvell, Roger, and Fraenkel, Heinrich, *Hermann Goering*, Heinemann, 1962.

Martel, General Sir Giffard Le Q., *Our Armoured Forces*. Faber, 1945.

Masefield, John, *The Nine Days Wonder*. Macmillan, 1941.

Mass Observation, *War Begins At Home*. Chatto & Windus, 1940.

Minney, R. J., *The Private Papers of Hore-Belisha*. Collins, 1960.

Montgomery, Field-Marshal Lord, *Memoirs*. World, 1958.

Morison, Samuel Eliot, *History of United States Naval Operations in World War II, Vol. I*. Little, 1960.

Morrison of Lambeth, Lord, *Herbert Morrison*. Odhams, 1960.

O'Brien, T. H., *Civil Defence*. H.M.S.O., 1955.

Owen, Frank, *Tempestuous Journey: Lloyd George, His Life and Times*. McGraw, 1955.

Padley, Richard, and Cole, Margaret, *Evacuation Survey*. Fabian Society, 1940.

Pickersgill, Hon. J. W., *The Mackenzie King Record 1939-1944*. University of Toronto Press, 1960.

Postan, M. M., *History of the Second World War, U.K. Civil Series: British War Production*. H.M.S.O., 1952.

Rawnsley, C. F., and Wright, Robert, *Night Fighter*. Holt, 1957.

Reith, Lord, *Into the Wind*. Hodder & Stoughton, 1949.

Reynaud, Paul, *In the Thick of the Fight*. Simon and Schuster, 1956.

Ribbentrop, Joachim von, *The Ribbentrop Memoirs*. Weidenfeld & Nicolson, 1954.

Roskill, Captain S. W., *The War At Sea, Vol. I*. H.M.S.O., 1954.

Rowse, A. L., *Appeasement: A Study in Political Decline, 1933-1939*, Norton, 1961.

Schellenberg, Walter, *Memoirs*. André Deutsch, 1956.

Scott, Sir Harold, *Your Obedient Servant*. André Deutsch, 1959.

Sherwood, Robert E., *Roosevelt and Hopkins*, Harpers, 1948.

Shirer, William L., *Berlin Diary*. Knoph, 1941.

—— *The Rise and Fall of the Third Reich*. Simon and Schuster, 1960.

Sillitoe, Sir Percy, *Cloak Without Dagger*. Abelard, 1955.

Slessor, Marshal of the Royal Air Force Sir John C., *The Central Blue*. Cassell, 1956.

Spears, Major General Sir Edward, *Assignment to Catastrophe*. Wyn, 1954.

Sykes, Christopher, *Orde Wingate*. Collins, 1959.

Templewood, Lord, *Ambassador on Special Mission*. Collins, 1946.

—— *Nine Troubled Years*. Collins, 1954.

Titmuss, R. M., *Problems of Social Policy*. H.M.S.O., 1950.

Waterfield, Gordon, *What Happened to France*. Musson, 1940.

Webster, Sir Charles, and Frankland, Noble, *The Strategic Air Offensive Against Germany*. H.M.S.O., 1961.

Wedgwood, Lord, *Memoirs of a Fighting Life*. Hutchinson, 1941.

Weizsäcker, Baron Ernst von, *Memoirs*. Regnery, 1951.

Welles, Sumner, *The Time for Decision*. Harpers, 1944.

Werth, Alexander, *Russia at War*. Barrie & Rockliff, 1964.

—— *The Last Days of Paris*. Hamish Hamilton, 1940.

West, Rebecca, *The Meaning of Treason*. Viking, 1947.

Weygand, General Maxime, *Recalled to Service*. Doubleday, 1952.

Whalen, Richard, *The Founding Father*. New American Library, 1965.

Wheeler-Bennett, Sir John W., *King George VI, His Life and Reign*. St. Martin's, 1958.

—— *The Nemesis of Power*. St. Martin's, 1954.

Women's Group on Public Welfare, *Our Towns*. Oxford University Press, 1943.

Wood, Derek, and Dempster, Derek, *The Narrow Margin*. McGraw, 1961.

Woolton, Earl of, *Memoirs*. Cassell, 1959.

The files of the London *Times, The New York Times, The Daily Telegraph, The Daily Mail, The Daily Express, The Daily Mirror, The Daily Herald, The Evening Standard, The New Statesman and Nation*.

INDEX

INDEX